Praise for Leisure with Dignity

"The greatest thinkers demand great students: read Charles Kesler and his Claremonsters carefully or not at all."

Peter Thiel, entrepreneur, investor, author

"Charles Kesler is a public intellectual, respected by millions. This book is a testament to the less visible core of his character, from which the rest flows. Charles is a knower and a teacher, better at each because of the other. In this book his students manifest what he has taught them and how much they love him. By reading it, you can join them in the privilege of knowing him. I have that privilege and commend it to you."

Larry P. Arnn, President, Hillsdale College

"This fine collection of essays by several of Charles Kesler's former students is a fitting tribute to his impressive ability to unite sound political judgment, intellectual acumen, and compelling teaching."

Mark Blitz, Fletcher Jones Professor
of Political Philosophy, Claremont McKenna College

"Charles Kesler is a philosopher and a gentleman, and has taught a generation of students to be companionable in the pursuit of difficult truths. Their essays collected here meet the highest standards of the festschrift, honoring Kesler by demonstrating his teaching in action on the great questions of politics and statesmanship. The result is a festival of engaging argument on the nature and fate of the American founding—a gift to a new generation of students."

Christopher DeMuth, Distinguished Fellow
in American Thought, The Heritage Foundation

"Scholar, teacher, and editor Charles Kesler has proven a national voice of reason well beyond his sterling reputation in academia. When national controversies arise, students, readers, and the public naturally look to Charles to calm tensions, to offer empirical analyses, and to explain where we are as a nation—and where we should be headed."

Victor Davis Hanson, The Hoover Institution, Stanford University

"Why is Kesler getting this festschrift? He's far too young, he isn't even vaguely near retirement, he was educated at that thing called Harvard, and he's from West Virginia. The problem seems to be that as a result of his exceptional brilliance, hard work, kindness, wit, and courage, he deserves it, having earned such deep affection and respect from so many. And don't forget, like Bill Buckley's, his qualities verge upon the magical."

Mark Helprin, Senior Fellow, The Claremont Institute, novelist

"A showcase of luminous essays by students of the eminent Charles Kesler proving how well he taught them. Featured is the relationship of ancient natural right to modern natural rights: is it dispute or comity? And how does political philosophy consider and address America?"

Harvey C. Mansfield, Research Professor of Government, Harvard University

"Charles Kesler is a national treasure. He has done immense and probably incalculable good for American politics through his many years of teaching, writing, and advising at the highest level. May his influence continue to grow at this most critical time for the country we all love so much."

Ryan Williams, President, The Claremont Institute

Leisure with Dignity

Leisure with Dignity

Essays in Celebration of

CHARLES R. KESLER

Edited by

Michael Anton & Glenn Ellmers

Encounter
BOOKS

NEW YORK · LONDON

First American edition published in 2024 by Encounter Books, an activity of Encounter for Culture and Education, Inc., a nonprofit, tax-exempt corporation.
Encounter Books website address: www.encounterbooks.com

Manufactured in the United States and printed on acid-free paper. The paper used in this publication meets the minimum requirements of ANSI/NISO Z39.48-1992 (R 1997) (*Permanence of Paper*).

FIRST AMERICAN EDITION

LIBRARY OF CONGRESS CATALOGING-IN PUBLICATION DATA IS AVAILABLE

Information for this title can be found at the Library of Congress website under the following ISBN 978-1-64177-349-2 and LCCN 2023053920.

Contents

Introduction

Michael Anton and Glenn Ellmers

In Hesiodic terms, Claremont's Golden Age was definitely the late 1960s, when Leo Strauss was there, along with his students Harry V. Jaffa, Harry Neumann, and Martin Diamond, who together trained the original pantheon of Claremonsters – Codevilla, Erler, Marini, Peterman, Uhlmann, West, and the great John Wettergreen – before Strauss decamped for St. John's and Jaffa and Diamond irretrievably fell out. The Silver Age flourished when the second generation, and some of the first – Arnn, Flannery, Garrity, Masugi, Schramm, and Silver – founded the Claremont Institute to preach and perpetuate the Old Man's teaching, as well as the grand strategic thought of his friend and colleague Harold W. "Bill" Rood.

The Bronze Age began with the arrival, in 1983, of Charles Kesler.

This is not in any way to short-shrift Charles. Bronze Ages can be great (just ask Hesiod himself), and Claremont's Kesler Era was definitely great – at least for us, who were mostly there in the 1990s. Not that we make any pretensions to the greatness of those mentioned above. Only that we were fortunate to be there at a propitious time, and to have benefited from such an outstanding teacher.

Jaffa was, in 1989, more or less forcibly retired from Claremont McKenna College and the Claremont Graduate School (as it was then called). He was still plenty spry and sharp enough to keep going, but he had also stepped on a lot of toes, and despite his being the grad school's number-one draw for students (his only competition on that score was Peter Drucker, in an entirely different field of study), many were glad to see him gone. (Except he never really left, but that's another story.)

Institutionally, a vacuum had to be filled – and Kesler filled it. Suddenly, scarcely thirty years old, Charles found himself, *de facto* as well as *de jure*, seniormost among a distinguished faculty of far older and more established scholars. *De facto* because, while no formal title attached to the role, Charles assumed Jaffa's place as the central figure in the Claremont graduate program that had been turning out so-called West Coast Straussians for the prior quarter century; *de jure* because he also took over the Salvatori Center, the institutional home of Jaffaism (though not anymore; again, another story) on the Claremont McKenna campus, replete with the largest and nicest corner office in the stately but now sadly demolished Pitzer Hall. In addition to all this, Charles was (and remains) a senior fellow at the Claremont Institute, in those days teaching most of the (then) six-week Publius program. We don't know if Charles left Harvard for Claremont expecting, within half a decade, to become a "new prince" while still barely needing a razor, but that's what happened – and we're all lucky it did.

Perhaps the uninitiated would benefit from a word on the differences between the Claremont Institute and the other nearby establishments that share the name. Claremont, California, is a city – really a suburb – thirty miles east of downtown Los Angeles on the far eastern border of Los Angeles County. Home to about 35,000 people, it is both a bedroom community and a college town, a distinction it gained with the opening of Pomona College in 1887. (To add to the confusion, there is also a neighboring city, much rougher than Claremont, named Pomona, but Pomona College has always been in Claremont.)

More schools would follow, but for our purposes, the two most important are the Claremont Graduate School (later University), founded in 1925, and Claremont McKenna (originally Men's) College, founded in 1946 with a focus on politics and economics to balance Pomona's emphasis on the liberal arts. These and three other schools eventually banded together to form the "Claremont Colleges" consortium, retaining their separate existences while sharing certain facilities, such as a central library.

The Claremont *Institute* was founded in 1979 by four of Jaffa's graduate students. Perhaps not coincidentally, that same year, Kesler published a cover story in *National Review* lauding Jaffa as conservatism's deepest and most consistent thinker. This was a bold move for such a young man: Kesler had graduated from Harvard only the year before (he was in the audience when Solzhenitsyn delivered his landmark commencement speech), had been a William F. Buckley protégé since age sixteen, and at Harvard had come under the wing of Harvey C. Mansfield, one of the three most distinguished conservative academics of the last half-century (the others being James Q. Wilson and Jaffa himself). To make the story even more improbable, at this point Charles hadn't even *met* Jaffa, but was invited for an audience on the strength of that article (Jaffa liked to be praised). The great man proceeded to greet his young admirer at the door to his hotel room dressed, let us say . . . informally. Charles can tell you the details if he likes, as for that matter so can several others who had similar experiences.

That meeting led to Charles's visiting Claremont the following year, as part of the second class of Publius fellows – a program of the institute, not any of the colleges – and three years after that being offered his first, and still only, full-time job: as assistant professor of government at Claremont McKenna (to be fair, he has been promoted since), with a joint appointment at the Claremont Graduate School.

By the time most of the contributors to this volume got to Claremont, Charles was well-established. *But* he also was still single, still lived in Claremont (he has since decamped to a spacious villa in the Oak Knoll section of Pasadena), and seemingly had nothing better to do than hang out with graduate students. And hang out we did.

Charles chose to teach all his grad classes at night – 7 P.M. to 10 P.M. – and always (really: *always*) came out with us for a pint or two after. In addition, every Friday, we would gather for happy hour at Lord Charley's, now long closed but back then the Cheers of the West Coast Straussians: everybody really did know our names. Weekday lunches (with Charles often picking up the check) and weekend movies were not infrequent. Somewhat rarer were excursions to Colorado Boulevard in Old Pasadena (a mere thirty minutes, but lots more action) or Newport Beach or the West Side (much further but *much* more action).

Charles was barely older than his students back then, so he could easily keep up, but in a sense he *seemed* older because he was (and is) so much more learned. Charles is the furthest thing from a pedant imaginable: he never shows off his erudition, and it's nearly impossible to drag deep thoughts out of him in a social setting. (Many continue to try, but we students learned long ago that the attempt annoys Charles and availeth us nothing). But in the classroom, Charles's brilliance shines through. He remains the single greatest lecturer we've ever encountered: prepared, polished, practiced. Three hours is a long time, but Charles could make it fly by, densely packing every minute with information, yet always within a scaffolding that made following along, if not easy, at least manageable – provided you were paying careful attention and taking notes.

Kesler's three main intellectual influences were, as noted, Bill Buckley, Harvey Mansfield, and Harry Jaffa. We believe this makes Charles unique among contemporary scholars and thinkers in having known extremely well, and learned from, the three most significant figures in intellectual conservatism of the last fifty years. (Nor does this exhaust the list of great minds Charles was privileged to know and study with, who also included the aforementioned Jim Wilson and the great Edward C. Banfield.) Each left an imprint too wide-ranging to summarize easily. But we may say that, from Buckley, Charles learned how to write and how to evaluate and influence contemporary politics; from Mansfield, the vast sweep of the history of political philosophy; and from Jaffa, the uniqueness of America within that story.

It would be wonderful, someday, to get Charles's personal recollections, assessments, and comparisons of all these great teachers. Yet we would not be the first to observe that extracting a piece of writing from Charles has become almost (though not quite) as difficult as getting him to philosophize in a bar. In recent years, Charles has mostly preferred to curate the thoughts of others while closely guarding his own innermost thinking.

One result of Charles's emphasis on quality over quantity is a C.V. that is noticeably shorter than the typical academic resume that rambles on for dozens, sometimes hundreds, of forgettable pages. But no one should get the wrong idea about our title. It is a phrase of Cicero's, Charles's favorite philosopher, and perfectly captures Charles's approach to life – as he himself recognized by invoking the words often in and out of class, even at times wearing a t-shirt bearing the phrase in Latin (of course): *cum dignitate otium*. Hard as it may be to imagine Charles in a t-shirt (these days, it's hard even to imagine him without a tie), the contributors to this volume were eyewitnesses, albeit long ago.

"Leisure" has come to mean "lounging" or "laziness," but it is derived from the Greek *scholē*, the root of our word "school." As the editors of this volume sometimes say to our students, "leisure" (*scholē*) is not lying on the couch binging Netflix; it's what you do with your finite time once all your necessities are met; leisure is the highest activity of the human being at his best.

Charles's most consistent, and still ongoing, output is the *Claremont Review of Books*, a highbrow quarterly of which he has been editor since its rebirth in 2000. Since then, the *CRB* has published (as of the time of this writing) ninety-one issues, each averaging seventy pages (more recent ones coming in at well over 100) with twenty to twenty-five articles – every single one, over twenty-three years, reviewed and edited by Charles – with each issue also carrying an editor's note penned by Charles and, occasionally, a longform essay by him. It's understandable, then, that Charles hasn't gotten around to writing the definitive Straussian take on the political philosophy of Cicero (though we think he should and hope he still will).

The roster of *CRB* contributors is a who's who of conservative academics and intellectuals, and even includes notable figures not on the Right. Charles remains, unlike some of his students (ahem), a unifying figure within the Right as well as an authority respected by mainstream scholars – at least those not utterly allergic to any hint of conservatism. This status has allowed him to maintain a "big tent" approach that has made the *CRB* a clearinghouse of must-read copy on all things Straussian, conservative, and American. That said, Charles also remains fiercely loyal. We know (because others, not Charles, have told us) that he is not infrequently rebuked by colleagues and old friends in such terms as "Did you see what that punk former student of yours said *now*?" And, may God continue to bless him, he defends us, still publishes us, and still hoists a pint (or, more commonly, a glass of wine) with us whenever he can.

We perhaps flatter ourselves in asserting that Charles publishes us because our writing is not bad. But if it isn't, we have him to thank. Charles is a grand exception to the rule that academics can't write. Not only is he great at it himself; even rarer, he knows how to teach the skill to others. The original Publius program was as much a crash course on writing as a seminar on political philosophy and American principles. Real work was assigned, which Charles (and others) then picked apart. (To cite just one example, Charles is the only reason we know the proper distinction between "that" and "which.") In grading for-credit work, he was just as interested in how ideas were expressed as in the accuracy of the expression. To remain Charles's grad student, you either learned to write well or you didn't make it.

Our only regret as editors is that the ten contributors to this volume were not more – for we ten do not comprise all the students whom Charles trained and sent out into the world. Whatever one thinks of us – whatever we think of ourselves – to have produced more than fifteen PhDs (or in some cases, near-PhDs) who've gone on to make something of a mark (not to mention one United States Senator, Tom Cotton) is a momentous achievement rare even in the academia of yesteryear; it is almost unheard of today.

Of course, as noted, quantity must be appreciated in terms of quality, and in the classroom and as an editor, Charles always aspired – and thereby inspired us – to disdain mediocrity. In his 2009 Opening Convocation lecture at CMC, he captured what might be called the distinctive Western Straussian approach to political philosophy, which prizes "a healthy love of honor and natural attraction to excellence." A proper education, he explained, should put

> these strivings into a larger, longer, and higher perspective. For there is, or at least should be, no greater balm for such noble desires than the serious study of the liberal arts and of the excellent men and women, across the ages, who nailed their lives to the cross of thought or of action.

We are all proud to be part of Charles's legacy, are grateful to have learned from him, and look forward to many years of learning more – and to continuing to enjoy Charles's always delightful company.

On First Looking into Plato's *Laws*

Bradley C. S. Watson

To the best of my recollection, I first read Plato's *Laws* in Claremont, California, in the fall of 1990. It was my first semester of graduate school and my first memorable graduate course. The lessons I gleaned from it have stayed with me over a long academic career. In that single and singular seminar, I was required for the first time to think seriously about things I have never stopped thinking (and writing) about: regime politics, nature versus convention, reason versus the passions, ancients versus moderns, the progressive rejection of both classical political rationalism and modern natural-rights claims. I also became fully aware of the attention to detail that is required to read, and learn, from great books. For me, the experience was a peak in Darien. The man who led me to that peak – as he would lead me to many others – was Charles Kesler.

As with most of Plato's writings, almost every page of this lengthy and fascinating work repays careful study. I recall being most struck by Plato's treatment of punishment – his highlighting of its fundamentally political character. If we know why and how a society punishes, i.e., what constitutes deviance and its control, we know much about the character of that society. If we know the dominant theory of punishment in an age, we know it will have consequences in the realm of practical politics that largely define those politics.

The *Laws* offers the first comprehensive penal theory in the Western tradition, matched only by that presented in Hobbes's *Leviathan*. But modern conceptions of state-inflicted punishment differ greatly from Plato's understanding. Even when the moderns maintain key elements of Plato's classical theory, they also depart radically from it as they move toward simplified utilitarian and rationalized understandings. The new utilitarian theories greatly affect the practice of punishment in liberal regimes, and their impact is by no means for the better.

Foremost in Plato's conception of legal punishment is a recognition that even the best possible polis – the one created in the *Laws* – must fall short of perfect virtue in all citizens. It ultimately falls short not because of what may rightly be called a defect in the laws concerning education to virtue, but because laws are for humans and the seed of humans, not for the sons of gods.[1] The book's central character, the Athenian Stranger, makes this clear in his discussion of criminal law beginning in Book IX, though it was implicit in his prior discussions of erotic temptations of all kinds. For the most serious crimes, at least, it can be said that laws are necessary because of original sin – or, in Plato's terms, "a certain gadfly that grows naturally in human beings as a result of ancient and unexpiated injustices."[2] The reality of human imperfection and corruptibility is as inexorable as it is lamentable. "It is indeed in a certain way shameful even to legislate all the things we are now about to lay down, in a city such as this, which we claim will be well administered and correctly equipped in every way for the practice of virtue."[3]

The best possible political order must ultimately come

to terms with the necessity of prohibition and punishment, precisely because that necessity is external to all possible political orders. There is a mystery to the human soul that is beyond the power of even the wisest and most just individuals, or cities, to penetrate. What is within the power of citizens and legislators is to recognize the unpredictable and destabilizing effects of this mystery, and to correct for those effects. Even the prelude to the law of temple robberies "and all other such things that are difficult to cure or incurable" will include exhortations to "try yourself to say, that every man must honor the noble and the just things. Flee, without turning back, the company of bad men."[4] This exhortation to virtue is critical to the definition of punishment, though not immediately reconcilable with the Stranger's later enunciation of the doctrine that no man commits injustice voluntarily. The Stranger takes it for granted that exhortations are bound in some instances to fail. In such instances it seems justice must diverge from the noble, because it must do what is shameful.[5] The Stranger could argue that undergoing just punishment is in fact noble, but he declines to do so. His abstruse treatments of voluntariness and nobility are matters to which we shall return.

The three causes of unjust acts or crimes are spiritedness, pleasure, and ignorance.[6] Spiritedness, at least, exists "by nature" and is by nature pugnacious and quarrelsome. It is the tyranny of spiritedness and pleasure within the soul that is injustice itself. Spiritedness, pleasure, and ignorance all cause the will to stray from its tendency toward the good, but they are not, strictly speaking, proofs of involuntariness.[7] In fact, the Athenian, after discussing the problem of voluntariness, soon reverts to an almost routine distinction between voluntary and involuntary crimes, proposing greater penalties for anything that "resembles" the former.[8] We are left to infer that unjust acts, whether voluntary or involuntary (in the sense of the will's deviation from its natural tendency), are never a mechanistic response to purely external, societal stimuli. At the very least, we cannot treat them as such for the purposes of the law. It might be that we are forever barred from understanding the internal workings of the soul when an injustice is committed.

In a larger sense, the majority of us have to be satisfied with "being puppets, for the most part, but sharing in small portions of the truth."[9] We do not, however, have to content ourselves with sterile doctrines of material causation; to do so would destroy the foundation of criminal law, which is far from the Stranger's intention. Even for crimes committed from ignorance, perhaps the closest to involuntary crimes, the criminal law must lower itself to something less than the noblest conception of justice. For even ignorance is not an exogenous factor with which man is confronted; it is a deficiency with which he must deal. While knowledge should rule, law must in fact do so.[10] Hence we can infer the reason for the Stranger's letting stand the contradiction between the just and the noble. Penal law by its nature is not utopian. It cannot be on earth as it is in heaven, for in heaven there is no need of it. Nor is it perfectly utilitarian in its ability to be an instrument of rehabilitation and deterrence, i.e., its ability to educate the criminal and other members of society.[11] Criminal justice and nobility are simply irreconcilable in the best possible state.

But not all aspects of the penal law are ignoble. Every man must accept the responsibility of convincing himself to honor the noble and just things because the soul is malleable to a certain extent, and indispensable to justice. In fact, it is subject to proper ordering for the sake of political justice, and is the *sine qua non* of that justice. Penal laws, in their preludes, thus have an educational function. In this sense, they can fulfill the highest aspiration of penal law, that of harmonizing justice and nobility.[12] If penal law can effectively guide men back to justice, taming the tyranny within their souls, it partakes of the noble process of education, rather than mere punishment, and becomes a natural extension of the education outlined earlier in the *Laws*.[13] It becomes but an aspect of the law as a whole, in all its justice and majesty.[14]

In addition, some laws, in their implementation, can be counted as the noblest even if they are not noble per se.[15] They might reach this plateau, at something less than the summit, with any combination of deeds and words that will "bring about hatred of injustice and desire, or lack of hatred, for the nature of the just."[16] The noblest laws will accomplish nothing less.[17]

But the penal law only *unites* justice with nobility in its prelude; in its implementation they are forever separate. Ignoble means must always be a part of the penal law's implementation. Victims must be recompensed, a variety of pleasures, pains, rewards, and penalties must be invoked, and the incurable must be put to death.[18] Every penal law has a rehabilitative and deterrent utility as mundane and deficient as the human nature which renders them necessary, for not even through the implementation of each in perfect measure would their necessity be obviated. Nevertheless, laws such as these can be said to be among the noblest aims of punishment. But they do not exhaust punishment's aims.

The Stranger's version of penal law, at its lowest and perhaps most ignoble level, finally reaches down to touch beasts of burden and inanimate objects.[19] By so specifying the law, the Stranger risks leaving himself open to questions on the inherent absurdity in his argument, but such questions never come. More fundamentally, the Stranger contradicts himself in the sense that he previously set down rehabilitation and deterrence as the goals of judicial punishment; beasts can hardly be rehabilitated.

But his argument concerning the beasts proves not to be quite the *reductio ad absurdum* it first appears. The Stranger follows it by enumerating the circumstances in which killers may remain unpolluted by sanction of the criminal law. They include matters as disparate as killing housebreakers and those who attack one's wedded wife. Capturing and killing either an errant animal or a housebreaker is unlikely to serve any high interest of the city *qua* city, much less be classified as noble. But such acts respond to human wrath and the need for revenge. Arguments of involuntariness, by equating virtue with knowledge, might be effective at mitigating this wrath in some cases, but perhaps not in the majority of them. The net of penal law must be cast very wide indeed, and should be permitted room to respond to the passions. Even "retributions from the gods" must form part of "the myth, or argument, or whatever it ought to be called" impelling individuals not to commit the heinous crimes that "presumably also would occur" in the best possible city.[20] The Stranger refuses to let criminal justice deny the ancient subterranean impulses that tug at the soul. The fatal flaw of reason is to see itself where it does not exist. Unless reason lowers itself, perhaps denies itself, in accordance with life as it is actually lived, it runs the risk of being forever held prisoner in a hall of mirrors.

One might encapsulate the primary or highest elements of the scheme of judicial punishment in the *Laws* by saying they point toward an education to virtue, which education is imparted to a soul that enjoys some freedom. In this sense, they reflect the argument of Protagoras that virtue is capable of being taught, and that he who would inflict punishment rationally does so not for the sake of a past wrong that cannot be undone.[21] They also reflect the argument of Socrates in the *Gorgias* that "The object of all punishment which is rightly inflicted should be either to improve and benefit its subject or else to make him an example to others, who will be deterred by the sight of his sufferings and reform their own conduct."[22] The *Laws* sets out to codify an important objective: if a man fails to run from intemperance and to condition his soul accordingly, "correction must be inflicted and the penalty paid if happiness is to be achieved."[23] However rational this aim, criminal sanctions can only strengthen that golden, ductile cord of reason in its battle with the Furies. In fact, "it is necessary always to assist this most noble pull of law because calculation, while noble, is gentle rather than violent, and its pull is in need of helpers if the race of gold is to be victorious for us over the other races."[24]

Plato's student, Aristotle, picks up on the ignoble nature of enforcing criminal sanctions. For him, the office "which is very nearly the most necessary as well as the most difficult ... [is] that connected with actions taken against persons found guilty or those whose names have been posted in notices, and with the guarding of prisoners."[25] There is an "odium" attached to this office such that "unless it is possible to make great profits, [men] will either not put up with being officials of this sort or, if they do, they will be unwilling to act in accordance with the laws."[26] Nevertheless, Aristotle insists that legal sanctions are needed for the purposes of deterrence and the rectification of ill-gotten gains.[27] Most tellingly,

Aristotle is much less inclined than Plato to blur the distinction between voluntary and involuntary action. For Aristotle, "if we have the power to act nobly or basely, and likewise the power not to act, and if such action or inaction constitutes our being good and evil, we must conclude that it depends on us whether we are decent or worthless individuals."[28] Aristotle sees clear reasons for distinguishing ignorance from incontinence:

> These conclusions are corroborated by the judgment of private individuals and by the practice of lawgivers. They chastise and punish evildoers, except those who have acted under constraint or due to some ignorance for which they are not responsible, but honor those who act nobly; their intention seems to be to encourage the latter and to deter the former.[29]

Thus for Aristotle ignorance is not a defense per se to criminal wrongdoing, for ignorance can itself be voluntary. The position of the *Laws* on this point is more ambiguous, but the argument on the whole is quite compatible with the Aristotelian view.

For Aristotle as for Plato, there is no "state of nature" in which man can exist or to which he may return. His nature is political or philosophic, his end is the virtuous life. Yet neither tolerable social interactions nor the pursuit of virtue are possible without an understanding of the innate capacity of man to be vicious as well as virtuous, and of the legal means that must be constructed to allow the pursuit of both community and virtue.

Before leaving the classical period, it is worth noting a remarkable political discussion recorded by Thucydides in his *History of the Peloponnesian War*. He records a debate over the punishment to be meted out by the Athenians to the rebellious Mytilenians. In addition to reiterating the intricacies of judgment that all regimes must confront when they punish, the debate introduces a new element to the equation. It is, from the point of view of a regime's authority to govern, a utilitarian element of the highest philosophical and practical import. Cleon argues that those in rebellion ought to be put to death because

> Their offence was not involuntary, but of malice and deliberate; and mercy is only for unwilling offenders.... To sum up shortly, I say that if you follow my advice you will do what is just towards the Mytilenians, and at the same time expedient; while by a different decision you will not oblige them so much as pass sentence upon yourselves. For if they were right in rebelling, you must be wrong in ruling.[30]

There is thus an inverse relationship between a city's unwillingness to exact punishment and the legitimacy of that city. If a city cannot or will not exact due punishment for the most serious assaults on its laws, it condemns itself to death. Cleon thus reminds us of a proposition of considerable logical as well as prudential power.

The Transition to Modernity

The first great expositor of penal theory in the modern era is Hobbes. He follows Plato to the extent his theory is utilitarian, i.e., insofar as he holds the view that the ends of punishment are future goods, generally rehabilitation or deterrence. But, as I have argued, there are elements of the thought of Plato that go well beyond conventional utilitarianism. So, if placing Plato and Hobbes in a single tradition of penal theory is not entirely spurious, neither is it particularly illuminating. The utilitarian view stands in contradistinction to the theories of Kant and Hegel that punishment ought only to be retributive in the sense of maintaining the balance on an abstract ledger of justice and injustice, regardless of consequences. At the most general level, "Theories of justification may be divided into the forward-looking and the backward-looking; the former finding the reason for punishment in its effects, the latter in its antecedents."[31]

In the Hobbesian world, atomized individuals naturally war against each other in the pursuit of their private interests. It is a world radically divorced from the classical one for the simple reason that, far from seeing in virtue a natural end toward which man tends or ought to tend, it reduces man's natural end ultimately to survival, resulting in the war of all against all. But Hobbes's vision is not entirely divorced from the classical world in its sense of the nature of just punishment. While starting from different premises, and designing the laws to suit different ends, Hobbes comes to familiar conclusions on the substance of state-inflicted punishments: "And seeing the end of punishing is not revenge, and discharge of choler, but correction, either of the offender, or of others by his example; the severest Punishments are to be inflicted for those Crimes, that are of most Danger to the Publique."[32] In this statement, Hobbes captures the essence of his penal scheme. It is one that confines itself strictly to elements of rehabilitation and deterrence. Wrath and revenge play no part, for they are not perceived to be in the interests of the sovereign. The scheme contemplates the maintenance of peace, which is always in the true interests of the sovereign and the people, "For the good of the Soveraign and the People, cannot be separated."[33] It is a peace maintained by a system of rewards and punishments geared to what men can understand. "The aym of Punishment is not a revenge, but terrour."[34] Thus, while it can be said that education to virtue plays no part in the aims of criminal law for Hobbes, the basic elements of that law are quite recognizable.

Other elements of Hobbes's scheme also parallel classical theory. "A Crime arising from a sudden Passion, is not so great, as when the same ariseth from long meditation."[35] He even sees the importance of what, in Platonic terms, would be a prelude: "The Perspicuity, consisteth not so much in the words of the Law it selfe, as in a Declaration of the Causes, and Motives, for which it was made. That is it, that shewes us the meaning of the Legislator."[36] Of course, in the Hobbesian conception, the meaning of the legislator is always a constricted one.

Rousseau is by far the most interesting innovator with respect to the Hobbesian view of punishment. He, too, can be viewed as a utilitarian in the sense his doctrine is forward-looking, denying the retributive aspect of justice. For Rousseau, even revenge is a social construct, man possessing no natural cruelty.[37] Since men are naturally good, it is impossible to imagine them warring against each other in a Hobbesian fashion. To the extent men do engage in war, they have been taught to do so. In his natural state, man is a sentimental being, purely. He is as far from the rational, calculating being of Hobbes's state of nature as it is possible to get. Starting from this romantic vision of innocence, Rousseau therefore posits a distinct hierarchy of utilitarian ends for the criminal law: first and foremost is the rehabilitation of the offender, followed, at a considerable distance, by deterrence. "There is no wicked man who could not be made good for something. One only has the right to put to death, even as an example, someone who cannot be preserved without danger."[38] This formulation stands in sharp contrast to Plato's notion that many wrongdoers are simply incurable and must be dealt with accordingly. Rousseau deals with the issue of effective deterrence, and the human demand for retributive justice, by ignoring them. In fact, it seems the main reference to deterrence in Rousseau is actually a call for effective preludes, which serves also as a searing indictment of Hobbes:

> The power of laws depend even more on their own wisdom than on the severity of their ministers, and the public will derives its greatest influence from the reason that dictated it. It is because of this that Plato considers it a very important precaution always to place at the head of edicts a well-reasoned preamble which shows their justice and utility. Indeed, the first of the laws is to respect the laws. Severity of punishments is merely a vain expedient thought up by small minds in order to substitute terror for the respect they cannot obtain.[39]

So both Hobbes and Rousseau echo some aspects of the classical tradition's "utilitarian" or "forward-looking" theories of punishment, but they differ substantively from each other and from the classical tradition as a whole.

Distinct from them, but not entirely distinct from the classical tradition, are the retributive theories of criminal justice of Kant and Hegel. As Hobbes and Rousseau are not entirely within the classical tradition based on their emphasis on utility, so Kant and Hegel are not fully outside the classical tradition because of their emphasis on retribution. One might say that the retributive aspect of justice, which for Plato reflects the irredeemably irrational or ignoble elements of political life, is fully rationalized in Kant and Hegel.

Both Kant and Hegel roundly denounce any view of punishment whose aim is other than upholding the moral law. For Kant, "The Penal Law is a Categorical Imperative; and woe to him who creeps through the serpent windings of Utilitarianism to discover some advantage that may discharge him from the Justice of Punishment." The abstract balance sheet on which this categorical imperative is calculated is "the Principle of Equality, by which the pointer of the Scale of Justice is made to incline no more to the one side than the other. It may be rendered by saying that the undeserved evil which any one commits on another is to be regarded as perpetrated on himself. … This is the right of RETALIATION … the only Principle which in regulating a Public Court … can definitely assign both the quality and the quantity of a just penalty."[40] For Kant, those who commit injustice are to be held responsible regardless of what preceded their actions, for reason can be regarded as a cause of behavior, and as essentially free.[41]

Hegel, in a further effort at rationalization, squarely addresses the distinction between retribution and revenge. In deeming the former to be a legitimate act of the rational state, and the latter an immoral act of the subjective will, Hegel distances himself from the *Laws'* codification of private vengeance. "When the right against crime takes the form of *revenge* … it is merely right *in itself*, not in a form that is lawful, i.e., it is not just in its existence. Instead of the injured party, the injured *universal* now makes its appearance, and this has its distinctive actuality in the court of law. It takes over the prosecution and penalization of crime, and these thereby cease to be the merely *subjective* and contingent retribution of revenge."[42] In Hegel, there is a positive *right* to punishment derived from the implied universal of the criminal's own action, and the necessity of bringing him under it. Accordingly, "in so far as the punishment which this entails is seen as embodying *the criminal's own right,* the criminal is *honoured* as a rational being. He is denied this honour if the concept and criterion of his punishment are not derived from his own act; and he is also denied it if he is regarded simply as a harmful animal which must be rendered harmless, or punished with a view to deterring or reforming him."[43]

The Liberal State

While Kant and Hegel are antithetical to Plato in their extreme rationalization of criminal behavior and their denial of the legitimacy of rehabilitation as an end of punishment, so too are they anathema to contemporary criminology insofar as it emphasizes, in the tradition of Rousseau, rehabilitation almost to the exclusion of other ends. James Q. Wilson and Richard Herrnstein argue that "Much of modern criminology, directly or indirectly, draws on Rousseau. It is indebted to him when it favors preventing crime through proper education and constructive social arrangements as well as when it prefers helping offenders by rehabilitation instead of preventing offenses by deterrence."[44] Even where modern criminology does not overtly advocate rehabilitation at the expense of deterrence, it advocates it as the primary means to that end. And it certainly advocates rehabilitation at the expense of retributive theories of justice, for what the criminal has done can never be undone. No matter how spurious modern rehabilitation theory might appear in light of recidivism rates and other factors, few of those treated by its tenets are ever deemed incurable. That the soul can be hopelessly out of balance, incapable of proper habituation, is an idea that has become, in the face of contemporary social science, the exception rather than the rule.

To the extent that some combination of state and society is viewed as being at the root of criminal conduct, a reverse habituation, in the form of reformation, is always implied. Standing the *Laws* on its head, the new criminology calls for a de-habituation. There are no injustices consequent on an unbalanced soul because there is no soul in the first place; thus there are no primordial "unexpiated injustices" to be contained. Rather, the only injustices to be expiated are those incurred in virtue of participating in the social life of the community.

Clarence Darrow, lawyer par excellence of the Progressive Era, remains one of the most direct and optimistic American spokesmen for this point of view:

> Nearly every crime could be wiped away in one generation by giving the criminal a chance. The life of a burglar, a thief, of a prostitute, is not a bed of roses. Men and women are only driven to these lives after other means have failed. Theirs are not the simple, natural lives of children, nor of the childhood of the world; but men and women can learn these professions or be

> bred to them. . . . Men are slow to admit that punishment is wrong, and that each human soul is the irresponsible, unconscious product of all that has gone before.[45]

The sentiments of Darrow and other progressive thinkers have many manifestations. They appear in the liberal state's near-obsessive concern with a complex mapping of the backgrounds and capacities of offenders, who are understood less as moral agents and more as pieces of flotsam bobbing on an ocean of antecedent causes. These concerns are the focus of attention in criminal courtrooms throughout the developed world. They are invariably justified on the basis of "fairness," but one cannot help but notice the deeper Rousseauian naturalism and determinism they incorporate, emphasizing as they do history and culture rather than nature.

The reality this modern theory of punishment chooses to ignore is the existence of the Furies, which the ancients knew so well. When a criminal is perceived to escape justice because his subjective condition, determined by exogenous cultural factors, prevents him from being properly punished, the very fabric of social life is directly attacked. Likewise, we have all borne witness to the anguish that descends on individuals and communities when a convicted felon, rehabilitated or deemed sufficiently "cured" to be released, once again wreaks havoc on innocent citizens. The justice system – the state itself – is viewed as impotent and incompetent. Under such circumstances, the more general bonds that join the individual to the polity cannot help but be strained. As the political sociologist Robert Nisbet noted, "Of all changes in recent American history, the most macabre and chilling is the breakdown of one of mankind's oldest and most salutary communities of will and purpose: that of crime and punishment. . . . In the community of crime and punishment there was a functional reciprocity between the deed and the punishment; the first aroused the thrill of horror; the second the thrill of retribution." There might never have been a rationalized reciprocity in the German philosophic tradition, but there was a "functional" reciprocity of retribution – an inadvertent but necessary means of sating the human wrath that Plato knew could not be avoided. In the stead of this community of retribution, there is in our age, according to Nisbet, "only the pseudo-community of sickness, victimization by society, and therapy."[46]

Groaning under the weight of decades of progressive thinking on such matters, the American polity currently finds itself in an untenable position. On the one hand, it seeks to deny the golden, ductile cord of reason that is at the heart of human culpability. On the other, it flees from the irrational elements of the soul that demand from the criminal law something more than mere utility. This is the paradox of contemporary penal theory, a theory that today seems on the verge of ignoring the lesson of Cleon that a regime that cannot punish cannot govern.

Lack of the ability to govern is perhaps the ultimate lot of regimes that fail to come to grips with the most fundamental fact that must be known by a wise legislator: "we aren't in the same position as were the ancient lawgivers who gave their laws to heroes, the children of gods . . . we're humans, and legislating now for the seed of humans."[47] Put another way, modernity, in its quest for the unlimited political and social horizon, has substituted idolatry for reason, seeking to reap the godlike powers that first tempted man when he ate from the forbidden fruit. It is instead reaping the whirlwind.

With good fortune and the grace of God, I will enjoy many more years of thinking about the directions of that whirlwind – and how best to contain and reverse the havoc it continues to wreak. And I will do so in concert with my teacher and dear friend, Charles.

Cicero: Statesman and Teacher of Statesmen

TIMOTHY W. CASPAR

MARCUS TULLIUS CICERO (106–43 BC), the ancient Roman philosopher, statesman, and orator, reached the pinnacle of Roman politics in 63 BC when he served as consul. A *novus homo* or "new man," he was elected to this highest and most prestigious office at the youngest legally permissible age. During his term of office, he was hailed as *pater patriae*, or father of his country, for successfully uncovering and foiling the revolutionary and murderous plot of the disaffected nobleman Lucius Sergius Catilina. On leaving office, Cicero was at the zenith of his fame and reputation. And yet a little over four years later, in early 58 BC, Cicero found himself at a political nadir – exiled from his beloved Rome and living in Greece. Ostensibly, exile was punishment for actions he took as consul, when, with the backing of the senate, he oversaw the execution of several of the Catilinarian conspirators without a trial. In fact, he was the victim of a vindictive political opponent, the tribune Publius Clodius Pulcher, acting as an agent of what is popularly known as the First Triumvirate – Pompey, Crassus, and Caesar.[1]

Following his death, Cicero's reputation in the West

experienced a similar rise and fall, reaching a peak in the late Middle Ages and Renaissance – Dante refers to Cicero as a philosopher multiple times and calls him Rome's "best Aristotelian"[2] – and continuing through the Enlightenment and the American Founding. Following a sustained and devastating attack launched in the nineteenth century by Hegel and his historicist students, whose ancient Roman hero was the world-historical figure of Caesar, Cicero's reputation declined rapidly and by the early twentieth century was in tatters. Scholars viewed Cicero as worthy of study only because of his role as an eclectic transmitter of the knowledge of his predecessors. D. R. Shackleton Bailey exemplified the lasting impact of this view when, at the turn of the twenty-first century, he wrote in the introduction to the Loeb Classical Library edition of *Letters to Atticus*, of which he was the editor and translator, that Cicero did not have "any pretensions to original thought" but rather "put the ideas he found in his Greek sources into elegant Latin."[3] Cicero's great value was in preserving and passing on to the West the ideas of the dominant philosophical schools of his day.

Nevertheless, just as Cicero eventually returned triumphantly from exile, landing in Italy in August 57 BC and then feted on his way back to Rome where he was greeted by adoring crowds, so did his philosophical reputation begin to undergo a gradual recovery starting in the second half of the twentieth century. The number of articles and books published since that time – and especially in the past generation or so – that take him seriously as a philosopher in his own right is remarkable.[4] Perhaps the least likely to be surprised by the vicissitudes of his posthumous reputation would have been Cicero himself, just as he would have been the most likely to foresee that the cycle of ups and downs he had experienced over the course of his political career would not end with his return from exile.

Cicero knew that such changes or cycles – whether of political fortunes or philosophical reputation – were endemic to human life.[5] Indeed, not long after his return to Rome he found himself defending the interests of the First Triumvirate, who, in their continuing struggle for individual preeminence at the expense of the common good, greatly damaged the tottering republic Cicero had worked so hard to save – not to mention the fact that they had been responsible for his exile in the first place![6]

How could Cicero have justified his actions on behalf of this gang of three? The question of consistency becomes even more pressing given the fact that during this same decade he penned some of his greatest works of political philosophy. He set forth his views on the best orator in *De oratore* (*On the Orator*), who possesses a broad range of knowledge and uses it to guide his republic through his speech.[7] In *De re publica* (*On the Republic*), he outlines the best kind of republic, and in *De legibus* (*On the Laws*), he considers the legislation required to bring about that best republic. The latter two books, along with the subsequent *De officiis* (*On Duties*)[8], are Cicero's three most political works, which taken together elucidate his natural-law teaching. While many politicians excuse apparently unprincipled actions on the grounds of necessity or self-interest, someone like Cicero – the great proponent of natural law – does not have that luxury. Rather, Cicero seems to have acted in a way that deliberately violated his understanding of natural law, making him at best hypocritical, at worst duplicitous and insincere.

Cicero attempted to explain himself in a December 54 BC letter to his fellow aristocrat Lentulus Spinther. His letters to Spinther were written, as D. R. Shackleton Bailey observed, "in as elaborate a style as his published works,"[9] and in this particular missive he defends his actions on the ground of Aristotelian prudence, the characteristic virtue of the statesman, whose task is to aim at a fixed end while adapting his methods to changing circumstances. Cicero writes that he is not

> for sticking fast to one set of opinions (*una sententia*), when circumstances have changed and the sentiments of honest men (*bonorum*) are no longer the same. I believe in moving with the times. Unchanging consistency of standpoint has never been considered a virtue in great statesmen (*re publica gubernanda viris*). At sea it is good sailing to run before the gale, even if the ship cannot make harbour; but if she can make harbour by changing tack, only a fool would risk shipwreck by holding to the original course rather than change and still reach his destination. Similarly, while all of us as statesmen (*administranda re publica*) should set before our eyes the goal of peace with honour (*cum dignitate otium*) to which I have so often pointed, it is our aim (*spectare*), not our language (*dicere*), which must always be the same.[10] (Glosses added.)

Given Cicero's reference earlier in the same letter to "our favorite Plato" (*Platonem nostrum*),[11] the sailing analogy might have prompted Spinther to recall another nautical image in Plato's *Republic*. In that book, Socrates portrays the philosopher as the "true pilot" of a ship full of sailors who ridicule his piloting knowledge as "useless" and who spend their time fighting among themselves for control of the ship.

The quarreling sailors represent "the statesmen now ruling" who care only about the struggle for political power but lack the knowledge required for just rule.[12] Cicero in his letter thus casts himself as one of the true pilots of the republic whose knowledge is essential for bringing the ship of state safely into port, but whose expertise and counsel are unappreciated by, or even seem inexplicable to, his shipmates.

The image of the prudent statesman as a pilot or helmsman of the republic recurs throughout Cicero's writings from this period, not only in his letters but also in his speeches and in his philosophical works.[13] Just as Cicero in his letter to Spinther conjures an image of himself as a pilot steering the republic safely through stormy waters, in his philosophical writings he sketches a picture of a master helmsman of the republic guided by the natural law, the lodestar of all just political communities. This correspondence suggests that if we want to understand Cicero's actions as a statesman, it would be helpful to consider his philosophic ideal of statesmanship.

He presents the main features or characteristics of this ideal in *De re publica*, the central book in a catalogue of thirteen of his philosophic works that he provides in *De divinatione* (*On Divination*).[14] The list begins with *Hortensius*, the now-lost exhortation to philosophy, and ends with *Orator*, which considers the idea of oratorical eloquence. This order implies that the best republic serves as the link between philosophy and rhetoric, between philosophy's timeless principles and the application of those principles to ever-changing political circumstances through the statesman's oratory.

One notable aspect of *De re publica* is the ambiguous nature of its presentation of the best way of life. Cicero begins with a preface in his own voice, offering one of the most robust defenses of the active life in classical philosophy. He is quite emphatic: "[V]irtue depends wholly upon its use. And its greatest use is the governance of the city and the completion in fact, not in speech, of the same things as these men shout about in corners." What "the philosophers" spend their time talking about, at least what they say "correctly and honorably," has been "accomplished and strengthened by those who have configured laws [*ius*] for cities."[15] Cicero is not thinking here of mundane or trivial laws, such as "the law about rainwater falling from the eaves of houses," which he scoffs at in *De legibus*.[16] Rather, his concern is laws laid down by founders and preservers of republics: "There is nothing in which human virtue more nearly approaches the majesty of the gods than either founding new cities or preserving ones that are already founded."[17] The case for the active life seems to be open and shut.

Yet this is not Cicero's final word on the matter. Having staked out a position that he says was necessitated by his rhetorical goal – he did not want his "argument about the republic" to "be in vain" so he "first had to remove doubt about entering public life" – he admits that there are some who have aided their republic through their thinking and writing about politics. He is now addressing those who remain unpersuaded by his oratorical barrage, but are still "moved by the authority of the philosophers." If they insist on pursuing the contemplative life, Cicero urges them to look to the example of those who may not have "managed the republic themselves" but who have nevertheless "performed some service for the republic because they have inquired, and written many things, about the republic."[18]

Thus Cicero's ire was directed only against those philosophers who "shout" in "corners" while contributing nothing, or nothing worthwhile, to the common good. These would have included the Epicureans, though the stricter Stoics would not have escaped the charge either.[19] However, he leaves the door open to philosophy that concerns itself with political things, to political philosophy. Those who think and write well about politics and provide prudent political guidance are performing their own statesmanlike service. When it comes to the question of the best way of life, Cicero thus offers two options: that of the statesman and that of the political philosopher. Insofar as the statesman acts upon the advice of the political philosopher, the political philosopher becomes a statesmanlike teacher of statesmen. Cicero, Academic skeptic that he is,[20] characteristically avoids an explicit endorsement of either option, though he does say that he has pursued both "simultaneously" in his own life.[21]

Cicero's ideal pilot or statesman first comes to sight later in the first book of *De re publica* when, in the midst of a discussion of revolution, the character Scipio Aemilianus says,

> There are wonderful cycles and, as it were, revolutions of changes and alterations in republics. While it is for the wise man to know them, it is for some great citizen and almost divine man, while governing (*gubernanda*) the republic, to foresee those that threaten and to direct (*moderantem*) its course and keep it in his power.[22]

The helmsman of the republic must be a "great citizen and almost divine man" who has the ability to govern or steer while being tossed about in the stormy waters of the cycle of regimes. In the midst of revolutionary change, his task is to direct or moderate that change.

Cicero emphasizes the importance of the moderating role of the statesman when in the following sentence Scipio introduces his notion of the best republic. Having assessed the strengths and weaknesses of the three simple types of republic – monarchy, aristocracy, and democracy – he concludes "that a certain fourth type of republic should be most approved, which is a moderation and mixing together" of the three simple forms.[23] This "moderately mixed constitution" takes advantage of the virtues of the simple republics and mitigates their vices. The constitution and the statesman will work in tandem to moderate the various claims to rule, with the goal of justice for the whole political community and not just a part.[24]

The statesman's moderating influence is not limited to traditional legislation – he must also act as a teacher of his fellow citizens. When Scipio mounts a defense of each of the simple "modes" of republic from the point of view of the partisans of each mode, he first treats democracy, then aristocracy, and finally kingship. What is distinctive about aristocracy is the rule of virtue, and, Scipio asks, "[W]hat can be more splendid than virtue governing (*gubernante*) a republic?" Through his invocation of the pilot image, he links his defense of aristocracy as the rule of virtue to the earlier image of the statesman as pilot of the republic. In the best republic, the leading men will not only compel their fellow citizens by means of legislation, they will also teach them through precept and example. Because each of the aristocrats "is a slave to no desire," all those things "in which he instructs his fellow citizens and to which he summons them" are things he has "embraced" himself, and "he puts forward his own life as a law for his own citizens."[25] In other words, the statesman's oratorical instruction and personal example together constitute a sort of informal law to supplement the formal kind. The statesman not only wields power but teaches the kind of virtue that is essential for the perpetuation of the best republic.

Scipio confirms the central importance of the statesman's virtue when he endorses the mixed republic for the third and final time as superior to the three simple forms.[26] Its superiority rests on the fact that it "has been brought to a condition of equilibrium, and tempered from the three primary modes of republics." This even-keeled republic embodies a moderate mix of three elements: "something preeminent and regal," "the authority of leading men," and "the judgment and will of the multitude." The "combined, moderately mixed constitution of the republic" is "usually" not susceptible to revolutionary change, although no human government is completely immune to it. The most effective antidote is the inculcation of virtue in the rulers who will in turn guide the entire republic toward virtue. If instead of virtue there "are great vices [*vitium*] in the leading men," then even the mixed republic is in serious danger of being overturned.

In the second book of *De re publica*, Scipio again invokes the image of the statesman as pilot or helmsman, though this time not during an abstract discussion of regime types but in the context of an idealized history of the Roman Republic. At the end of the first book he claimed that the republic "that our fathers received from their ancestors and left to us from that time ... is the best," and that consequently their "own republic" would be "explained as a model" to which he would "tailor" his "entire speech ... about the best form of the city."[27] Now, to understand how Rome could be such a model – what Walter Nicgorski calls "the best exemplification among actual regimes of the best practicable regime"[28] – he turns to examine Roman history.

Scipio's idealized account of Rome's first six kings overlooks or obscures a number of uncomfortable aspects, such as the fratricide at the country's foundation. However, he has no such reservations about criticizing Lucius Tarquinius Superbus, Rome's seventh and final king. Scipio offers an unstinting assessment of his turn from kingship to tyranny, "the lowest type" of regime.[29] Indeed, "no animal more horrid, foul, or hated by gods and human beings can be thought of than" a tyrant.[30] His sketch of the tyrant's dark and repulsive vices stands in stark contrast to his portrayal of the statesman's virtues and has the salutary effect of throwing a bright light on those virtues.

Scipio begins his account of regime change by alerting potential statesmen that they "must learn to recognize from the beginning" the "natural motion and revolution" of the "circle" (*orbis*) of republics, a study that is the "source" of their "political prudence," which virtue is the subject of "this entire speech." If the statesman can "see the paths and bends of republics" and knows "how each thing inclines," he "can hold it back or run to meet it first."[31] This exhortation recalls Scipio's earlier comparison of the statesman to a pilot, tasked with foreseeing regime "cycles" (*orbes*) and acting to moderate them.[32] He returns to the image here in the second book after the tyrant Superbus emerges.[33]

By summoning the pilot as a kind of mediator between the rise of tyranny and the subsequent birth of the Roman Republic, Cicero implies that statesmanship at the highest level involves the founding or re-founding of republics. Also worth noting is the fact that the tyrant makes his "appearance" not in the abstract dress of Scipio's theoretical consideration of the simple republics but only after donning a

Roman toga. The interlocutors have "discovered" the "origin of a tyrant" in an actual city, not in the city in speech that "Socrates himself depicted" in Plato's *Republic.*[34] While Cicero frequently acknowledges his debt to Plato, he also insists on his independence. He may imitate the title and the dialogue form, but the content is distinctively Ciceronian.[35]

With Rome in the hands of the worst kind of tyrant, the cycle has turned, and Scipio introduces his political savior. It is true that, in a nod to Plato, the helmsman who will stand in opposition to the named tyrant is unnamed, and in that sense is an abstract figure. Yet it is the legendary Roman statesman Scipio who summons him to do his work. The unnamed statesman may be a timeless and universal figure, but he operates only within a specific political context; any republic in any time that finds itself in crisis should seek this man's aid:

> Let there be opposed to this man another, who is good, wise, and knowledgeable about the advantage and reputation of the city, a protector and manager (*tutor et procurator*), so to speak, of the republic. Let those be the names for whoever will be a guide and helmsman (*rector et gubernator*) of the city. Make sure you can recognize this man, for it is he who can protect the city by judgment and effort.[36]

In his preface, Cicero says the "greatest use" of virtue "is the governance (*gubernatio*) of the city," and later he chastises those "educated men" who refuse "to govern (*gubernare*) ... in a tranquil sea" but nevertheless believe they could "approach the helm (*gubernacula*) during the greatest floods."[37] Cicero there hints at what Scipio here makes explicit: the statesman, the preeminent practitioner of political prudence, is akin to the pilot or helmsman of a ship. Yet that is not all. Scipio adds several key elements, pairing "helmsman" (*gubernator*) with "guide" (*rector*) and "protector" (*tutor*) with "manager" (*procurator*).

Scipio's use for the first time in *De re publica* of the word *rector* links this passage to later passages that further elucidate "the type to which this human being belongs."[38] Insofar as this human type embodies a combination of the apparently equal qualities of guide (*rector*) and helmsman (*gubernator*), this passage also links the statesman of *De re publica* to his institutional home in the senate as described in *De legibus*. In *De legibus*, the character Marcus says that the senate should serve as the "master of public deliberation" and that the republic should "be governed (*gubernari*) by the deliberation of the leading order."[39] His use of the verb *gubernari* indicates that the human type who will populate the senate will be the *gubernator* and *rector* of the *De re publica*.

In Scipio's republic, the senate is at the helm and composed of senators who are "without every vice." Indeed, "no one who has a share in vice will even come into that order."[40] It is essential that senators exhibit virtue, because the senate as a whole will serve as a "model" for – and so shape the character of – the other orders of the republic, whether for good or for ill. Marcus observes that just as the "leading men" of a republic have "regularly stained" it by their "desires and vices," so they have also "regularly improved and corrected [it] by their self-control."[41] The greatest task of the *rector* and *gubernator* is to lead the republic away from vice and toward virtue, which he will accomplish not only by means of legislation but also through the powerful example of his own character. As Marcus says of the Roman past: "[W]hatever was the quality of the highest men of the city, such was the city." What follows is a lesson for the future: "[W]hatever change of customs emerges among the leading men, the same will follow among the people."[42] Demonstrating just how important character is, he makes an explicit break with Plato's emphasis on the role music plays in regime change. In contrast to "that divine man," Marcus believes "that the customs of cities change along with changes in the nobles' lives and ways."[43] As the character of the leading men goes, so goes the republic.[44]

Marcus emphasizes the statesman's role as a teacher, which points to Scipio's statesman, whose titles include *rector* and *tutor*. Often translated as "guide" and "protector," both words also have the connotation of "teacher."[45] Scipio later explicitly agrees with Marcus regarding the importance of good character: the statesman must ensure "that he never cease instructing and observing [*contemplari*] himself, that he call others to the emulation of himself, that he show himself to his fellow citizens as a mirror through the brilliance of his spirit (*animi*) and life."[46] Through his own virtuous example, the statesman will encourage a life of virtue.

Scipio returns to this theme in the fragmentary fifth book, where he again compares the statesman to the pilot of a ship. Just as "a favorable course" is the goal of the "helmsman" (*gubernatori*), so also the "director" (*moderatori*) of the republic aims at "the happy life of citizens," whose happiness consists above all in the fact that they are "honorable in virtue."[47] Whether we call him a *moderator, rector, gubernator, tutor,* or *procurator* (Cicero likes to say that he often uses more than one word to refer to the same thing in order to clarify its meaning),[48] his goal is the same – the inculcation of virtue, an essential ingredient in the happy life of the republic. Scipio adds: "I want him to be the perfecter of this work, which is the greatest and best among human beings."[49] While the founders and preservers of cities exhibit the kind of "human virtue" that most closely "approaches the majesty of the gods," as Cicero said in the preface, the perfecting or teaching of virtue, which for human beings is the "greatest and best" work, is essential to the success of their political enterprise.[50]

In everything he does, Cicero's statesman aims to secure justice and the common good, the two goals that originally brought the political community into being, guided all the while by a higher or natural law.[51] While Cicero's focus is on the natural-law statesman who rules in an actual regime, i.e., Rome, he is not unaware of the Platonic alternative, which is proposed and rejected by the interlocutors of *De re publica,* at least as a standard for the best republic.[52] Consider that the theoretical conversation about the apolitical topic of astronomy at the opening of the dialogue leads to a definition of the natural law virtually indistinguishable from Socratic natural right and in a subsequent disparagement of politics. If, as Scipio says, "the common law of nature ... forbids that anything belong to anyone except to him who knows how to handle and use it," then it follows that there is no political office or power "more preeminent than a man who looks down on all human things and regards them as inferior to wisdom."[53] But Scipio's dear friend Laelius responds by chastising him for caring more for things about which "we can know nothing" – even if we could, we would not be "better or happier" – than he does for his own divided and troubled city. His reprimand has its intended effect, and Scipio agrees to a discussion "about the republic."[54]

In the third book of *De re publica,* the book devoted to a

discussion of justice, it is Laelius who offers a political definition of natural law, the standard against which all conventional laws should be measured: "True law is correct reason, congruent with nature, spread among all persons, constant, everlasting. It calls to duty by ordering; it deters from mischief by forbidding." Nature – fixed, universal, and timeless – is the source of this law. As Laelius says, there is "one law both everlasting and unchangeable [that] will encompass all nations and for all time."[55] The statesman's task is to obey the law's commands and prohibitions while applying them to his particular political circumstances.

Likewise in *De legibus*, Marcus defines a natural law that will guide the promulgation of the law codes he says are necessary to bring Scipio's republic into being[56]: "[L]aw is highest reason, implanted in nature, which orders those things that ought to be done and prohibits the opposite."[57] This definition differs from Laelius's, though the identification of law and reason, as well as the ruling authority of nature, remain central for both. For Laelius, natural law is "correct reason" that is "congruent with nature." For Marcus, it is "highest reason" that is "implanted in nature."

What explains this difference? In Laelius's account, the natural law is the only kind of law, and insofar as there is "one god" who is the ultimate source of nature, he "will be the common teacher (*magister*) and general (*imperator*), so to speak, of all persons." For Laelius, the "one god" apparently rules directly over "all persons": he is said to be "the author (*inventor*), umpire (*disceptator*), and provider (*lator*) of this law."[58] By contrast, Marcus the legislator must distinguish between higher and lower laws, between "highest reason" and lower forms of reason. In other words, he introduces the notion of a hierarchy of laws, which the prudent statesman is especially well qualified to rank. Consequently, Marcus equates law with "the mind and reason of the prudent man."[59] He has "implanted" law or "highest reason" in the nature of a statesman who gives voice to the natural law, just as the magistrates who rule in the mixed republic give voice to his natural-law legislation.[60]

While Scipio and Marcus agree that the statesman should hew to a natural-law standard, all too frequently, as in the case of the First Triumvirate, human beings reject the dictates of reason and seek their own self-interest at the expense of justice and the common good. As Scipio admits, "the nature of republics itself often overcomes reason."[61] In such a situation, how should a pilot of the republic respond?

Both Scipio and Marcus address this question through a consideration of the office of the tribunes. While they agree that the institution's establishment marks a decline, both defend it as the best possible outcome given the circumstances. Scipio sees the episode as a case study in both failed and successful statesmanship. Prior to the crisis that sparked the plebeian demand for formal representation, the republic was properly mixed: "all things were maintained by the leading men possessed of the highest authority, as the people yielded."[62] However, the leading men failed to maintain this proper mix, which requires "an evenhanded [*aequabilis*] balancing of rights, duty, and service, so that there is enough power in the magistrates, enough authority in the deliberation of the leading men, and enough freedom in the people."[63] They did not take the necessary steps – as leading men of the past had done – to alleviate the crushing debt disproportionately and unjustly burdening the people. They were not prepared with the appropriate "medicine" to restore the "health of all," because they "overlooked" the need for a "plan" to resolve the crisis. Consequently, "a cause arose for the people," who demanded tribunes "in order to diminish the power and authority of the senate."[64] The senate had failed to act in its role as doctor of the body politic to cure what ailed it, thereby initiating a turning of the political "circle."[65]

Nevertheless, due to its outstanding virtue, the senate's guiding authority "remained heavy and great, with the wisest and most courageous men in arms and deliberation protecting the city." Indeed, Scipio says the senate's authority "greatly flourished" at this time because the senators, who possessed the greater share of honor, "had a smaller share of pleasures and a hardly larger one of wealth." In addition, in "private matters" each senator worked "most diligently" to protect "individual citizens."[66] Far from being diminished, the leading men enhanced their authority through a combination of wisdom and courage in their public roles and moderation and justice in their private lives. The institution of the tribunes may have made the republic *de iure* more democratic, but this concession to the plebeians, combined with the great public and private virtue of the leading men, had the result of making the republic *de facto* more aristocratic. Although the tribunes represent a decline in principle, their establishment preserved the "harmony" of the "orders" essential to the republic's health; given the circumstances at the time, this was the best possible outcome.[67]

Marcus offers precisely this defense in response to a vehement and lengthy attack on the tribunes by his brother Quintus. What really galls Quintus about an office that "arose in sedition and for sedition" is the effect it had on the standing of the leading men. It "snatched away all honor from the Fathers," "made all the lowest things equal to the highest," and "demolished the weight of leading men."[68] In response, Marcus chastises his brother for unjustly cataloging the institution's "defects" without acknowledging "the good things" it wrought. Even the consulship itself, an office held by leading men, would not escape censure if it focused only on the flaws of those who have held the office. Though Marcus does not agree with his brother's wholesale condemnation, he "confess[es] that there is something bad in that power itself." Nevertheless, he urges Quintus to be mindful of the fact that "without this bad we would not have the good that was sought in it." What is more, the alternative is worse. True, the tribunes have too much power, but that is greatly preferable to the ferocity and ardor of the "violence of the people."[69]

In an actual republic such as Rome, in which the leading men – and the people – are not fully virtuous and not without flaws, the establishment of the tribunes embodies the kind of "political prudence" that the *rector* and *gubernator* must possess.[70] This prudent act should not be condemned but praised as an example of "our ancestors' wisdom (*sapientiam*)," a demonstration of the kind of political wisdom needed to save the mixed republic in times of crisis. As Marcus says, "When the Fathers conceded this power to the plebeians, the weapons fell, the sedition was extinguished, a compromise was found so that the less important men thought that they were equalized to the leading men. In that one thing was the salvation of the city." The Fathers' "compromise" was redeemed by the fact that it restored harmony to the republic.[71] Scipio and Marcus agree that such a compromise may not be perfect, but, insofar as it is the best possible choice given the political circumstances, it should be considered truly wise.[72]

Likewise, Cicero's actions on behalf of the First Triumvirate represented a prudent acknowledgment of the necessary constraints within which he would have to operate if he hoped to affect the direction of Roman politics. Though he may not have had his hand directly on the tiller as he did when he was consul,[73] he could help to pilot the ship of state through the exercise of his political influence. As Cicero knew all too well, he was not living in Plato's *Republic* or even Scipio's, but rather in "Romulus' cesspool."[74] Thus, political success depended on "the goodwill of the powers that be" (*potentium benevolentiam*).[75]

Cicero's comparison of himself to the pilot of a ship in his letter to Spinther demonstrates a consistency of thought in his private and public writings on the theme of statesmanship. The pilot image also connects his political actions to the kind of political prudence that is a central theme of his philosophical books on the best republic and its laws. Like his characters Scipio and Marcus, Cicero understands that his political situation is not perfect; indeed, far from it. However, like them, he also understands that his task – the task of every statesman – is to help steer the republic as best he can. The serious study of Cicero's words and deeds reveals timeless lessons about political prudence that are applicable in every age. Such a study is therefore essential for anyone who aspires to be a philosophical statesman or a teacher of statesmen.

The Messiah of the Machiavellian Moment

The Reluctant Tyranny of the Good Man in the Corrupt Republic

Murray S. Y. Bessette

Niccolò Machiavelli's reputation remains controversial in part owing to the perceived discontinuity between "the politics of *The Prince* and the values of the *Discourses*."[1] The politics of the former are literally Machiavellian, subject to blame and not to praise. Those casually acquainted with his works, including "many people who have never read him," would identify him as the source of the political principle that "the end justifies the means."[2] That nearly every political problem has the same homicidal solution; that the ultimate guarantee of the safety and security of princely rule so often involves the death of one, few, or many; that Machiavelli seems "to teach maxims of public and private gangsterism," has given rise to the view that at best Machiavelli is "a teacher of evil," and at worst he "was an evil man."[3] This view of the prince of princes extends even to his republican teaching. According to this view, often associated with the Straussian School, Machiavelli's is a "rapacious" republicanism wherein the people are deceived by the elite concerning their respective "rule" within the regime.[4] In short, Machiavelli's modern republic is republican in appearance, but oligarchic in reality. Those friendlier to the philosopher, most notably the scholars associated with the Cambridge School, perceive Machiavelli's republicanism as a continuation of the classical tradition.[5] In their story, the character of Machiavelli appears praiseworthy, as a partisan of civic (or citizen) virtue dedicated above all to the cause of liberty.[6] If some in the Straussian School see the politics of *The Prince* dominating the values of the *Discourses*, then those of the Cambridge School see the values of the latter leading to a rejection of the politics of the former. Neither school, however, adequately wrestles with the puzzle "posed by Machiavelli's repeatedly claiming that if one wishes to create or maintain 'a republic in corrupt cities,' then 'it would be necessary to turn it more toward a kingly state than toward a popular one' (*Discourses* I.18), despite his adoption, throughout most of his writings, of a staunchly pro-popular government stance."[7] Nor does John P. McCormick, who has ventured a populist or democratic interpretation of Machiavelli that portrays him as a partisan of the people over and against the patrician elite – Machiavelli not as modern, but as contemporary.[8] Ryan Balot and Stephen Trochimchuk correctly note that "revisionist accounts" – such as those provided by McCormick and Miguel Vatter – fail to help us "confront the untimely challenges of past thinkers," and instead "often reinforce our prevailing sensibilities or dominant prejudices."[9] I would add that such reinterpretations merely elide the problems they claim to resolve. The controversy that surrounds Machiavelli's reputation cannot be resolved by bringing him up to date; rather, one must pin down precisely why a philosopher dedicated to liberty would at the same time counsel tyranny.[10] To put this another way, one must ask whether there is a fundamental continuity between the politics of *The Prince* and the values of the *Discourses*.

Roger D. Masters is undoubtedly correct when he states, "Because Machiavelli so openly endorses republican regimes in the *Discourses*, if he is consistent, *The Prince* must also contain a republican political teaching despite its superficial endorsement of autocratic princely rule."[11] But the logic of his statement cuts both ways. If Machiavelli is consistent, then the *Discourses* too must contain an autocratic princely teaching. To solve this puzzle the following essay generally approaches Machiavelli's teaching in the *Discourses* from the perspective of its addressees: good men. More particularly, it examines this teaching within the specific context of what John Pocock terms the "Machiavellian moment," which is "the moment in conceptualized time in which the republic was seen as confronting its own temporal finitude, as attempting to remain morally and politically stable in a stream of irrational events conceived as essentially destructive of all systems of secular stability."[12] According to Pocock, the Machiavellian moment – that is, the moment when one is faced with a corrupt republic containing a corrupt people – calls for the "Machiavellian Messiah," the "paradoxical figure of a leader who 'heads' a headless body that desires not to be ruled."[13] In sum, by explicating Machiavelli's advice for the good man – which, to state it briefly at the outset, is that the good man must seize rule within the corrupt republic with the intent of reestablishing a civil and political way of life; that is, the good man must become Machiavelli's Messiah – the following will reveal the fundamental continuity between the politics of *The Prince* and the values of the *Discourses,* or rather, it will show that Machiavelli is consistent by placing his politics at the service of his values.

The Political Reluctance of Good Men

Machiavelli addressed the *Discourses* "not [to] those who are princes but those who for their infinite good parts deserve to be" (Letter).[14] That there are those who deserve to be princes but are not raises the possibility of those who are princes but do not deserve to be – the addressee of *The Prince.* It is the "infinite good parts" of the *Discourses'* addressees that make them deserving of rule, which indicates a connection between goodness and political merit. That good men deserve to rule highlights the connection between politics and justice; that they might not rule while the undeserving rule in their stead highlights the limits of the realization of justice in political life for both the individual and the city. Since the addressees are not princes but private individuals, as such they have the time to read, unlike princes who only have time for a short treatise.[15] Although they live a private life, they nevertheless are interested in political things; they "forced" Machiavelli to write the *Discourses* (ibid.).[16] The philosopher qualifies this: he was not so much "forced" as "encouraged" to undertake the "enterprise" despite its "difficulty"; there is freedom in Machiavelli's undertaking (I.Preface.2). Similarly, The *Discourses* seeks to encourage those who are deserving of being princes to undertake freely a difficult enterprise that the nature of politics and men nevertheless will force them to do. "Men of quality," such as those to whom the *Discourses* is addressed, live "in continual danger" (III.2.1). They cannot "say: 'I do not care for anything; I do not desire either honors or useful things; I wish to live quietly and without quarrel!' For these excuses are heard and not accepted" (ibid.). Good men, men of quality, excellent men, cannot choose to abstain from politics because they are "not allowed to abstain by others" (ibid.). For them politics is like nature: *administrationem expellas furca, tamen usque recurret.*[17] The private lives of the addressees, thus, cannot remain so. Politics will enter their lives in one of two modes: either such men will be "constrained to be princes" (III.5.1), or princes will constrain them "either to distance [themselves] from or to bind [themselves] to them" (III.2.1). (The former mode almost never occurs[18] – a notable and important example thereof, however, is Timoleon of Corinth.) As a result, good men must choose the character of their relation to politics (i.e., to both the princes and the peoples of their cities); to fail to choose is to fail to be free and to be a subject of necessity. The teaching of the *Discourses* seeks to guide this free choice.[19]

From the outset, Machiavelli shows his awareness of the reason why his addressees are content to be private men: "the envious nature of men" results in their being "more ready to blame than to praise the actions of others" (I.Preface.1).[20] As a first effort to overcome his young friends' reluctance to engage in the troublesome activity of politics that arises from envy, Machiavelli appeals to their "good parts." He speaks of his own "natural desire ... to work, without any respect, for those things [he] believe[s] will bring common benefit to everyone" (ibid.), that is, of his own overcoming of the reluctance caused by the envious nature of other men. Machiavelli's point is that the "respect" – and by implication the "envy" – of certain men is, or at least should be, irrelevant to good men. Good men ought to be content with the possibility that their efforts on behalf of the common good "could bring [them] reward through those who consider humanely the end of [their] labors" (ibid.). In tacitly appealing to "the mode that all things from friends are taken, where one always considers the intention" (Letter), Machiavelli subtly identifies whose respect ought to matter: that from other good men, for one cannot possess complete friendship except with one's peers.[21] He calls on his friends to imitate the works of the great political men of the past as he himself is imitating the works of the great authors of the past. He calls on them not simply to admire but also to imitate "the most virtuous works the histories show us, which have been done by ancient kingdoms and republics, by kings, captains, citizens, legislators, and others who have labored for their fatherland" (I.Preface.2).

Founding as Re-Founding

The greatest among these acts, that which generates the greatest honor by providing the greatest common good (security), is founding a city.[22] Machiavelli invokes this example in the first chapter, the heading of which indicates that he will treat the universal "Beginnings of Any City Whatever."[23] His adding "and What Was That of Rome" leads one to question whether Rome is an exception – which it turns out to be. While "all cities are built either by men native to the place where they are built or by foreigners," both a foreigner and a native built Rome: Aeneas chose the site; Romulus ordered the laws (I.1.1; cf. I.1.5). In immediately including Numa (I.1.5), who reordered the laws of

Romulus when they were found to be insufficient "for such an empire" (I.11.1), Machiavelli indicates "opportunity" is not confined to that which fortune provided to Moses, Cyrus, Romulus, or Theseus. One need not build the city to be a founder thereof; one can be a founder of a city by maintaining it.[24] Perhaps rather than speaking of founders and maintainers, it is more appropriate to speak simply of re-founders; every founding, insofar as it begins with and reforms people who are preexisting and, thus, informed by a particular regime, is a re-founding.[25] The matter limits the form that may be impressed thereupon, the orders that may be arranged therein, or, at the very least, the modes by which this can be completed (cf. I.17; I.18; I.25; I.26; I.55).[26]

Rome, thus, was a republic that was given laws "by chance and at many different times" (I.2.1). In every city there is "some degree of unhappiness," and as a result it "is forced by necessity to reorder itself" (ibid.), a task both difficult and dangerous. "[B]ecause enough men never agree to a new law that looks to a new order in a city unless they are shown by a necessity that they need to do it," a people must be constrained for the founder to be free (ibid.; cf. I.1.4).[27] The task of maintaining a regime entails understanding its degeneration (or corruption) with an eye toward its future regeneration (or re-founding), and thus presupposes an understanding of the cycle of regimes. Machiavelli's account of this cycle reiterates that security is the origin of cities (I.2.3).[28] The people come together to place one at their head.[29] This elective principality soon becomes hereditary. Machiavelli explains the reason for this change: from "the fact that the fathers of such have been great men and worthy in the city, . . . it is believed that their sons ought to be like them" (III.34.2). The shift from choice to succession diminishes the freedom of the people: no longer can they choose "the one who would be more prudent and more just" (I.2.3). The end result of this transformation is that "at once the heirs [begin] to degenerate from their ancestors" and "tyranny quickly [arises]" (ibid.). The people together with the powerful subsequently rebel and establish an aristocracy. This in turn falls prey to the problem of "hereditary exhaustion," whereby the government of those few who care only or mostly for money arises, resulting in rebellion and the birth of the popular state.[30] Hereditary exhaustion undoes this state as well: "once the generation that had ordered it [is] eliminated ... it [comes] at once to license, where neither private men nor public [are] in fear, and each living in his own mode, a thousand injuries [are] done every day" (ibid.). With the corruption of the popular state the people again finds itself dispersed and, like beasts, without common standards.[31] Machiavelli now for the first time introduces the "good man" and equates him with the founder: "So, constrained by necessity, or by the suggestion of some good man, or to escape such license, they [return] anew to the principality" (ibid.; cf. I.58.4). He indicates the action the good man takes when faced with a dispersed (thoroughly corrupt) people:[32] the good man reintroduces a political or civil way of life by moving the people from the licentious form of popular government to principality through providing new common standards; he does not reintroduce the popular form.[33]

What is a Good Man to do?

Machiavelli's account of the cycle of regimes raises two questions. First, is it possible to prolong the good and to abridge the bad intervals of the cycle? And second, must the good man wait until the people are thoroughly corrupt before he can act? The answer to the latter questions is no: "The desires of free peoples are rarely pernicious to freedom because they arise either from being oppressed or from the suspicion that they may be oppressed. If these opinions are false, there is for them the remedy of assemblies where some good man gets up who in orating demonstrates to them how they deceive themselves" (I.4.1). According to Machiavelli, the good man acts to check a free people when its desires are pernicious to freedom, that is, he acts to preserve its free character.[34] The acceptance of the good man's orations appears to rest not on the recognition of his goodness, but on the fact that he is "a man worthy of faith" (ibid.), which may point toward a religious foundation of authority (cf. I.54).[35]

If one individual can work such benefits for the public, could not more working together produce even greater public goods?[36] Recall that Machiavelli's addressees here in the *Discourses* are two, not one. Furthermore, they are the sole source of respect and potential reward for each other. It would seem natural that friends might wish to work together in a common enterprise, but as Machiavelli's examples imply, and as the heading to *Discourses* I.9 makes explicit, this capacity to benefit the public in this manner may require that one be alone, not one of few.[37] A necessary implication of this is that the good man (i.e., either of the particular addressees of the *Discourses*) must forego the companionship of other good men, at least insofar as they could have been *equal* companions in a common enterprise. The Machiavellian good man and his companions could mutually pledge to each other their lives, their fortunes, and their sacred Honor, but only if the enterprise were under his ultimate direction, were to "depend on his mind" (I.9.2). In the event his compatriots will not freely yield this preeminent position to him, if there is competition for the honor, as there was between Romulus and Remus, it is likely that the outcome will not differ from that example. Given the aforementioned reluctance of good men to engage in politics, perhaps this is unlikely to occur. Regardless, Machiavelli offers this advice and then excuses the necessary conclusion drawn: "So a prudent orderer of a republic, who has the intent to wish to help not himself but the common good, not for his own succession but for the common fatherland, should contrive to have authority alone; nor will a wise understanding ever reprove anyone for any extraordinary action that he uses to order a kingdom or constitute a republic" (ibid.). It seems the good and the wise are also friends, for the wise understanding examines and evaluates such actions by looking to the intent; the best intentions *always* excuse extraordinary actions, whether it is killing a brother or killing a good friend.[38] In the immediate sequel this excuse is characterized as "suitable," not just – perhaps because "knowledge of justice" arises not until laws are made, punishments ordered, and common standards established (I.2.3). The question of the maintenance of that which is ordered is taken up next, with the "prudent and virtuous" orderer delegating this responsibility to the many. The reason Machiavelli provides for entrusting this necessary function to the many is related both to the reason why a free people so easily falls under the sway of the authority of the good man and to the need of moving them toward something new: "For as the many are not capable of ordering a thing because they do not know its good, which is because of the diverse opinions among them, so when they have come to know it, they do not agree to abandon it" (I.9.2; cf. I.2.3 and I.2.1). It appears the prudent and virtuous orderer establishes principality to found a republic.[39]

The Good Must Anticipate the Bad

Lurking in the background of this discussion of the role of the individual of good intent is the issue of the individual of ill intent, the individual who acts "for his own succession" and not "for the common fatherland," who seeks to order not "a civil and free way of life" but "an absolute and tyrannical one" (I.9.2). Machiavelli brings this problem to the fore within the context of individuals who are praised and blamed. For our purpose the important contrast is between individuals "who have founded either republics or kingdoms" and the "squanderers of kingdoms and republics" (I.10.1). A good man might expect Machiavelli to contrast the founder with the tyrant, that is, the creator with the destroyer, as he does in the chapter heading; however, since every founding is a re-founding, properly speaking, every creation is also at the same time a destruction of that which was there previously. The founder and the tyrant share in both creation and destruction; it is in the end (i.e., their intent) that they differ. The political "sin" is not to destroy the kingdom or republic, but to squander it, that is, to hasten through the good period of the cycle of regimes instead of prolonging it by devolving the necessary task of maintenance upon the people.[40] Thus, Machiavelli tacitly answers the first question raised by his account of the cycle of regimes. To squander the kingdom or republic is to pave the way for tyranny; it is not to establish it. The wise understanding consists in seeing that "no one will ever be so crazy or so wise, so wicked or so good, who will not praise what is to be praised and blame what is to be blamed, when the choice between the two qualities of men is placed before him" (ibid.). Machiavelli is preparing the good man for a proposition: will he accept the necessary task of seizing rule within a kingdom or republic that has been squandered with the intent of reestablishing a civil and political way of life? If he will not take the opportunity, the man of ill intent will, and an absolute and tyrannical way of life will result (cf. the acts of Dionysius of Syracuse at the beginning of Plutarch's "Life of Timoleon").[41] As an incentive, Machiavelli highlights the glory associated with taking up this task: "And truly, if a prince seeks the glory of the world, he ought to desire to possess a corrupt city – not to spoil it entirely as did Caesar but to reorder it as did Romulus" (I.10.6).[42] But there is glory in the example of Caesar nonetheless. Perhaps Machiavelli seeks to imply that any order is preferable to the disorder of a corrupt city. Regardless, our author's criticism of Caesar is that he could have both reordered Rome *and* held the principality and, therefore, "he does not merit any excuse" for not doing so (ibid.).

There is something divine in the longing to be a founder. The individual simply "born of man" is "terrified" of the "wicked times" (ibid.): he longs for the peace and quiet of the "golden times when each can hold and defend the opinion he wishes" (I.10.5), and he does not see or does not desire the opportunity for glory that corruption presents. As Machiavelli further indicates, it is the "heads and orderers of religions" who are "most praised" (I.10.1). Recall that "a man worthy of faith" is most effective at checking the desires of a free people that happen to be pernicious to freedom (I.4.1). The authority of faith seems to depend upon the strength of religion within the people; the examples of Numa and Savonarola, however, demonstrate that it is a question of having enough virtue to ensure the people believe you when you pretend to be an intimate of the gods. In other words, the one who doubts of the sufficiency of "his authority" – or virtue – to introduce "new and unaccustomed orders" must have recourse to god if he is to be successful; while "his authority" is not sufficient for the end, it is, nevertheless, necessary to the means (I.11.2; cf. I.11.5).[43] The fear of god both depends upon and supplements the fear of man.[44] The appeal to religion depends upon the ability of the people to recognize virtue; since a corrupt people without common standards no longer possesses this capacity, one sees the necessity of necessity.[45]

A corrupt people, nevertheless, could obtain its freedom by accident – "as Rome acquired it after the expulsion of the Tarquins" (I.16.1).[46] The rape of Lucretia was accidental only insofar as it did not occur by necessity; that is, Sextus Tarquinius was not driven by necessity to conquer this particular woman's honor, but by lust, which in turn was aroused by her virtue.[47] It was necessary, however, that such an accident would eventually occur (III.5.1; cf. II.28).[48] The weakness of the prince provides the opportunity to the good man to seize rule provided he properly displays his virtue (cf. the actions of Brutus immediately following the suicide of Lucretia).[49] Virtuous actions, especially at such times, appear miraculous and have an attractive (or persuasive) force of their own.[50] In overthrowing the prince, "[w]hoever takes up the governing of a multitude" is faced with the choice of Caesar: to do so "either by the way of freedom or by way of principality" (I.16.4; cf. I.10.6). Brutus had to foreswear princely power in Rome; "to order [the] city well [he] had of necessity to lay down the principate," or rather not take it up in the first place (I.10.6). This was necessary in order to make the people friendly to him, for "[e]very man had his own complaint to make of the prince's crime and his violence."[51] The real lesson here is that the good man will of necessity have to eliminate those who benefited under the previous regime – even if they are his sons – and who, therefore, "are enemies to that new order" (I.16.4). Machiavelli then notes his departure from the subject of the chapter heading, shifting his discussion from those good men who take the way of principality to "those princes who have become tyrants over their fatherlands" (I.16.5). This is the thirteenth explicit reference to tyranny in the *Discourses*. Such a man "should examine first what the people desire; and he will always find that it desires two things: one, to be avenged against those who are the cause that it is servile, the other, to recover its freedom" (ibid.). The former is complementary to the need to kill the sons of Brutus; the latter is complementary to the longing to found. To see this complementarity "he should examine what causes are those that make [peoples] desire to be free," wherein "[h]e will find that a small part of them desires to be free so as to command, but all the others, who are infinite, desire freedom so as to live secure" (ibid.), which is to say, the few desire to oppress, the many desire not to be oppressed.[52] Recall it is the need for security that constrains the people at the end of the cycle of regimes (I.2.3); those who desire security "are easily satisfied by making orders and laws in which universal security is included, together with one's own power" (I.16.5). In other words, one satisfies the desire of the infinite many by bringing order.[53]

Murray S. Y. Bessette

The Character of the Man Gives Color to the Law

Machiavelli emphasizes the necessary role of the good man in creating a free people out of a corrupt one in the chapter "Having Come to Freedom, a Corrupt People Can with the Greatest Difficulty Maintain Itself Free" (I.17). This heading is a modified repetition of the previous one; Machiavelli replaces "a people used to living under a prince" with "a corrupt people," eliminates the role of accident, and increases the difficulty of the task at hand. Each of these modifications arises from a proper consideration of the two chapters: one cannot consider a people used to living under a prince simply as corrupt, for the Roman people was not corrupt (I.17.1); a corrupt prince who tyrannizes his people will eventually induce them to rebellion or conspiracy, as such this reaction is not accidental but necessary (I.16.1; cf. II.28, III.5.1, and III.6); and maintaining the freedom thus acquired requires an act of founding, which is the greatest political act. A corrupt city "without the creation of a new lord ... never settles down, unless indeed the goodness of one individual, together with virtue, keeps it free" (I.17.1). While our author says "such freedom will last as long as the life of that one" (ibid.) – with the city returning to tyranny with his death – the example he selects (Timoleon) proves otherwise.[54] At the end of Plutarch's "Life of Timoleon" we find the following words: "And they themselves [the people of Syracuse], using the civil polity and the laws which he [Timoleon] had ordained, enjoyed a long course of unbroken prosperity and happiness."[55] The settlement of a corrupt city requires the creation of a new lord; the character of the city, be it political and free or tyrannical and unfree, depends upon the character of the new lord, on whether he is a good and virtuous man or a tyrant. Corrupted matter (i.e., a dispersed, disordered people) requires ordering, but "where it is corrupt, well-ordered laws do not help unless indeed they have been put into motion by one individual who with extreme force ensures their observance so that the matter becomes good" (I.17.3). Good laws are not enough in themselves, "[f]or the prudent individual knows many good things that do not have in themselves evident reasons with which one can persuade others. Thus wise men who wish to take away this difficulty have recourse to God" (I.11.3). But as Machiavelli indicated earlier, the appeal to god ultimately is an appeal to virtue. Good laws require a virtuous founder to be effective – assuming the founder also rules. However, if the founder were to perish – like Caesar – then a forceful ruler would also be necessary. This greatest task – ordering or maintaining freedom in a corrupt city – is the subject of the next chapter. It is a subject "almost impossible to give a rule for" (I.18.1), because corruption, like disease, is infinitely variable. Just as many goods do not have evident reasons that can persuade others, so too unseen evils or evils that can only be "shown ... by conjecture" lack persuasive force (I.18.4). Once the evil is sufficiently developed so that all can see, it can no longer be addressed within the ordinary modes "since the ordinary modes are bad; [and so] it is necessary to go to the extraordinary, such as violence and arms, and before everything else become prince of that city, able to dispose it in one's own mode" (ibid.).[53] Machiavelli must disabuse the good man of his mistaken belief that goodness always or necessarily entails lawfulness. "Because the reordering of a city for a political way of life presupposes a good man, and becoming a prince of a republic by violence presupposes a bad man, one will find that it very rarely happens that someone good wishes to become prince by bad ways, even though his end be good, and that someone wicked, having become prince, wishes to work well, and that it will ever occur to his mind to use well the authority that the has acquired badly" (ibid.).[57] To be good is to follow good laws when they are present; to be "perfectly good" is to enter into "malice [when it] has greatness itself or is generous in some part" (I.27.1), that is, to provide and enforce good laws through extraordinary means when they are lacking. The good man also sees himself as a conservative, one who wishes to maintain or return to that which is or was good in the city. Machiavelli is teaching him: "From all the things written above arises the difficulty, or the impossibility, of maintaining a republic in corrupt cities or of creating it anew. If indeed one had to create or maintain one there, it would be necessary to turn it more toward a kingly state than toward a popular state" (I.18.5). In other words, "a *reversion*, a return in any sense or degree is simply not possible ... one *must* go forward";[58] the cycle of regimes only turns in one direction, as a republic becomes more and more corrupt, kingship becomes more and more necessary (I.2.3). Simply put, taking up an almost kingly power in a corrupt republic is necessary to further the good. Moreover, it is the lesser evil, for "[t]o wish to make [the people] become good by other ways would be either a very cruel enterprise or altogether impossible" (I.18.5).

The Second Coming: Re-Establishing Republican Values Through Princely Politics

The conservative character of the good man leads him naturally to prefer maintaining freedom within a free city (cf. I.10.5). As a free city is corrupted, it is necessary to make new orders as well as new laws (I.18.1; cf. I.18.4). Machiavelli treats this subject in the chapter entitled "He Who Wishes to Reform an Antiquated State in a Free City May Retain at Least the Shadow of Its Ancient Modes." Reform admits of degrees; it is limited by "the necessity of retaining at least the shadow of [the] ancient modes" (I.25.1) – how dark of a shadow must be retained is an open question. Setting that question aside, the would-be reformer must still contend with the fact that many good things and conjectural evils lack persuasive power (I.11.3; cf. I.18.4). Machiavelli's solution here – retaining the shadow of ancient orders – conceals the radical nature of what precedes its adoption: the kings were expelled before the consuls were created; the ancient way of life is suppressed prior to making the needed alterations. The only true option, then, is "to make an absolute power, which is called tyranny by the authors," in order to "renew everything" (I.25.1). Just as wishing to possess gives way to wishing to acquire (I.5), ordering a republic for narrow limits gives way to ordering a republic for empire (I.6), and as seeking not to be offended gives way to offending (I.46), so too wishing to maintain the freedom of a city gives way to the complete refounding of the city: "in sum, not to leave anything untouched in that province, so that there is no rank, no order, no state, no wealth there that he who holds it does not know it as from you" (I.26.1). Machiavelli counsels, "any man whatever should flee [these modes] and wish to live in private rather than as king with so much ruin to men. Nonetheless, he who does not wish to take this first way of the good must enter into this evil one if he wishes to maintain himself" (ibid.). But the difficulty for good men of keeping to private life, or rather the impossibility of their being allowed to keep to private life, is the reason why Machiavelli is teaching them that it is better to rule than to be ruled by worse men, and that the good men who recognize this ought to enter into rule "as a necessity and because they have no one better than or like themselves to whom to turn it over."[59] A certain author, moreover, has taught that reluctant rulers – such as these good men would be – lead to a freer and more secure government.[60] I suspect, given the character of his teaching, Machiavelli agrees. If good men were to follow Machiavelli, they would "desire good princes and tolerate them, however they are made" (III.6.1), that is, they would recognize that the extraordinary means necessary for the good prince to come to rule are legitimized by the political and civil order established thereby – "wherever the end is required, the means are authorized."[61] Inconveniences will develop within the city that do not warrant action on the part of good men; Machiavelli's example of such an inconvenience is the rise of a single individual in a republic (I.33.2). If a good man rises, other good men ought to tolerate his rule – in fact they should embrace it. The desire of good men *not* to rule, however, may result in an erroneous evaluation of rising men; good men may be prone to wishful thinking. The question, of course, is what is the good man to do when the individual who rises merely appears to be of good intent. Machiavelli teaches the good man to take the "much more secure policy" when faced with such circumstances: "to temporize with it [rather] than to attempt to extinguish it" (ibid.). It should be noted, however, that this teaching only holds when "the error is allowed to run on so far that it is a more harmful policy to wish to remedy it than allow it to continue" (ibid.). In other words, this teaching only holds when a mistake has been made, when the man "very expert in civil affairs" (I.33.3) has failed to recognize the danger early enough to snuff it out quietly. Sometimes the cure is worse than the disease, but not always; when it is not, "if you see you have enough to cure it, set yourself at it without hesitation" (I.33.5). Other times, by temporizing, diseases "are eliminated by themselves or at least the evil is deferred for a longer time" (ibid.). If the time is not ripe for action, or if the good man failed to recognize the ripeness of the time, Machiavelli does not want the good man to waste himself in futility; he wants him to have patience. Implicitly understood here is that the elimination of the inconvenience cannot be effected by ordinary modes. Thus, in doing good through the necessary extraordinary modes, the good man establishes a precedent that may provide future coloring for others to do ill (I.34.4; cf. I.46).[62] Such inconveniences arise as a direct result of the restlessness of men who "are wont to worry in evil and to become bored with good" (I.37.1), which leads to a desire for innovation, a "desire [that] makes the doors open to everyone who makes himself head of an innovation in a province" (III.21.2).[63] While temporizing with an inconvenience is a much more secure policy than extinguishing it once it has arisen, there is no more secure mode than anticipating the ways by which another individual will rise (I.52). In a corrupt republic this entails "favoring the collectivity" (I.52.2; cf. I.16.4); the good man must favor the collectivity so as to prevent another from doing so. One must pander to the people, otherwise the excellent man will be treated as an enemy out of "envy or . . . other ambitious causes" (II.22). In gaining the favor of the people, the excellent man cultivates the envy of the great; he must, therefore, seek "to eliminate the nobility," only then will he "turn to the oppression of the people" (I.40.5).[64] The elimination of the great serves a tripartite purpose: it cultivates the favor of the people, it eliminates those who are envious of this favor (cf. III.30), and it leaves one alone to dispose of the city in one's own mode (cf. I.9 and I.18).

In the final analysis, Machiavelli is encouraging the good man to be the inconvenience that arises in his corrupt republic since it is necessary both that inconvenience arise and that the effects thereof depend upon whether the individual is "good or bad" (I.35.1; cf. I.16, I.46, I.58.4, and III.1).[65] As such, he places the politics of *The Prince* at the service of the values of the *Discourses*. In teaching the good man, Machiavelli is also teaching the man of ill intent how to arise in his city – he advises the Machiavellian Messiah and Anti-Christ alike. In recognition of this, our author has provided incentives toward moderate rule; Machiavelli seeks to maximize freedom in every stage of the cycle of regimes. It is precisely because men are so easily corrupted (I.42) that one must come to understand how to reform a corrupt people, that is, how to make it once again good; for if a corrupt people cannot be reformed and cannot live free, then freedom ultimately will be extinguished and servitude will be the universal condition.[66] The good man must be shown that the orders of every republic, once they have become corrupt (and corrupt they will become), are insufficient to reconstituting a free people (cf. III.1.2); the good man is the necessary condition – so too is the wise man, assuming Machiavelli is wise. In teaching the good man, Machiavelli seeks to make him the good *and* wise man (cf. III.30.1).[67] Such a man, however, is not sufficient unto himself to reform a corrupt people in his own time. Fortune may prevent him from acting – what is the good man then to do? Machiavelli claims this as his situation: "For it is the duty of a good man to teach others the good that you could not work because of the malignity of the times and of fortune, so that when many are capable of it, someone of them more loved by heaven may be able to work it" (II.Preface.3). In communicating the good that he knows to the good men to come, Machiavelli shows "that fortune does not have power over" him (III.31.1); while he could not work this good in his lifetime, nevertheless, he is the ultimate source of the freedom that will arise again.

"Wind up the untuned and jarring senses"

Shakespeare's King Lear *as* Psychologia Kai Psychagogia

Glenn Ellmers

Homer and Hesiod ... created for the Greeks their theogony; it is they who gave to the gods the special names for their descent from their ancestors and divided among them their honors, their arts, and their shapes."

Herodotus, *History*, 2.53

The legislator has to learn to understand men by studying the poet. Otherwise he will be a very poor legislator.

Leo Strauss, *On Plato's Symposium*, 173

In his writings on Shakespeare, David Lowenthal was fond of quoting the words inscribed on Shakespeare's gravesite monument in Stratford:

JUDICIO PYLIUM, GENIO SOCRATEM,
ARTE MARONEM:
TERRA TEGIT, POPULUS MAERET,
OLYMPUS HABET.

Him who was Nestor by his judgment, Socrates by
his genius, Virgil by his art:
The earth covers, the people mourn,
Olympus possesses.

Can this extravagant praise be defended? In this essay, I offer an interpretation of *King Lear* as the psychological key to Shakespeare's dramatic universe that might offer some justification for this claim. It is commonplace to regard *King Lear* as the greatest tragedy of the greatest English poet, perhaps the greatest poet simply. In what follows, I suggest that *Lear* is Shakespeare's most Platonic play, and the one that unlocks his highest ambition.

As with the Platonic dialogues, each of Shakespeare's plays has a place within a larger, coherent whole. Unlike *The Tempest, King Lear* is not autobiographical. And while Lear is a great king, Shakespeare's models of statesmanship and magnanimity are probably more to be found in *Coriolanus* and *Henry V*. Apart from the history plays, Shakespeare's political views are perhaps explored most fully in *Othello* and *The Merchant of Venice* considered alongside *Julius Caesar* and *Antony and Cleopatra*: Shakespeare's political philosophy bridges the ancient and modern worlds. Nor is *Lear* the most philosophical play; that designation perhaps goes to *Macbeth,* Lincoln's favorite and the only one (as Leon Craig has noted) in which the word *metaphysical* appears. Yet for all that, *King Lear* is the play where Shakespeare displays his greatest poetic powers because, as I wish to argue, it is the unparalleled emotional and psychological effect of this drama that creates in his audience the soul-turning experience necessary for his vast project. Numerous scholars in the Straussian orbit have drawn out the political content of Shakespeare's dramas, including many fine commentaries on *King Lear*, which I won't recapitulate here. What has perhaps been neglected is the possibility that, as with Plato, the medium is part of the message. My purpose in this essay, then, is to suggest that Shakespeare's arguments are inseparable from the artistry of his dramas. Properly developed, this thesis would require a book. This essay must suffice for the present purposes as an introduction and overview.

Two observations by Harry Jaffa supply a launching point for these reflections. The first appears in his most wide-ranging essay on this topic, where Jaffa claims, "Shakespeare's deepest intention [is] to be the poet-philosopher of the English-speaking peoples, the teacher of its citizens, statesmen, and legislators."[1] The second is from "The Limits of Politics: An Interpretation of Act I, scene i of *King Lear*." Jaffa notes:

> One might paraphrase Machiavelli by saying that the founders of religions are the true founders of civil society; Numa, rather than Romulus, is the founder of Rome. Another expression of the same thought, which is classical as well as Machiavellian, is that to found a state is an act of human virtue, but to perpetuate it requires divine assistance. It is the thesis of this essay that Lear's incomprehension of this truth was his tragic flaw.[2]

Despite many commentaries on *King Lear* that have drawn upon Jaffa's essay, no one has ever developed or even (as far I can determine) remarked upon this astounding statement.

"Wind up the untuned and jarring senses"

Puzzles about the play

King Lear exacts a heavy psychological toll on its readers and viewers, which some find not only exhausting but disorienting. Critics have identified many features that seem odd or even inexplicable. Paul Cantor has observed, "As convinced as critics are of the greatness of *King Lear* as a work of art, they evidently have a hard time giving an account of the play that explains that greatness."[3] The eminent nineteenth-century Shakespeare scholar A. C. Bradley famously described the play as "too huge for the stage." There is, he claimed,

> something in its very essence which is at war with the senses, and demands a purely imaginative realization. It is therefore Shakespeare's greatest work, but it is not what Hazlitt called it, the best of his plays; and its comparative unpopularity is due, not merely to the extreme painfulness of the catastrophe, but in part to its dramatic defects. ... For this reason, too, even the best attempts at exposition of *King Lear* are disappointing.[4]

Bradley notes that the play is not only unsettling, but often leaves one feeling "bewildered." Time and location are frequently indeterminate. He concludes that perhaps Shakespeare "deliberately chose to be vague." Lear's prehistoric British kingdom has a dreamlike quality. The plot is tremendously rich, but the details often seem to tumble together, such that even attentive readers find it hard to reconstruct the orderly progression of the action. Thus, says Bradley,

> the number of figures, events, and movements, while they interfere with the clearness of vision, have at the same time a positive value for imagination. They give the feeling of vastness, the feeling not of a scene or particular place, but of a world; or, to speak more accurately, of a particular place which is also a world. This world is dim to us, partly from its immensity, and partly because it is filled with gloom; and in the gloom shapes approach and recede, whose half-seen faces and motions touch us with dread, horror, or the most painful pity – sympathies and antipathies which we seem to be feeling not only for them but for the whole race.

These features not only "inspire in us emotions of unusual strength, but they also stir the intellect to wonder and speculation. How can there be such men and women? we ask ourselves."[5]

One commentator has even found a kind of postmodern absurdism in the play's jarring mathematical distortions: the play is "notable for the prominence of mathematical language, and for the imprecision of that mathematical language. *King Lear* presents its textual information in such a way that all experience of it, from inside or outside the play, renders logical coherence impossible."[6]

Although the dramatic action centers on the question of succession and the kingdom's perpetuation, the words *posterity, eternal/eternity,* and *immortal/immortality* never appear. Everything, as Sylvia Bigliazzi notes, takes place "in the now."[7] Both the kingdom and its families are disturbingly barren. Lear not only has no sons, but no grandsons, and in fact no grandchildren at all. Though neither Goneril nor Regan is a newlywed, there is no indication that either has ever been pregnant. (Consider Lear's curse at I.vi.)[8] Lear's wife is dead and Gloucester's is never mentioned. The play is entirely devoid of motherhood. In the final scene, when virtually all the major characters are expired, Edgar's only claim to the throne is as Lear's godson; there is no one in the royal house left to wed. The single enlargement of a family that occurs, apart from the marriage of the doomed Cordelia, is a union of two of the vilest characters, when Edmund is effectively adopted by Cornwall.

So intense is the emotional suffering of the major characters, that more than a few critics have found a nihilistic message in the play. Though Shakespeare makes Christianity an explicit theme in many other dramas, Lear's kingdom is overtly pagan. Yet numerous commentators have seen a story of Christian redemption, perhaps in order to salvage what would otherwise be a sense of unrelenting despair. Themes and language about "nothing," "never," "nobody," and "no cause" recur constantly. Convention is ruthlessly repudiated or discarded; stripped and naked bodies reveal man as a "bare, forked animal." Yves Bonnefoy, the most eminent French interpreter of Shakespeare, writes: "Nature herself appears shaken and drawn into the vortex; her own convulsions beat physically upon the unprotected, and symbolize the moral storm afflicting a chaotic world . . . "[9]

In fact, with the exception of *Hamlet,* which serves as its counterpoint, *King Lear* is unique in depriving its audience of seeing the normal moral order vindicated. All the evil characters perish, but so do most of the virtuous ones – including Cordelia, whose death is so wrenching and apparently unnecessary that otherwise discerning readers see it as an inexplicable dramatic failure. Pervasive dissatisfaction with Shakespeare's final scenes led Nahum Tate in the late seventeenth century to create a fraudulent but highly popular replacement ending, in which Cordelia lives and marries Edgar – an emotionally satisfying fraud that gratified audiences for 200 years. We consider below whether Shakespeare had good reasons to prefer his own version.

Shakespeare as political thinker

Almost six decades since the publication of Allan Bloom and Harry Jaffa's *Shakespeare's Politics*, it is now well established that Shakespeare was a keen student of politics and a philosophically astute thinker. Like Machiavelli, he was interested in how Christianity, as the universal religion of the West, contributed to what Leo Strauss called the theological-political problem. John Alvis notes that in terms of diagnosis, Shakespeare and Machiavelli seem to be in substantial agreement. Christianity

> elevates the life of passivity, humility, and contemplation of other worldly rewards over the life of spirited activity, politics, and honor-seeking in this world. Christianity thus disposes men more to suffer than to perform deeds of strength. Machiavelli argues that Christianity makes men servile in two ways: first, by diverting hopes of happiness toward an afterlife, Christian piety weakens our devotion to the here-and-now; second, by extolling the nobility of patiently enduring one's lot in life, Christian teaching discour-

> ages men from undertaking a manly contest with fortune.... The political consequence of this outlook is that contemporary Europe finds itself exposed to the mischief of wicked rulers who alone accept the invitation to enter upon a struggle with fortune....

In the way he portrays the "acquiescence of Christian realms to usurpers, tyrants, or corrupt rulers," Shakespeare appears to "focus upon the same malady Machiavelli had claimed was afflicting Christendom."[10] But whereas "Machiavelli would loosen moral restraints, Shakespeare's play appears to intend a strengthening of Christian audiences by teaching the dangers of passivity." Machiavelli may be seen as anticipating certain aspects of Nietzsche's critique that "Christianity is called the religion of pity. Pity stands opposed to the tonic emotions which heighten our vitality: it has a depressing effect."[11] Alvis argues that Shakespeare aims to ameliorate some "defects of Christian education by offering as models of conduct" characters that combine spirited patriotism and magnanimity. "Shakespeare may have thought his Christian audience required an education that would revive a proper care for things of this world [and] a deeper regard for their earthly city."[12] Alvis devotes a fine book to showing how Shakespeare resurrects an understanding of honor that celebrates classical nobility commensurate with Christian sensibilities.

These claims would be remarkable enough for many nineteenth-century critics. Yet, I would argue that even this does not quite capture the full scope of Shakespeare's genius. His poetic art, especially his use of tragedy, represents a unique form of philosophic rhetoric and "indirect rule."

Glenn Ellmers

Philosophic Poetry

I propose to supplement the many excellent commentaries on Shakespeare's political thought with an argument that has four main parts:

- Socratic and Christian devaluing of the body, elevation of the mind or soul, and emphasis on the primacy of the eternal suggest that grief is unreasonable. But tragedy loses its power and essential public function when death loses its sting.

- Plato assumed that popular belief in the gods and their role in upholding the prephilosophic view of healthy politics is natural to man and would always be with us. He did not foresee the extent to which Socratic philosophy, with its rational, cosmopolitan theology, would contribute to destroying the ancient polis and its civic piety.

- Shakespeare, like Machiavelli, had a political project focused on certain political, moral, and even philosophic challenges posed by medieval Christianity. By modifying the classical understanding of tragedy, and developing his own form of poetic rhetoric, Shakespeare creates for the English-speaking world a superior cosmology – not laws (*nomoi*) as such, but what Plato calls "preludes."

- *King Lear* occupies a unique place in Shakespeare's dramatic universe. It aims to reach the whole soul, including those aspects beyond or below philo-

> sophic *logos*, to effect a radical reorientation or turning (*pyschagogia*), intended to counteract excessive universalism – both Platonic/Christian and Machiavellian – and rehabilitate the noble passions along with sacred honor.

Vile Bodies and Socratic Imperialism

In his long essay on Shakespeare's "moral universe," Jaffa remarks on a notable instance of Socrates laughing, which "comes near the end of the *Phaedo*, when Crito asks Socrates, 'How shall we bury you?'" Socrates responds mirthfully that they must catch him first, meaning that his true self cannot be buried. "The entire burden of the long dialogue in the prison, on the day of the execution," Jaffa writes, "is that the soul is immortal and that death is no more than a separation of the soul from the body."[13]

A similar attitude toward the mortal coil can be found in the New Testament, expressed perhaps most memorably by St. Paul, in his First Letter to the Corinthians: "O death, where is thy sting? O grave, where is thy victory?" Whatever the merits or flaws of Nietzsche's critique of Socratic rationalism, he was not wrong to argue that a powerful version of Platonism and Christianity glorifies the eternal as the true reality, over the transience of flesh-and-blood existence. Elaborating on the passage quoted above, Jaffa asks, "Are we invited to laugh at the death of Jesus?"

> Jesus' prayer to his Father, to forgive his persecutors – for they knew not what they did – reminds us of the Platonic-Socratic thesis that, since virtue is knowledge,

> wrongdoing is ignorance, and hence involuntary. The death of Socrates is not tragic, because there is no catastrophe – indeed, no suffering either – and hence neither pity nor terror in the spectacle of his trial or execution. But neither is there catastrophe in the death of Jesus if we take his death to be a necessary means to the glorious end of his resurrection. If, through his death, Jesus is united with the Father, even as Socrates is united with the Idea of the Good, death is for both a consummation devoutly to be wished.[14]

Both Socrates's rational cosmology and Christianity's One God of the universe stand in sharp contrast to the piety of the ancient cities. In the world of the *polis,* all gods were local – the founders and protectors of each particular city, and implacably jealous of alien gods. As Jaffa's teacher Leo Strauss explains in *What Is Political Philosophy,* "Plato replaces the law enforcing belief in the existence of the gods of the city of Athens by a law enforcing belief in the existence of the gods of the universe, thus laying the legal foundation for the freedom of Socratic philosophy, if not for the freedom of philosophy as such."[15] But this freedom of philosophy, Strauss suggests elsewhere, may have been "too successful."[16]

The overriding concern of the classical philosophers regarding belief in the gods seemed to be the irrationality and excesses of piety, which had to be tamed and refined in any properly constituted city. Strauss, however, seemed to wonder if that perspective gave sufficient weight to the central importance of the sacred or the holy in political life. In this respect, Thucydides may have understood the pre-philosophic perspective of citizenship better than Plato or Aristotle. (Athens won the Peloponnesian War, according to Strauss's interpretation of Thucydides, because its spirit conquered Greece and the world. I take that to mean the spirt of Socrates.) At the end of *City and Man*, Strauss says that Thucydides shows more clearly the "concern with the divine" that is primary "for us" as citizens. What is "first for us," Strauss adds, "is not the philosophic understanding of the city but that understanding which is inherent in the city as such, in the pre-philosophic city, according to which the city sees itself as subject and subservient to the divine in the ordinary understanding of the divine or looks up to it."[17]

When Plato discusses the varieties of regimes, therefore, Strauss notes that

> he never makes an observation about the differences between these regimes in regard to religion. I disregard now certain subtle observations which are uninteresting in terms of the broad observation. When Aristotle gives an analysis of the regimes, he takes for granted that there will always be religious institutions and a certain religious spirit. This matter is neutral to the differences between regimes. I draw your attention to this fact because it deserves really serious consideration. The notion of a secular polity, which, as polis, has no religious institutions, did not exist. I think this is a notion which does not come up until the modern era.[18]

Plato was certainly aware of the limits of reason in political life, and the need for myths or noble lies. Thus, while poetry's emotional and populist appeal is initially disparaged in the *Laws* and the *Republic,* in each work Plato revises his view through a second sailing, which offers a more subtle appreciation for poetry's virtues. Poetry's power to "charm" (a power that philosophic *logos* lacks), along with a keen insight into the human soul, means that at the highest level the poet can "legislate" – shape the authoritative opinions of the people – more comprehensively than the philosopher.

In his seminar on the *Laws,* Strauss remarks,

> Now Nietzsche said the poets are artists, have always been valets of a morality, of an established morality. That is what Plato means: the poets imitate that "truth," those opinions which the legislator authoritatively has laid down. He glorifies the ideals of a society merely because they are the ideals of a society.... I do not believe that this can be applied to the poetry on the highest level, and I think Plato knew that. Herodotus had said before Plato that Homer and Hesiod, so far from imitating ancient legislators regarding the gods, created the Greek theology. So the poets are not imitators of imitators but rather originators of such things, at least on the highest level. Now what then the difference [is] between philosophers and poets becomes a very difficult question....[19]

Yet Plato, in Strauss's judgement, nevertheless seems to insist in the end that the poetic art must remain ministerial to philosophic reason. In a 1958 lecture, Strauss explains that a good regime demands self-control and a certain equanimity toward mortal life. Thus,

> the most striking rule laid down by Socrates [in the *Republic*] is the prohibition against presenting the terrors of death and the suffering from the loss of a man's dearest. The poets are not permitted to state in public what they alone can state adequately when everyone else is made speechless through suffering, grief, or sorrow. They must write poetry on the principle that a good man, by virtue of his self-sufficiency, is not made miserable by the loss of his children, his brothers, or his friends. The poets may present the lamentations of inferior women and still more inferior men, so that the best part of the young generation will learn to despise lamentation.

Left to its own natural inclinations, poetry – and especially tragedy – "gives expression to the passions by poetically imitating the passions, it consecrates the passions." The "ministerial poetry" regulated by philosophic reason, "on the other hand, helps man in learning to control the passions."[20] In Nietzsche's view, this amounted to nothing less than the end of tragedy and its life-giving spirit. Strauss explains that according to this Nietzschean critique:

> Socrates' praise of knowledge means that the whole is intelligible and that knowledge of the whole is the remedy for all evils, that virtue is knowledge and that the virtue which is knowledge is happiness. This optimism is the death of tragedy....[21]

The spirit of tragedy, for the Greek poets, was inseparable from the religious outlook of the polis. In that world, "Divine power and authority – the basis of human law, morality, and politics – were not abstract and omnipresent, but were essentially local and emplaced," as David Janssens notes. "Literally, the law was experienced as being 'the law of the land': it assigned a proper place to both human beings and gods inside and outside the city."[22]

The regime of Socratic rationalism, including "Platonism for the masses" (Nietzsche's disparaging term for Christianity), vanquishes the spirit of tragedy and with it the pious patriotism of ancient citizenship. As Harry Jaffa notes, when republican Rome, in this respect still an ancient city, was replaced by Christian, imperial Rome – a universal regime with a universal religion – the public heroism of ancient tragedy was replaced by the private passion of the calculating administrator.

> It is from the ashes of Caesarism that the phoenix of Christian empire arises, the empire in which this-worldly rule is subordinated to the rule of another world. Shakespeare's understanding of the problem of honor is to be found above all in his understanding of the perplexity befalling human affairs when men's duties as husbands, fathers, and citizens are interpenetrated with their duties as citizens of the city of God.[23]

One more point before we return to Shakespeare, who differs from the Greek tragedians by being open to philosophy, and thus does not threaten "to seal the cave and then tell us that living in it is unbearable," as Michael Davis puts it.[24]

"Wind up the untuned and jarring senses"

Machiavelli

Plato's world-changing rationalism is the focus of a series of lectures Strauss gave in 1958 on "The Problem of Socrates." In the first lecture Strauss addresses the question of modern rationalism *vis-à-vis* its origins in classical political philosophy.

> The modern project stands or falls by science, by the belief that science can in principle solve all riddles and loosen all fetters. Science being the activity of reason par excellence, the modern project appears as the final form of rationalism, of the belief in the unlimited power of reason and in the essentially beneficent character of reason. Rationalism is optimism. Optimism was originally the doctrine that the actual world is the best possible world because nothing exists of whose existence a sufficient reason cannot be given. Optimism became eventually the doctrine that the actual world can and will be transformed by man into the best imaginable world, the realm of freedom, freedom from oppressions, scarcity, ignorance, and egoism, heaven on earth.[25]

This view would take a radical, and politically destructive, turn in modern philosophy and the utopian tyrannies of the twentieth century. But its roots run much deeper.

If Socrates and St. Paul turn the body into mere bone and sinew, Shakespeare refused to embrace the opposite extreme of seeing the human as nothing *but* bodies, which was the solution, in somewhat crude terms, of Shakespeare's great challenger. In his *Thoughts on Machiavelli* Strauss observes that it is possible to see elements of Machiavelli's teaching in Thucydides, because some

> find in both authors the same "realism," i.e., the same denial of the power of the gods or of justice and the same sensitivity to harsh necessity and elusive chance. Yet Thucydides never calls in question the intrinsic superiority of nobility to baseness, a superiority that shines forth particularly when the noble is destroyed by the base. Therefore Thucydides' *History* arouses in the reader a sadness which is never aroused by Machiavelli's books. In Machiavelli we find comedies, parodies, and satires but nothing reminding of tragedy. One half of humanity remains outside his thought. There is no tragedy in Machiavelli because he has no sense of the sacredness of "the common."[26]

In one sense, Machiavelli appears as the inveterate opponent of both Christianity and classical philosophy. Yet from another perspective, when Strauss refers to the sacredness of the common, we see that Machiavelli shares the universalist outlook that emerges with the death of the polis. Strauss several times comments on the Florentine's universal science of politics, including Machiavelli's observation that the common people are sensible on specific issues, but "sound judgment regarding particulars is impossible if it is not protected by true opinion about generalities."[27] This is not to dispute that political life is indeed governed by or subject to general or universal principles – as Shakespeare would certainly affirm by pointing to the permanence of human nature. The problem is rather that Machiavelli's depreciation of the soul and the sacred is too liable to treat the satisfied bodies of his new politics as merely interchangeable monads. As Strauss notes, Machiavelli's realism did not lead him to accept Thucydides' argument that pre-philosophic political life, as it appears to the citizen, depends on the sacredness of the common. Every citizen who is expected to make patriotic sacrifices must believe to some degree that *this* land and *this* regime is the holy city, the city of righteousness.

Shakespearean Tragedy and Sacred Place

According to Aristotle's *Poetics*, poetry is more philosophical than history, "For poetry speaks rather of the general things while history speaks of the particular things." But this does not mean that poetry is inherently abstract or generic, only that the poet is not bound by the necessities that limit human action in the real world. The poet's dramatic freedom allows him to display explicitly those broader lessons that history can only indicate by inference: for example, "that it falls to a certain sort of man to say or do certain sorts of things." To be effective, however, the tragedian must invoke specific people and places to reach the emotions and predispositions of the audience. It is this universality, Aristotle continues, that poetry aims for when using proper names: "the particular is what Alcibiades did or what he suffered." Therefore, the tragedians "cling to actual names. The cause of this is that the possible is persuasive." This credible realism requires characters and places the audience will recognize and empathize with, if the poet is to succeed in "the greatest things by which tragedy guides the soul [*pyschagogei*]."[28]

It is not surprising, then, that almost every Shakespearean

play is particular, replete with proper nouns: "a local habitation and a name" (*Midsummer Night's Dream,* V.i). Civic and religious obligations, loves and hates, wars and friendships, are guided by specific traditions and customs, and an underlying metaphysical theology or cosmology. The typical Shakespearean figure, as Alvis notes, "finds himself born into an order of authoritative opinion supported by political power. His neighbors share a public creed, declaring themselves hospitable to a given view of human and divine affairs and unfriendly to others."[29] *Lear* is a notable exception, a point I will address in a moment.

The emphasis on place and particularity is one element of Shakespeare's art. Another is the poet's ability to charm or enchant by appealing to the imagination. Tragedy allows us to see the truth "feelingly," as *Lear*'s Gloucester says. Strauss says that the gulf separating the philosopher from the *demos* or common people "can be bridged only by ... a certain kind of noble rhetoric which we may call for the time being accusatory or punitive rhetoric." Because philosophy is "incapable of supplying this kind of rhetoric" but can only "sketch its outlines, the execution must be left to orators or poets."[30]

I believe a version of Strauss's accusatory or punitive rhetoric appears in Shakespearean drama as an ethical and political pedagogy, compatible with robust Christianity, emphasizing what Jaffa calls "the inexorability of the moral order." This teaching appears with striking clarity in *Macbeth*. The title character, as Jaffa notes, is

> a man who is certainly proud, but who has demonstrated on the field of battle, in the face of temptation and treachery, that his great pride is justified by his great virtue. And it is his fall that we witness. More

> than that, we witness the inextricable intertwining of crime and punishment. There is no tincture of salvation resulting from Macbeth's crime – only damnation. . . .
>
> Macbeth's soliloquy in Act I tells us with perfect clarity why the murder must fail. The action that follows bears out the truth of that soliloquy. Not only does the plot fail, but neither Macbeth nor Lady Macbeth is allowed one moment of enjoyment of the fruit of their crime. Their punishment begins almost immediately with the murder.[31]

But this moral order is not merely punitive; it contains lessons in nobility, valor, and magnanimity – as well as good sense. Canvassing the primary literary influences on the habits and institutions of the Anglo-Saxon world, George Anastaplo argues that "Shakespeare was the one who probably provided early Americans with a comprehensive moral and political account of things." In the history plays, especially, they encountered an "entertaining instructor in constitutional principles, an obviously wise man who could teach them about the most important temporal things (just as the Bible was generally believed to guide them with respect to spiritual things)." Shakespeare died well over a century before the drafting of the American Constitution, but the way he "spoke about the things he described – the moral presuppositions underlying what he said – helped shape generations of Americans."[32]

For this teaching to succeed, Shakespeare must first reach his audience. "What if I could persuade you to let me go?" Socrates asks Polemarchus at the beginning of the *Republic*. "How can you persuade us if we won't listen?"

comes the reply. Shakespeare transcends the rational *logos* of the philosopher which can speak only to an aristocratic elite: Tocqueville saw the Bible and Shakespeare in many an American log cabin. The ability to charm or enchant makes Shakespeare's audiences willing and even eager to listen. This brings us then to the concluding point: Shakespeare's art as essential to his argument.

King Lear represents Britain itself – a powerful and even admirable monarchy. Yet "Britain" lacks the wisdom to ensure its perpetuation. Recalling Jaffa's remark at the beginning of this essay, Lear does not comprehend that perpetuation, even more than founding, requires divine assistance, i.e., a civil religion that not only unites the people, but instills the virtues and opinions necessary for political vitality. Lear is blind to the role of political theology because he cannot distinguish nature from convention: "They told me I was everything. 'Tis a lie" (IV.vi). As the Fool reminds him, he became old before he was wise. The play's second plot, which confounds so many critics, is essential because it shows the great danger to which the kingdom is exposed by its discredited religion, represented by the kind but feckless and superstitious Gloucester. The bastard Edmund, who in good Machiavellian style would create his own legitimacy, is the only character who appeals to nature as the source of law (I.ii). But Edmund's law of nature is the rule of "brains" and "manliness" – "the kind of virtue praised by Callicles in Plato's *Gorgias*."[33]

Shakespeare, I contend, wishes to counteract that danger, and provide Britain with the prudent and just civil religion it lacks – to make the regime of the English-speaking world wise before it grows old. Machiavelli's new modes and orders founded a new "moral continent," as Strauss notes: the modern era. But he has a rival. Anastaplo's observations above confirm Strauss's remark: the United States "may be said to be the only country in the world which was founded in explicit opposition to Machiavellian principles."[34] Yet Shakespeare's education, however moderate it may be in its political lessons, is in its own way as radical and demanding as the Florentine's solution.

"Off, off, you lendings!" – Lear's Psychagogia

What Jaffa calls Shakespeare's inexorable moral order, so persistently instructive in most of the plays, appears shockingly incomplete in *King Lear*. But the desolation and dislocation mentioned above, which critics and audiences alike have attempted to overcome through tendentious interpretations or even fabricated endings, serve a crucial purpose. Shakespeare reserved his greatest artistic effort for the play that goes furthest in stripping his audience of accepted opinions and emotional attachments, leaving them spiritually raw, as it were – reduced to a moral-political nakedness that is as painful yet as necessary as the *periagoge* of Plato's cave. Only through such a radical confrontation with, and break from, convention – enacted through Lear's anguished self-discovery in the storm – can Shakespeare cleanse or "purge" (in Aristotle's term) the souls of his audience, and prepare them for the revivifying education supplied in the other plays. Man's connection to eternity is then recovered, but grounded in the emphasis on particularity discussed above. (There is an important ancillary role for *Hamlet* in this scheme, discussed very briefly below.)

Such an ambitious goal can be achieved only if Shakespeare successfully navigates a narrow passage. His audience must connect with the play, find it sufficiently familiar and appealing, such that they will vicariously share in the characters' suffering and transformation. Yet he must be politic enough to leave his clues partially submerged. Directly assailing Elizabethan or Jacobean England and its subjects would be both personally reckless and dramatically obtuse. Thus, while Lear's kingdom is overtly British – indeed, at "a peak of prestige and political excellence," in Jaffa's words – it exists in the far distant pagan past, deliberately vague in many details. A longer treatment of this thesis would allow examination of many of the devices Shakespeare uses to advance his purpose. Let me mention only the Fool's prophecy about a future utopia (III.ii), which serves, via a joke, to establish an unmistakable connection with his audience:

> When priests are more in word than matter;
> When brewers mar their malt with water;
> When nobles are their tailors' tutors,
> No heretics burn'd, but wenches' suitors;
> When every case in law is right,
> No squire in debt nor no poor knight;
> When slanders do not live in tongues,
> Nor cutpurses come not to throngs;
> When usurers tell their gold i' th' field,
> And bawds and whores do churches build:

This gentle mockery of the England well known to his contemporaries offers some relief from the intensity of the play as a whole, by which Shakespeare seeks to expunge the excessive equanimity or dispassionate otherworldliness fostered by Plato and Christianity. As we read or watch the play, we feel Lear's suffering so keenly because Shakespeare wants to rehabilitate the natural feelings of grief over the death of those we love. Such grief, acknowledging the permanence and reality of death (which is diminished in Plato's *Republic* and *Laws* and even in some readings of Corinthians) allows us to care more deeply about the fate of this world, and thus attend to our duties, friendships, and loves here on earth.

That is the reason for the *almost* unbearable barrenness and despair of the play. The vacuum – emotional, political, and metaphysical – created at the end of *King Lear* points in a way to a philosopher-king. But that figure is not Edgar, whose education is, like ours, incomplete.

> Men must endure
> Their going hence, even as their coming hither;
> Ripeness is all. (V.ii)

> The weight of this sad time we must obey,
> Speak what we feel, not what we ought to say.
> The oldest hath borne most; we that are young
> Shall never see so much nor live so long. (V.iii)

Edgar's two memorable epigraphs are indeed profound – perhaps all the more so because of their brilliant ambiguity. There seem to be as many interpretations of "ripeness" as there are critics. But consider those passages alongside Cordelia's single prayer:

> O, you kind gods,
> Cure this great breach in his abused nature!
> Th' untuned and jarring senses, O, wind up,
> Of this child-changed father! (IV.vii)

She asks "kind gods" to heal the breach in Lear's – *viz.,* Britain's – abused nature by winding up (as an instrument) the jarred senses to "tune" them. If Shakespeare was not familiar with Plato's *Laws,* it is an extraordinary coincidence that the Athenian Stranger, in Books IV and V, discusses "preludes" to the laws that help to "tune" the souls of the citizens. (Plato is making use of the dual meaning of *nomos* as both law and music. These preludes are metaphysical and theological accounts of man's relation to nature and the gods, which we might call civil religion, and which Avicenna referred to as "prophecy." See *Laws,* 722dff.)

Yves Bonnefoy, in an essay comparing *Lear* and *Hamlet,* argues that Shakespeare is confronting "a deep fissure" in the West, "when technology and science" challenged "the structures of traditional meaning [and] the established order fell into fragmentation." *Hamlet* represents fatalism. "Our condition is in nonmeaning, nothingness," and this might be "one of the possible 'solutions' proposed" for "the great crisis in values" appearing in the Elizabethan era. By contrast, the idea of ripeness "emerges in *Lear* as a potentiality for everyone, as the existential starting point from which the protagonists of this tragedy of false appearances begin to be something more than mere shadows." The end of *Lear* is decisively a beginning. Bonnefoy says the "cracking of the cosmos, might well seem to suggest the collapse of meaning." And the play seems to end without answering that challenge. But for that very reason it serves as the gateway to the rest of the Shakespearean universe. "It is here," Bonnefoy adds, "that true reflection begins again, here that the idea of justice takes shape once more."[35]

Too many critics, seeing what might be called the empty stage at the end of *King Lear,* want to backfit their own preconceptions and prejudices on to the play. But my suggestion is that the command Lear issues to Cordelia in the opening scene – "Speak again" – is the one that Shakespeare gives to himself. He will take up the perpetuation of Lear's realm: he will fill with noble images and enlivening scenes the theater occupied by the English-speaking peoples, and perhaps indeed the whole world.

The Founders and Classical Prudence

Matthew Spalding

Poor George Washington. Once "first in war, first in peace, and first in the hearts of his countrymen," today he is widely recognized but rarely seen beyond the stoic figure of Gilbert Stuart's iconic paintings. Most scholars agree he was an indispensable figure, but they are quick to peg him below those who voiced the ideas and wrote the pamphlets that define the Founding Era. Washington looked good in uniform and even better on a horse, they grant, and shrewdly placed himself in the right place at the right time to achieve everlasting fame. Beyond that, America's *pater patriae* has become little more than a founding facilitator.

Just how did the dominant figure of America's opening chapters come to be held in such low regard? One clue worth exploring is in a thoughtful description of the man written by Thomas Jefferson after Washington's death. It is direct and candid: "His mind was great and powerful, without being of the very first order, his penetration strong, though not so acute as that of Newton, Bacon or Locke," Jefferson wrote, adding, "and as far as he saw, no judgment was ever sounder." A bit of a backhanded compliment from the effete Jefferson, who preferred that philosophical triumvirate, but the distinction made between abstract thinking and practical reasoning goes to the heart of the matter. Washington's contemplative mind, "slow in operation" by Jefferson's measure, was nevertheless "sure in conclusion."

Jefferson is more effusive about his compatriot's character: "his integrity was most pure, his justice the most inflexible I have ever known, no motives of interest or consanguinity, of friendship or hatred, being able to bias his decision." Central to understanding Washington was the virtue that elevated his sound judgment and sure conclusions to a type of wisdom: "Perhaps the strongest feature in his character was prudence, never acting until every circumstance, every consideration was maturely weighed; refraining if he saw a doubt, but, when once decided, going through with his purpose whatever obstacles opposed." Washington was not a theorist but a man of practical wisdom, which made him, "in every sense of the words, a wise, a good, and a great man."[1]

An old word of classical origins – the Greeks called it *phronesis*, the Romans *prudentia* – prudence is the virtue that has to do with deliberation, judgment, and decision based on experience and the knowledge of particulars. Despite its honorable pedigree, however, prudence has a bad reputation nowadays. It is sometimes thought of as a form of prudish moralism wrongly associated with temperance; recall Dana Carvey's *Saturday Night Live* impersonation of the elder George Bush's timidity: "wouldn't be prudent." More troubling, prudence is often perceived as a rhetorical façade to mask the calculations of self-interest and political pragmatism. While it may be a useful tactical skill, prudence is by no means what it used to be – and certainly no longer the highest virtue of political life and the central characteristic of statesmanship.

Indeed, it was the destruction of prudence, part of the

lowering of politics to the competition for power and the concomitant rise of abstract moralism, that has made Washington, and the American Founding generally, largely unintelligible in the calculus of modern political thought. And yet the American Founding, and Washington in particular, cannot be understood apart from the cardinal virtue of prudence.

Classical Prudence

The classic articulation of prudence is in Aristotle, who founded the discipline of political science, particularly in the *Politics* and the *Nicomachean Ethics,* the latter of which lays out the concept of prudence or practical wisdom, as *phronesis* is often translated. Indeed, it is fair to say that prudence plays the central role in all of Aristotle's politics and ethics. At the beginning of the *Politics,* we learn that man is by nature political, drawn to political associations by speech and reasoning for the purpose of living well.[2] At the beginning of the *Ethics,* we learn that all human action is oriented toward some good, and that the good is that at which all things aim.[3] The overarching virtue that is proper to politics and looks toward the highest human ends is prudence.

Though it is an intellectual virtue, prudence is not about contemplating the unchanging truths associated with abstract wisdom or the fixed forms of scientific knowledge such as mathematics. There are those such as Socrates who are wise about the highest forms of truth, but that is not prudence. Indeed, Aristotle distinguishes between those who are wise simply and those that have practical wisdom. Some "know things that are exceptional and wondrous and difficult and miraculous, but useless, because they do not inquire about human goods."[4] Those focused on universal truths to the exclusion of the particulars of human activity lack practical wisdom. Prudence is the rational capacity that deals with human things which are variable and capable of change and subject to deliberation, choice, and decision. The realm in which prudence operates is the realm of contingency, uncertainty, and changing circumstances – that is, politics.

The close relationship between thinking and acting is the crux of the matter. Unlike other forms of knowledge, the object of practical reason is always action – to know what to do and how to do it. Prudence recognizes what is universally true but always attends to the particulars that pertain to action. Indeed, prudence is directed at the "ultimate particular" of which there can be no universal knowledge. Prudence connects universals and particulars, and the need to maintain the proper relationship between universals and particulars is what calls forth prudence in the first place. And since its key elements – deliberation, judgment, decision – cannot be separated from action, we can say that practical wisdom is reason in action.

The focus on relating universals and particulars emphasizes deliberation and especially experience. Skilled deliberation is thinking matters through in order to develop a clear conception of the proper end, and of the appropriate means and their likely success in achieving the correct end. Experience, more particularly concrete experience lived over time, is the ripening agent of practical wisdom. The variety of available means and possible contingencies in human affairs is incalculable; the solution is not theoretical reasoning or scientific expertise in a futile attempt to overcome unpredictability but more reflective experience of human events, of learning from trial and error over time and circumstances. This is why the young (in addition to being prone to follow their passions rather than their reason), even the smartest of them (despite their raw intelligence), do not possess prudence.

It is important to understand that, for Aristotle (and the whole classical and Christian tradition that followed him), prudence is always connected to the good. It is the mark of someone of practical wisdom to be able "to deliberate beautifully about things that are good and advantageous for himself, not in part, such as the sort of things that are conducive to health or strength, but the sort of things that are conducive to living well as a whole."[5] Prudence is an activity involving reason that governs action, always concerned with what is good and bad for human beings; it is that connection which raises practical judgement to the level of practical wisdom. Cleverness is the capacity to choose the best means to any morally neutral outcome, but prudence, though it requires one to be clever, is always oriented toward achieving the good in each situation: "if one's object is something beautiful this capacity is to be praised, but if it is base, it is shamelessness."[6]

A word must be said about the great importance of Aristotle's teleological approach, which is to say the orientation of everything toward its *telos* or end. By this he means to describe both the end to be sought as well as the standard of measurement relative to the end. In both cases, *telos* is defined by the distinctive and fundamental good or function (*ergon*) of a thing found in its nature. Man's distinctive and fundamental nature is reason, understood as both the essential characteristic of man and the activity that will lead to man's flourishing and happiness (*eudaimonia*). Man's natural end, the human good, is an activity of the soul in accord with reason and human actions in accord with virtue.[7]

As the virtue of directing action to good ends, prudence is central to every moral habit; prudence is the activity that makes virtue in the abstract a virtue in fact. One may understand the good of courage in theory, as opposed to rashness and cowardice, but the virtue does not exist until prudence determines the courageous act in particular circumstances. Moral virtue in general sets the sights right, while practical wisdom determines the actual target and wills the action. This is why one must be of good character to be prudent: "So it is clear that it is impossible to be possessed of practical judgement without being good."[8]

In general, prudence deals with individual moral decisions; it is fundamentally self-regarding, focused on the individual achievement of ends and the perfection of the individual actor. Nevertheless, we may identify a more specific form of prudence that is associated with politics proper. Aristotle speaks of this practical judgement "applied to the city" as the art of lawmaking generally and as deliberative or judicial politics when the activity deals with particular actions.[9] Because the city's purpose is not merely survival or even self-sufficiency but living well in a community, it requires a larger and higher prudence in those responsible for its well-being. Aristotle compares those individuals to the master builder who has a comprehensive or architectonic view of the regime and its overarching good. The virtue of prudence – made up of the deliberation, judgement, choice, and decision of individual actors – remains the key ingredient of politics proper, which explains and defines political statesmanship. The statesman, in accord with Aristotle's larger understanding of ethics and politics, must deliberate and act for the good of the regime, alive to the strategic necessities of the regime but also justice and the moral well-being of its citizens. The end of the statesman, the object of political prudence, is the establishment and maintenance of the regime that is the best possible regime under particular circumstances, understood in light of the best regime simply.

Who Killed Prudence?

Niccolò Machiavelli's teaching is a clear departure from the classical political thinkers, and an overturning of their ethical and political ideas. The ancient view of man, he writes in *The Prince*, aimed too high and thus overshot man's true nature, making the classical conception of politics both unrealistic and improbable. Machiavelli is not interested in the "imagined republics and principalities that have never been seen or known to exist in truth" – think of Plato's city in speech, or the idea of Aristotle's best regime – but will "go directly to the effectual truth" of politics.[10]

Machiavelli's view is that man is not directed toward virtue or some concept of the good drawn from nature – there is no natural *telos* directing man toward anything beyond the immediate. Machiavelli's effectual truth is that men live with the constant requirement to satisfy their basic needs, under constant threats to their well-being. Man's whole life is defined by necessity, which causes man ceaselessly to seek not the good life but to keep ahead of his rivals. Politics is transformed by all-consuming necessity: it is not an activity of justice and good that fulfills man's political nature but is the lower-end product of constant struggle.[11]

Basing politics on necessity transforms the idea of virtue into an instrument in man's defense against the rapaciousness of man. It may be useful to have a reputation for the old virtues, but, given the sheer dominance of necessity, it is much better to have the ability to act unreservedly as one must to survive. Machiavelli therefore makes his own list of virtues and vices that, without a hierarchy of ends to orient them, is instead a menu of "qualities" neither good nor bad but which bring praise or blame depending on their use. "[I]f all men were good, this teaching would not be good," Machiavelli admits, "but because they are wicked and do not observe faith with you, you also do not have to observe it with them."[12]

Likewise, nation-states, in order not to be weak and vulnerable, require leaders who are liberated to practice this new understanding of virtue. To the extent that there remains a "common good" it is no longer defined in the old terms of natural human ends but is instead based on the lowest common denominator desired by all societies: independence, power, prosperity, stability, empire. Justice is what is concretely beneficial to the new, more limited ends of the political order. Machiavelli famously concludes that "it is necessary to a prince, if he wants to maintain himself, to learn to be able not to be good, and to use this and not use it according to necessity."[13] And the prince must be "so prudent as to know how to avoid the infamy of those vices that would take his state from him."[14] The new ends justify and determine the appropriate means: "So let a prince win and maintain a state: the means will always be judged honorable, and will be praised by everyone."[15]

In this world, prudence becomes the servant of necessity.

It is still focused on making the right choice in particular circumstances: "Prudence consists in knowing how to recognize the qualities of inconveniences, and in picking the less bad as good."[16] But rather than deliberation and judgment for the sake of achieving good ends, prudence becomes the ability to toggle back and forth between virtue and vice without recourse to any higher ends or standard of justice. Prudence is the ability to distinguish between what appears to be a virtue and what appears to be a vice and then choosing whichever is necessary to maintain power.

One may conclude that there is something here vaguely akin to classical prudence, choosing from a range of actions to achieve an outcome. But it is no longer a deliberative process to navigate between available options to find the particular act in each situation to best advance the higher good – because it is disconnected from any conception of the good in the first place. In short, a narrow component of classical prudence – cleverness – has become the thing itself, an amoral *techne* of decision-making in service to an amoral politics of achieving and maintaining power.

Machiavelli notes that it is the opinion of some that the unpredictability of human affairs is such that "men cannot correct them by their prudence." Holding this opinion causes men to become fatalistic and to leave politics to be "governed by chance."[17] Machiavelli here means those such as Aristotle (and his many followers) who recognized the undeniable role of chance in politics. But Machiavelli also wants man to gain far greater control over chance, or what he calls fortune, than Aristotle ever dared dream was possible. And one way to do that is to reject any sense of caution associated with the old notion of prudence in favor of impetuosity. One must act quickly and without hesitation according to one's perception of necessity. The best approach depends on "the times": caution for quiet times, impetuosity for tumultuous times. But since impetuosity is more likely to produce results than caution, and since few (if any) men can adjust their accustomed mode of proceeding as times change, most are better off simply being impetuous – more ferocious and more audacious than cautious or tepidly prudent.[18]

It was Thomas Hobbes who fleshed out a theory of politics based on Machiavelli's perception of political reality. Hobbes agreed with Machiavelli that the classical thinkers failed by being too high-minded and idealistic: man was not the thoughtful being of the ancients but is a pre-political, calculating animal who is hedonistic by nature: "For the Thoughts are to the Desires, as Scouts, and Spies, to range abroad, and find the way to the things Desired."[19] As a result, politics – tracking Machiavelli's emphasis on necessity – is a war of all against all, making life "solitary, poore, nasty, brutish, and short."[20] Hobbes constructed a political theory for this harsh world to replace the instabilities of Machiavelli's politics of necessity with the stable but complete rule of the absolute state. By Hobbes's logic, the only way to escape all this mayhem (and avoid man's fear of violent death) while precluding reliance on Machiavelli's impetuous ruler is through "the Generation of the great Leviathan."[21] As his was a "scientific" treatment of Machiavelli's "effectual" truth, Hobbes can be said to be the founder of political science in the modern sense.

Like Machiavelli, and likewise rejecting any higher good or ends in favor of immediate wants and needs, Hobbes disdained the classical understanding of prudence. Indeed, the concept is even less significant in Hobbes's theory than in

Machiavelli's politics. Prudence, for Hobbes, is "a Praesumption of the Future, contracted from the Experience of time Past" and, ultimately, is nothing but experience, "which equall time, equally bestowes on all men, in those things they equally apply themselves unto."[22] Indeed, prudence "is not attained by Reasoning, but found as well in Brute Beasts, as in Man; and is but a Memory of successions of events in times past, wherein the omission of every little circumstance altering the effect, frustrateth the expectation of the most Prudent."[23] For Hobbes, prudence is merely a reflexive urge, like the trained instincts of Pavlov's dog, to avoid pain and seek reward.

Machiavelli separated politics from morality, and Hobbes devalued moral reasoning to the point of its functional elimination; both made prudence serve the low ends of their harsh politics. The idealistic morality of Immanuel Kant was a reaction against the realism and egoistic morality of early liberalism. According to Kant, the problem with classical thinkers such as Aristotle as well as early modern thinkers such as Machiavelli and Hobbes is that they understood the good of man to be focused on personal interests and practical existence. But only a purely rational being – abstracted from the brute facts and harsh experience of the world that gives rise to the realism of Machiavelli and Hobbes – is capable of being moral. In order to create a pure ethics unadulterated by any such reality, Kant completely severed reason from the experience of politics. In doing so, he removed practical wisdom from the moral equation and destroyed the concept of prudence altogether.

Kant's moral philosophy turns on the distinction between *a posteriori* and *a priori* reasoning. Reasoning that proceeds from experience to the deduction of knowledge (*a posteriori* reasoning) is personal, particular, and situational. Knowledge based on experience is always hypothetical and burdened by doubts arising from circumstances. Reasoning that proceeds directly from theoretical deduction independent of experience (*a priori* reasoning) is disinterested, universal, and categorical. This knowledge applies to all rational beings equally and in all circumstances without exception. For Kant, experience should have no bearing on moral principles. The categorical imperative "concerns not the material of the action and its intended result but the form and the principle from which it results. What is essentially good in it consists in the intention, the result being what it may. This imperative may be called the imperative of morality."[24]

To be a moral person is to act only according to universal and categorical principles, following an impersonal, impartial, and theoretical rule of reason without regard to practical circumstances or real-world consequences. Only the form of the will matters and constitutes morality. Prudence is self-regarding, concerned with outcomes, and based on individual experience – thus selfish and not rational. Because it is less than rational, based on experience and directed at particulars, it cannot, for Kant, be moral.

The result of all this is that politics is usually perceived either as a struggle for power separated from the pursuit of justice, or derided by a high, apolitical moralism. One view is driven by a low realism that excludes any moral considerations and the other by an abstract idealism that rejects all practical concerns. Both share the assumption that moral principle and political power are incompatible. Either way, both the means and the ends of politics are widely and deeply confused and misunderstood. For all their criticism of the ancients' alleged naivete, these modern thinkers are the ones who look at man apart from how human beings actually live their lives. They posit an abstract individual in a state of nature (in Hobbes's term) or as universal rationalism (to use Kant's terminology). Their politics is an unchanging theory that is valid and effectual always and everywhere, and their universal ideas always lead to universal conclusions.

Prudence, Indeed, Will Dictate

In a letter written soon after becoming the first president of the United States, George Washington recorded his thoughts on the establishment of the new nation. The introspective Washington was well aware of his unique role: "In our progress towards political happiness my station is new; and, if I may use the expression, I walk on untrodden ground. There is scarcely any part of my conduct which may not hereafter be drawn into precedent." Washington's succinct statement of the situation underscores the extraordinary achievement:

> The establishment of our new Government seemed to be the last great experiment for promoting human happiness by reasonable compact in civil Society. It was to be, in the first instance, in a considerable degree a government of accommodation as well as a government of Laws. Much was to be done by prudence, much by conciliation, much by firmness. Few who are not philosophic spectators can realize the difficult and delicate part which a man in my situation had to act.[25]

Who might be Washington's philosophical spectator? Not the idealistic Kant, given Washington's defense of accommodation and conciliation, not to mention his uncategorical assertion that this particular government was among the best in the world, "though not absolutely perfect."[26] What about Machiavelli? Washington understood many of Machiavelli's lessons. He knew the value of "one's own arms," for instance, and warned of a slavish dependence on foreign countries and the dangers of foreign entanglements. And Washington was often quite bold, as when he ordered his soldiers to arrest the British mayor of New York for treason even before the Declaration of Independence. The difference is that Machiavelli's point of reference is always the extreme situation driven by necessity, while Washington looks to justice and the good as the object and deviates reluctantly for the sake of those ends.[27] For Washington, there is always a connection between public policy and private morality as "there exists in the economy and course of nature, an indissoluble union between virtue and happiness," which means the activity and the end of politics are to be found in nature itself.[28] That is hardly Machiavellian.

In deference to the constitutional rule of law, Washington refused the calls of leaders in the army and in Congress to use military force to reform the national government at the end of the war, and rejected outright the pleas of his own officers for Washington to make himself king. Twice when Congress was forced to abandon Philadelphia in the face of advancing British troops, Washington was granted near dictatorial powers to maintain the war effort and preserve civil society. On both occasions, he briefly used and then quickly returned the authority to Congress. In the end, Washington's prudential statesmanship is decidedly not Kantian and markedly points away from rather than toward the political science of Machiavelli or Hobbes.

The Declaration of Independence is a powerful example of prudential thinking. Its very purpose is to give reasons for actions taken, to declare the causes that impel the American colonies to separate from England. It begins with a statement of ends in the form of four self-evident truths: that all men are created equal, that they have certain unalienable rights, that governments are created to secure these rights and derive their just powers from consent, and that when government becomes destructive of these ends the people may alter or abolish it and institute a new government to effect their safety and happiness. The document ends by declaring the united American colonies free and independent, absolved of all allegiance to the British crown, and possessed with the power to do what independent states may of right do. The crucial argument in between begins with the first word after the long sentence proclaiming those self-evident truths: prudence.

Only the last self-evident truth is itself a right to action, and that right (to alter or abolish and institute new government) is invoked only when government becomes destructive of the ends of civil society. Revolution is not justified for light and transient reasons, but only after a long train of abuses becomes insufferable tyranny and the *right* to act becomes a *duty* to act. Or as the Declaration says, "Prudence, indeed, will dictate . . . " How does prudence dictate? According to Aristotle, prudence "gives orders" in that it "makes one enact the things related to the end."[19] The Declaration's statement of ends is insufficient by itself to create a political obligation. It is prudence that connects knowledge of the end with an assessment of the facts on the ground in order to come to the right decision. Only when prudence dictates does declaring independence become a duty.

Indeed, the whole founding can be seen as the work of prudent statesmen and practical, not theoretical, wisdom.[30] The Constitution is the means to achieve the ends found in the Declaration. Its republican structure, according to *The Federalist,* is designed carefully to secure the "fundamental principles of the revolution" – equal natural rights and government based on the consent of the governed – in light of "the transcendent law of nature and nature's God, which declares that the safety and happiness of society are the objects at which all political institutions aim."[31] The Constitution's solution to the challenge of faction – "sown in the nature of man" – is not to abolish liberty in order to extinguish the problem (a "remedy ... worse than the disease"), nor to follow abstract views an ingenious theorist might "bestow on a constitution planned in his closet or in his imagination."[32] Publius instead speaks of auxiliary precautions – the separation of powers, legislative checks and balances, an independent judiciary, the enlargement of the orbit – that are "powerful means, by which the excellences of republican government may be retained and its imperfections lessened or avoided."[33] These auxiliary precautions are described as "inventions of prudence," improvements in the *means* not the *ends* of government.[34] The ends remain those abstract truths proclaimed in the Declaration of Independence.

The serious study of a great political figure like George Washington and a momentous event like the American Founding makes apparent the inadequacy of modern political science to comprehend politics and appreciate the human condition. Theory must always be supplemented by practical wisdom because reason detached from reality is manifestly unable to guide human activity and is innately prone to tyranny. The single-minded archetypes that emerge out of the politics of Machiavelli, Hobbes, and Kant are not statesmen such as Washington, Jefferson, and Madison but ideological monsters such as Hitler, Stalin, and Mao.

What is needed today is a conception of politics that is not only realistic about human nature but appreciates the higher and ennobling truth about moral virtue and the political good. Recalling Aristotle's distinction between theory and practice is the place to begin this recovery. Theory contemplates the universal and unchanging truths that are ends in themselves. But there is also an infinite variety of circumstances in political reality calling for deliberation, judgment, and action. Politics is the art of the practical, focused on what can best be done here and now. There is a kind of reason that guides moral and political choices, that connects universals to particulars, abstract truth to concrete circumstances.

By its embrace of the dictates of prudence, the American Founding is the very antithesis of Kant's categorical imperative. By positing a cognitive function of mind preceding and guiding the exercise of the will toward a proper natural end beyond immediate survival and power, the principles of the founding reject Machiavelli and Hobbes. While what prudence dictates can be bold in action, it is ultimately moderate in its aims, aware of the limits of man's knowledge as well as the frailties and ambitions of human nature. The founding is both modern and liberal in many ways but remains grounded in the classical understanding of practical reason. The manifestations of prudence change, but the virtue remains the same.[35]

The Founders and Classical Prudence

The Athenian stranger of Plato's *Laws* notes that "lawgiving and the founding of cities is the most perfect test of manly virtue" and that "the natural genesis of the best regime, and laws to match" occur only when great power coincides with a divine sense of moderation and prudence.[36] Aristotle describes the working alliance of moral character and prudence as the "eye of the soul."[37] It is in the classical principles of statesmanship and political life and not modern political science that one will find a philosophic spectator to understand the phenomenon of Washington and the American Founding.

The Federalist and the Ancients

MICHAEL ANTON

STANLEY ROSEN once wrote that Leo Strauss "used to endorse Nietzsche's remark that the student's duty to his teacher is to kill him."[1] Assuming Rosen's account is accurate, Strauss certainly did not mean that literally.[2] (Nietzsche . . . well, one never knows.)

The point is that the student, whatever debt he owes his teacher for truths conveyed, owes him the further debt of moving beyond parrotry. Whether all teachers welcome this spreading of the wings, I cannot say. I *can* say with some certainty that the conclusion of this chapter will alarm my teacher Charles Kesler, who might wonder whether I learned anything from him at all. I believe I did (whether Charles wishes to claim this distinction for himself is another matter), even if I have taken that learning in directions he may not approve. But as Charles well knows, a teacher's ability to chart – and thus his responsibility for – a student's subsequent direction is limited. "All you can do is raise them," Elizabeth Taylor (as Leslie Benedict) says of a wayward daughter in *Giant*.[3] Charles raised us well; if any of us have gone astray, that's on us.

The Federalist and the Ancients

Modern or Ancient?

In the introduction to his most recent book, Kesler explains that its unifying purpose is to vindicate America against those who doubt that the country "was ever that great, or could be made so again."[4] One of the central arguments of Kesler's career concerns the question of the ancients' influence on the American Founding. This issue rises well above a mere scholarly controversy over "sources" and goes to the heart of what kind of regime the American Founders were trying to build, to what America *is*.

To sum up as briefly as possible, those who argue that the American regime is purely modern – that is, derived wholly and self-consciously from modern political philosophy – conclude that this origin makes America, and *a fortiori* Americans, "low but solid,"[5] concerned more with comfortable self-preservation than with the soul. Kesler cites the influential political scientist Joseph Cropsey, who declared America "an arena in which modernity is working itself out" and "the microcosm of modernity, repeating in its regime, on the level of popular consciousness, the major noetic events of the modern world."[6]

Kesler identifies this view's most prominent exponents as Douglass Adair and Martin Diamond – somewhat ironically, both of them his predecessors in Claremont.[7] Like these two scholars, Kesler focuses much attention on *The Federalist*. Indeed, one of Kesler's earliest scholarly efforts was an edited volume of fourteen essays to commemorate the two-hundredth anniversaries of the drafting and ratification of the Constitution and publication of the eighty-five essays that would shortly be collected into a single volume.[8]

He also wrote the introduction and notes to *The Federalist*'s best-selling edition.[9]

Kesler credits Diamond especially with establishing the centrality, not just to *The Federalist*'s argument but to the American Founders' whole political science, of the "extended sphere"[10]: the claim that great size is not only *not* an impediment to republican success but is *necessary* to that success.[11]

Yet despite this genuine admiration, Kesler ultimately finds Diamond's view of the founding "terribly one-dimensional."[12] In Kesler's telling, Diamond reduces the founding to a mere product of theory, and a constrained theory at that, with no room for deeper principles or for the prudence necessary to apply those principles to specific circumstances to produce good outcomes. In all this, the Harvard-educated Kesler respectfully – but firmly – criticizes what might appear to be his own team, whom he refers to (following the usage of our mutual teacher Harry V. Jaffa) as the "Eastern" Straussians.[13] Indeed, Charles once quipped that "The American Founding or the American regime is not a chapter in the Strauss-Cropsey *History of Political Philosophy*, and should not be treated as if it were."[14] That is, while modern political philosophy may inevitably degenerate into pointless production and consumption (what Leo Strauss called "the joyless quest for joy"[15]) and culminate in anti-rational nihilism, political *practice* follows its own logic and course – influenced, to be sure, by philosophy, but in the last analysis decided by citizens and statesmen.

As to philosophy's influence, for Kesler the American Founders relied just as much on ancient wisdom as on modern theory. He is fond of quoting Thomas Jefferson's 1825 letter to Henry Lee, which explains that the authority of the Declaration of Independence rests primarily on the "the harmonizing sentiments of the day" and only secondarily on "the elementary books of public right, as Aristotle, Cicero, Locke, Sidney, &c." – two ancients and two moderns and, as Kesler notes, all republicans.[16]

Not that one Jeffersonian reference to ancient authors can or should settle the question. But Kesler finds many others and, more to the point, explains in detail the founders' debt to the classics, the similarities between ancient thought and the founding principles, and the relevance of ancient political science in evaluating the American Founding not as mere theory but as the act of practical statesmanship that it was.

Let me say up front that Kesler long ago convinced me on this point and I consider the matter settled, if not in the scholarly literature, at least to my own satisfaction. Herewith, nonetheless, is my own contribution to that literature, in keeping with my teacher's teaching. I shall attempt to illuminate the ancient elements of the founders' political theory. For the sake of simplicity, and to show due consideration to one of the two poles of Kesler's scholarship (the other is Cicero), I shall limit my remarks to *The Federalist*.

What Not to Do

To begin where Charles himself begins his course on *The Federalist*,[17] that work presents itself as the product of one "Publius," i.e., Publius Valerius Publicola, one of the founders of the Roman Republic.[18] In other words, *The Federalist*'s authors wish to claim for themselves some degree of the authority and majesty of the ancients, and in particular of ancient Rome, history's most successful republic.

In part, this choice was in keeping with common practice

in the Founding Era, when pseudonyms proliferated and often took Roman (e.g., Agrippa, Brutus, Cato, Cincinnatus, Helvidius Priscus, Marcus, Tullius) or Roman-sounding (e.g., Americanus, Philadelphiensis) forms. It also reflected the elite education of the time. As Kesler explains,

> education in the colonies and in the new nation was anchored, from the primary school to college, in the study of classical languages and literature. By comparison with much instruction in the classics today, this study was serious: it did not regard Greece and Rome as two unusually interesting cultures, an acquaintance with which was mildly diverting and sometimes useful in decoding highbrow literature and middlebrow crossword puzzles. For the founders, instruction in the classics was, to a great extent, the study of living wisdom that happened to have been written centuries ago in different languages.[19]

From all this (and more), one might expect a respectful, even reverential treatment of the ancients in *The Federalist*. Yet that expectation is at first glance not met.

In recanvassing *The Federalist* to write this chapter, I find that twenty-three of its eighty-five papers discuss the ancients.[20] In nearly all cases, they are cited for the lessons taught by their examples, not for their theoretical insights. Plato and Socrates are mentioned once each, the former to dismiss the possibility of "a nation of philosophers" and a "philosophical race of kings" (No. 49), the latter with the pungent and memorable observation that "[h]ad every Athenian citizen been a Socrates, every Athenian assembly would still have been a mob" (No. 55). The only other ancient authorities cited are Plutarch (in Nos. 6, 18, and 38) and Polybius (No. 63), both in their capacities as historians rather than for their philosophical or moral teachings.

The Federalist's very first mention of the ancients, in No. 4, cites the "history of the states of [ancient] Greece and of other countries" to illustrate the dangers of disunity. Those "other countries" are not specified to be either ancient or modern; it is likely that both are intended. In other words, the founders are not "historicists" (to cite a concept that would emerge a few decades later): they did not believe that ancient examples were inapt to their situation simply for being old, nor did they see a fundamental discontinuity between antiquity and modernity in all things. They rather believed that, because human nature remains more or less constant (more on this below), ancient examples have just as much to teach as modern ones.

Unfortunately, nearly all of those lessons appear to be negative. A cursory look at the discussions of the ancients in *The Federalist* seems to reveal a long and almost unrelieved litany of failures. The reader is early on confronted with "the petty republics of Greece and Italy" (No. 9) and "the turbulent democracies of ancient Greece" (No. 14). The entirety of *Federalist* 18 is given over to a discussion (for whose length Publius apologizes) of the failures of the Amphictyonic Council and the Achaean League, two ancient defensive confederacies cited by opponents of the proposed Constitution as models for the loose defensive alliance that (these critics argue) would be sufficient to ensure American security. Of foreign corruption, we are reminded of "[h]ow much this contributed to the ruin of the ancient commonwealths" (No. 22). "Greece was undone," Publius quotes Montesquieu, "as soon as the king of Macedon obtained a seat among the

Amphictyons" (No. 43), i.e., as soon as the latter confederacy unwisely admitted a state with a regime radically different from those of its existing members. But homogeneity alone was not enough to save the ancient confederacies: "We have seen, in all the examples of ancient and modern confederacies, the strongest tendency continually betraying itself in the members, to despoil the general government of its authorities, with a very ineffectual capacity in the latter to defend itself against the encroachments" (No. 45). Anti-Federalists who charge that the Constitution's less popular elements portend tyranny, and who therefore insist on a more radically democratic structure, should remember that "[i]n the ancient republics, where the whole body of the people assembled in person, a single orator, or an artful statesman, was generally seen to rule with as complete a sway as if a sceptre had been placed in his single hand" (No. 58). Those who fret about vesting executive power in one man are reminded that "Roman history records many instances of mischiefs to the republic from the dissensions between the Consuls, and between the military Tribunes, who were at times substituted for the Consuls" (No. 70). Even the most spectacular ancient success carried a more spectacular downside: "the liberties of Rome proved the final victim to her military triumphs" (No. 41).

Damning with Faint Praise

Even when Publius appears to pay a compliment, it is more likely than not backhanded. The Romans are praised in *Federalist* 5 – but for their skill in turning allies into conquests so imperceptibly that their victims didn't notice until far too late. The Lycian and Achaean Leagues are damned with the faint praise that these confederacies "appear to have been most free from the fetters of that mistaken principle" (i.e., of loose confederation; No. 16). Number 45 delivers the punchline: both were ruined anyway.

Roman bicameralism is praised in *Federalist* 34, but not as an end itself or for its good effects. Rather, Rome's two independent legislatures – one patrician, the other plebian – are cited to vindicate the coexistence in America of federal and state authority, to show that practice often trumps theory, i.e., that something which on paper may appear impracticable often works in real life.

Rome is subsequently cited for her martial valor, but more as a reminder of the unfortunate necessity for states to remain armed in the face of potential predation (No. 41). For all of Publius's Roman pretentions, America is not to become another Rome; she is not to seek empire.[21] She will have enough on her hands defending her own territory and interests while maintaining a balance between a military strong enough to deter and (if necessary) meet aggression, but not so strong as to threaten domestic liberty.

The closest Publius ever comes to unqualified praise of the ancients is the statement that "history informs us of no long-lived republic which had not a senate" (No. 63). Sparta, Rome, and Carthage are said to be "the only states to whom that character can be applied." Here, finally, appears to be an ancient innovation worth copying. But even here, Publius makes a momentous change.

Whereas no ancient senate (to say nothing of hereditary legislatures such as the British House of Lords) rested on a popular foundation, Publius's proposed senate will. Indeed, in *The Federalist*'s fourteenth essay (which concludes the book's first section),[22] Publius declares that the American Constitution proposes a government that will be "unmixed" and "wholly popular." Granted, the United States Senate will function something like the aristocratic ancient bodies from which it takes its name, and the presidency will have monarchical-like powers.[23] But, in contrast to all known predecessors, ancient or modern, American senators and presidents alike will depend, ultimately, entirely on the people for their selection and legitimacy. When Publius uses the word "mixed" as praise for his new constitution, he means the mixture of federal and state sovereignty (cf. Nos. 39 and 40), not ancient political philosophy's recommendation of a mixed regime with popular, aristocratic, and monarchical elements.

Size Matters

A wholly popular regime is not an innovation; there were numerous such governments in the ancient world. But in all of them, the people assembled "in person" (Nos. 10, 14, 48, 52, and 58) to administer the government's functions. This Publius defines as "democracy" (or "pure democracy"; Nos. 10 and 63). He rejects this form of government as impracticable for a country as large as the United States, and also as a bad regime simply, because prone to majority tyranny.

The proposed American Constitution by contrast is representative. This too is not an innovation: Publius acknowledges that "we owe" to modern Europe "the great principle of representation" (No. 14). What *is* an innovation is placing representation on a wholly popular foundation. America will be the world's first-ever wholly popular (or unmixed) *and* wholly representative republic.[24] This is the first of two unique contributions to political theory and practice that Publius claims for America.

The other is that America will be the largest republic ever conceived as such; that is, not as the result of expansion but designed as such from the beginning. As noted above, in the famous tenth *Federalist*, Publius seizes upon an alleged objection or downside to the adoption of the proposed constitution and boldly proclaims it an advantage. Not only, he asserts, is the great size of the United States no bar to the country's remaining republican; that size will rather *help* or even *ensure that* the country remain republican. Indeed, he argues that the "extensive republic" is the only way to avoid the chief danger from a wholly popular government – i.e., majority tyranny. Returning to *Federalist* 14, Publius boasts that "America can claim the merit of making the discovery [of the principle of representation] the basis of unmixed and extensive republics. It is only to be lamented that any of her citizens should wish to deprive her of the additional merit of displaying its full efficacy in the establishment of the comprehensive system now under her consideration."

As Kesler has shown,[25] the issue of the "extensive republic" is the key to *The Federalist*. The strongest headwind facing advocates of the new Constitution was the popular belief (or prejudice) that only small countries could sustain republicanism and that, conversely, large countries would inevitably descend into tyranny. Perhaps one reason Publius never cites ancient political science is because nearly all the ancients argued that republics must be small. Be that as it may, Publius does, we recall, admit that "the liberties of Rome proved the final victim to her military triumphs," i.e., that size, at least if it is the product of military expansion, can indeed be deadly to liberty – domestically no less than externally.[26]

But in support of the view that republics must be small, the Constitution's opponents looked less to the ancients than to Montesquieu, the philosopher by far most oft-cited in *The Federalist*.[27] Hence, when Publius first refers to Montesquieu (in No. 9), it is to show (or assert) that those who cite him as an authority against the possibility of the large republic do not understand him. Publius equates Montesquieu's "CONFEDERATE REPUBLIC"[28] – i.e., a defensive confederacy of otherwise sovereign states that vest power over foreign affairs in a central government while reserving to themselves authority over domestic matters – with *The Federalist's* extensive republic. In other words, he turns Montesquieu back against those critics of the Constitution who cite the French philosopher in support of the argument that the state governments are alone sufficiently republican to secure Americans' liberty. To the contrary, Publius replies: the state governments are already *too large* to fulfill Montesquieu's requirement for small republics, and yet at the same time *too small* to serve as proper "extended republics" that can secure liberty for the long term.[29]

At any rate, Montesquieu's argument that republics must be small of course channels the ancients.[30] Publius must therefore vindicate the large republic tacitly against ancient theory, explicitly in contrast to ancient practice, as well as (he claims) against a mistaken interpretation of modern theory.

"New" or "Improved" Science?

Advocates of the founders-as-moderns thesis sometimes attribute to Publius (or other American Founders) the phrase "new science of politics." The passage most often cited in support of this assertion is from *Federalist* 9:

> *The science of politics,* however, like most other sciences, *has received great improvement.* The efficacy of various principles is *now well understood,* which were either *not known at all, or imperfectly known* to the ancients. The regular distribution of power into distinct departments; the introduction of legislative balances and checks; the institution of courts composed of judges holding their offices during good behavior; the representation of the people in the legislature by deputies of their own election: these are *wholly new discoveries,* or have *made their principal progress towards perfection in modern times.*[31] [Emphases added]

If this were not enough to establish the Constitution's novelty, and hence modernity, we may add this passage from *Federalist* 14:

> But why is the *experiment* of an extended republic to be rejected, merely because it may *comprise what is new?* Is it not the glory of the people of America, that, whilst they have paid a decent regard to the opinions of former times and other nations, they have *not suffered a blind veneration for antiquity,* for custom, or for names, to overrule the suggestions of their own good sense, the knowledge of their own situation, and the lessons of their own experience? To this manly spirit, posterity will be indebted for the possession, and the world for the example, of the *numerous innovations* displayed on the American theatre, in favor of private

> rights and public happiness. Had no important step been taken by the leaders of the Revolution for which a precedent could not be discovered, no government established of which an exact model did not present itself, the people of the United States might, at this moment have been numbered among the melancholy victims of misguided councils, must at best have been laboring under the weight of some of those forms which have crushed the liberties of the rest of mankind. Happily for America, happily, we trust, for the whole human race, they pursued *a new and more noble course.* They accomplished a revolution which has *no parallel in the annals of human society.* [Emphases added]

One hallmark of modern political philosophy is its assertion that it alone is grounded or scientific, that all prior political teachings "had been built in the air" whereas modern political science "reduces" "justice and policy ... to the rules and infallibility of reason."[32] In *Federalist* 31, in the midst of a relatively mundane discussion of taxation, Publius all but compares political science to math:

> Though it cannot be pretended that the principles of moral and political knowledge have, in general, the same degree of certainty with those of the mathematics, yet they have much better claims in this respect than, to judge from the conduct of men in particular situations, we should be disposed to allow them.

To this we might add Publius's defense in *Federalist* 38 of the Constitutional Convention's reliance on an "assembly of men" rather than "some individual citizen of preeminent wisdom and approved integrity" as was customary in the ancient world.[33] The collective wisdom of many is bound to be superior to the judgment of one alone, especially since the latter avowedly depends on divine inspiration which, even if not knowingly fabricated, is at a minimum "unscientific."

All this, and much else beside, might seem to settle the question in favor of the Constitution's being wholly modern. And yet I declared at the outset that I agree with Kesler on the founding's ancient admixture. Must that judgment now be abandoned? Or can it be defended? And if so, how?

First of all, as Kesler points out, Publius never actually uses the phrase "new science of politics."[34] In one of Charles's many witticisms that convey important truths, he explains that, as "readers of cereal boxes know, 'new' and 'improved' are not the same, and hence cereal companies like to use both terms to communicate the sheer magnificence of their work. Publius, on the other hand, claims only to have added new elements to an already existing science, to have improved but not remade it."[35] That is, Publius sees himself as building on insights already known, supplementing and improving them with subsequent discoveries learned through investigation and experience.

Because nearly all of Publius's references to the classics are to failures of practice that teach lessons to avoid, one might suspect that he entirely rejects ancient wisdom. Yet Publius nowhere criticizes ancient political philosophy in *The Federalist*.[36] He does, however, levy one criticism against *modern* political philosophy that I believe has received insufficient attention. In No. 14, he writes:

> To this accidental source of the error may be added the artifice of some celebrated authors, whose writings

> have had a great share in forming the modern standard of political opinions. Being subjects either of an absolute or limited monarchy, they have endeavored to heighten the advantages, or palliate the evils of those forms, by placing in comparison the vices and defects of the republican, and by citing as specimens of the latter the turbulent democracies of ancient Greece and modern Italy. Under the confusion of names, it has been an easy task to transfer to a republic observations applicable to a democracy only; and among others, the observation that it can never be established but among a small number of people, living within a small compass of territory.

The "error" in question is the opinion "which limits republican government to a narrow district." Its "accidental source" is the inability or refusal of "some celebrated authors" to see the key difference between a democracy and a republic, viz., that "in a democracy, the people meet and exercise the government in person; in a republic, they assemble and administer it by their representatives and agents." These authors "confound" the two – whether from incomprehension or artifice, Publius does not aver – in a way that flatters the monarchies under which they live. In other words, certain influential modern political philosophers either *do not understand* or *deliberately obfuscate* a fundamental political distinction.

Nature, Modern v. Ancient

This criticism by itself cannot establish that Publius is not, or does not understand himself to be, a modern: he might be criticizing modernity from a more modern position.

I believe the solution to this difficulty can be found in Publius's statements on "nature." It would be a whole 'nother chapter just to summarize Publius's views on this vast topic ("nature" or a variant appears in *The Federalist* 247 times). Suffice it to say for present purposes that Publius explicitly bases his entire political science on his views of human nature, the nature of human understanding, the nature of government, and the comprehensive "nature of things."[37]

But neither is this observation in itself decisive, since early modern no less than classical political philosophy claims to take its bearings from nature. It would be less a book than a life's work (and in a sense *was* Leo Strauss's life's work) to demonstrate the many and profound differences between ancient and modern thought. I present instead the barest summary, focusing on those features that bear directly on Kesler's disagreement with earlier scholars' characterization of *The Federalist* and, *a fortiori*, the founding.

Taking a quick stroll through the moderns' statuary hall, we first find Machiavelli, who argues – contra the ancients – that man is not the social and political animal; he is instead radically selfish, but his selfishness can be the basis of a just political order if channeled through institutions forged by the right kind of founder, who is himself motivated by the selfish passion of glory.[38] We next find Hobbes, who disparages glory (and any higher or aspirational impulse) as "Pride," a "Selfe-Conceipt; or great Dejection of mind" which he includes with "Injustice, Ingratitude, Arrogance, . . . Iniquity, Acception of persons, and the rest" which "can never be made lawfull."[39] We then find Locke, who elevates Hobbes's imperative for self-preservation to men's "comfortable, safe, and peaceable living . . . in a secure enjoyment of their properties"[40] acquired through diligent industry. And we find Publius's "celebrated Montesquieu" who, in the course of rejecting ancient virtue in favor of modern "trade and finance,"[41] declares that "[c]ommerce cures destructive prejudices" and that the "natural effect of commerce is to lead to peace."[42] (Quick glances at Harrington, Spinoza, Sydney and others yield not dissimilar results.)

Is this picture true to Publius's estimation of man? It may at first seem so, considering his apparently jaundiced view of human nature. For instance, he says it is "human nature" for nations to "make war whenever they have a prospect of getting anything by it" (No. 4); that the "causes of faction are . . . sown in the nature of man" (No. 10); that no one with a "tolerable knowledge of human nature" needs reminding that "personal considerations" often produce "great national events," i.e., wars and other destructive quarrels not in the national interest (No. 6); that "the constitution of human nature" includes a "love of power" which induces men occupying lower offices to disobey the lawful edicts of those above them (No. 15); and that "the frailty of human nature" prevents men from sorting truth from falsehood (No. 24). He also advises "making the proper deductions for the ordinary depravity of human nature" (No. 78) and observes that "[i]n the general course of human nature, a power over a man's subsistence amounts to a power over his will" (No. 79).

We find in addition references to "inhumanity and cruelty" (No. 6), "human avarice" (No. 12), "the capriciousness of the human mind" and "human selfishness" (No. 15), "the unruly passions of the human heart" (No. 31), "the imperfection of the human faculties" and "the infirmities and depravities of the human character" (No. 37), "the caprice and wickedness of man" (No. 57), as well as "the vanity, . . . conceit, and . . . obstinacy of individuals" and "the effects of this despicable frailty, or rather detestable vice, in the human character" (No. 70), among others.[43]

In *The Federalist*'s most famous statement on this theme, Publius asks:

> what is government itself, but the greatest of all reflections on human nature? If men were angels, no government would be necessary. If angels were to govern men, neither external nor internal controls on government would be necessary. (No. 51)

This litany of vices might seem to mirror Publius's litany of ancient failures and cause one to conclude that he takes a dim view of man. To the extent that Publius holds out hope for better behavior, he might seem to do so only on the basis of modern premises, viz., that it is foolish to count on man's alleged higher motives, which are unreliable (if they even exist); that "institutions with teeth in them"[44] rather than character formation through education will deliver justice; and that the purpose of those institutions should to be to channel selfish passions toward productive ends. For instance, Publius declares in *Federalist* 71:

> It is a general principle of human nature, that a man will be interested in whatever he possesses, in proportion to the firmness or precariousness of the tenure

> by which he holds it; will be less attached to what he holds by a momentary or uncertain title, than to what he enjoys by a durable or certain title; and, of course, will be willing to risk more for the sake of the one, than for the sake of the other.

In the very next essay, Publius adds that "the desire of reward is one of the strongest incentives of human conduct." In this vein, he also specifically refers to the United States as a "commercial republic" (No. 6), speaks of the "commercial character of America" (No. 11), and describes Americans as a "commercial people" (Nos. 24 and 34).[45] In other words, the key to political success is aligning human passions, especially acquisitiveness, with earthly incentives. If modern (or at least early modern) political philosophy could be boiled down to one tenet, this would be it.

Yet once again, this is not the whole picture. Some of Publius's observations about human nature simply reflect common sense. For instance, in *Federalist* 17 he notes:

> It is a known fact in human nature, that its affections are commonly weak in proportion to the distance or diffusiveness of the object. Upon the same principle that a man is more attached to his family than to his neighborhood, to his neighborhood than to the community at large, the people of each State would be apt to feel a stronger bias towards their local governments than towards the government of the Union . . .

Others evince a keen, noncynical awareness of the higher virtues. Indeed, as Kesler has shown, the movement of *The Federalist* overall is from lower to higher: from "safety" in *The*

Federalist's first part to "happiness" in its second.[46] The first part (Nos. 1–36)[47] focuses on union, or more precisely on the necessity of union to self-preservation. As Kesler explains,

> It is only in *The Federalist*'s second [part], which turns to the merits of the proposed Constitution as such, that Publius begins consistently to look at matters from a higher point of view. Here we learn that the Constitution strives to secure "the common good of the society," "the happiness of the people," and a complex "public good" that incorporates such elements as "a due sense of national character," the cultivation of "the deliberate sense of the community," and even "extensive and arduous enterprises for the public benefit" that will be championed by future presidents.[48]

Hence Publius's assessment of human nature turns out to be much more balanced than his account of ancient political practice, and more in keeping with ancient political philosophy, which sees the low but also the high, and the former always in the light of the latter.[49]

"The supposition of universal venality in human nature," Publius declares in *Federalist* 76, "is little less an error in political reasoning, than the supposition of universal rectitude."[50] In No. 55, he observes that "[a]s there is a degree of depravity in mankind which requires a certain degree of circumspection and distrust, so there are other qualities in human nature which justify a certain portion of esteem and confidence. Republican government presupposes the existence of these qualities in a higher degree than any other form." Among these qualities, "[t]here is in every breast a sensibility to marks of honor, of favor, of esteem, and of confidence, which, apart from all considerations of interest, is some pledge for grateful and benevolent returns" (No. 57). And: "Ingratitude is a common topic of declamation against human nature; and it must be confessed that instances of it are but too frequent and flagrant, both in public and in private life. But the universal and extreme indignation which it inspires is itself a proof of the energy and prevalence of the contrary sentiment" (No. 57).[51]

To these "qualities" (or "virtues"),[52] thoroughly familiar to the ancients, Publius adds one of his own which, despite its relative novelty, is perfectly in keeping with the basic premises of classical political philosophy. As Kesler was the first to show in one of his most famous and influential explications of *The Federalist*, Publius gives the new(ish) word "responsibility" "its classic definition." In Publius's usage, "responsibility" has two meanings. First, government must be responsive to what the people want, responsible to them for delivering it, and its officers subject to punishment (e.g., losing elections, impeachment) for failure. The second, higher meaning goes "beyond mere responsiveness" and encompasses serving "the people's true interests or their reasonable will,"[53] i.e., giving them not merely what they want or demand but what they ought to want or what is good for them. "Responsibility" thus enters the pantheon of virtues to help further elevate the founders' political science, and their regime, above mere concern for mere life to facilitation of the good life.

Publius even relies – perhaps naïvely – on higher motives to uplift the thoughts and actions of office-holders: "Every consideration that can influence the human mind, such as honor, oaths, reputations, conscience, the love of country, and family affections and attachments, afford security for [senators'] fidelity" (No. 64). And: "There are strong minds in every walk of life that will rise superior ... and will command the tribute due to their merit ... and I trust, for the credit of human nature, that we shall see examples of such vigorous plants flourishing in the soil of federal as well as of State legislation" (No. 36).[54] Naivety is, to say the least, not a hallmark of modern political philosophy.

Returning to Publius's criticism of modern political philosophy in *Federalist* 14, the chief reason he rejects direct democracy is that it allows and even encourages human vices to predominate. His solution is representation, which is not only necessary in a large republic, but also choiceworthy in itself because it encourages the better angels of human nature to come to the fore. The election of representatives – in addition to being the only way to maintain popular government in an extensive country – will "refine and enlarge the public views, by passing them through the medium of a chosen body of citizens, whose wisdom may best discern the true interest of their country, and whose patriotism and love of justice will be least likely to sacrifice it to temporary or partial considerations" (No. 10). Kesler compares this to Aristotle's identification of election as "the aristocratic way of choosing office holders. Lot, or chance, is the democratic way."[55]

Even in matters of epistemology, Publius turns out to be closer to ancient circumspection than to modern certitude. *Federalist* 37 – the beginning of the work's second of two main parts – is mostly a long lament on the limits of the human mind and the difficulty of human prudence to address concrete problems. And in *Federalist* 55 Publius retracts his earlier comparison of political science to math: "Nothing can be more fallacious than to found our political calculations on arithmetical principles."[56]

In sum, Publius does not think human nature has changed from ancient times: it remains just as bad, but also just as good, as it always was. Nor does he give any indication that he thinks ancient writers understood human nature or politics incorrectly. He is concerned rather with correcting practice, and not just ancient practice but *all* practice, modern emphatically included. This chapter has not focused on (because that is not its intent) Publius's criticisms of modern political practice, but they are often just as pointed as his recounting of ancient failures.[57]

How Did Things Come to This?

The argument that there is an ancient element to the American Founders' political philosophy, and to the country they built, is typically advanced against the notion that America is solely or mostly focused on getting and spending, and thus is a fundamentally flawed regime whose decay into its present condition was inevitable. If Kesler is right, as I believe he is, that the founding contains a significant ancient admixture, then the question of why things turned out the way they did – by which I mean, as badly as they have – looms like a circling vulture.

We come, finally, to the allegedly obligatory praecepticide. Here is a real point of disagreement between Charles and me.[58] To be blunt, these days I find *The Federalist* to be, in the words of my fellow Kesler student (and co-editor of this volume) Glenn Ellmers, "the owner's manual for a car that no longer runs."

Those who believe the founding's sole basis was "low but

solid" modernity cannot find the present outcome surprising. But those of us who believe the founding was a noble work crafted by wise and great men cannot but find the present dismaying. It also means, to borrow from Ricky Ricardo, that we have some 'splainin' to do.

Kesler's answer – and the answer of the sect of which he is, if not the founder, at least now the head and defender – is that the alien import of Progressivism corrupted and supplanted the founding. I know the argument well; one does not study with Kesler without learning it. (It is also the subject of his 2012 book *I Am the Change*.)[59] And certainly I'm convinced that Progressivism did, and was intended to, fatally weaken and eventually overturn the founding. But I have to ask: does not this explanation rather beg the question, or force us to wonder what it was about the founders' regime that made it susceptible to the worst elements of modernity?

There is no question that the American Founding was a stunning achievement – among the greatest political achievements, if not *the* greatest, in history. Those of us who lament its present state and fear its passing should ask ourselves whether, in the course of human events, and especially amidst the acid wash of late modernity, 250 years is not in fact a very long time over which to deliver liberty, security, justice, prosperity, and happiness to hundreds of millions (to say nothing of what this country has done for foreigners).

Recall that Publius himself defines one criterion of a successful republic as being "long-lived" (*Federalist* 63). The three republics he cites in that passage – Sparta, Rome, and Carthage – all lasted about 500 years as republics (longer if one counts their other regimes). Would Publius be dissatisfied with half as long for his handiwork? Or did he know or believe that there is something about modernity that speeds history along, thwarting the attempts of even the wisest men to hold things steady?

Whatever his answer, Publius must perforce, as I do – as Charles does – lament the end whenever it comes. I, at any rate, do not know what or how he and his fellow founders could have done better.

The Federalist on Enterprise, War, and Empire

Anthony A. Peacock

Charles Kesler has been a superb friend, colleague, and mentor for over a generation now. As many have recognized, Charles has mastered the craft of teaching like few others today in the political science profession, combining insightful interpretations of texts of political philosophy with shrewd observations about their relevance to modern American politics. Unlike the many specialists who dominate the discipline of political science today, Charles has an exceptionally encyclopedic mind. He is as comfortable discussing ancient Greek and Roman political thought as he is the arcana of present-day American politics. And he typically does this through the vehicle of a highly refined, irreverent sense of humor that makes his lectures both insightful and entertaining. He is, as they say, the complete package.

It is from Charles's encyclopedic repertoire that I draw for the chapter below. Charles is the editor of the most popular edition of *The Federalist,* has written some of the most enlightening essays on *The Federalist,* and has done as much as anyone to demonstrate the connectedness of *The Federalist,* not only to the modern understanding of republican governance but to ancient understandings as well. The very pseudonym under which *The Federalist* was written, "Publius," makes clear this continuity with antiquity.[1] Charles recognized this in one of the earliest essays he wrote on *The Federalist*. In *Saving the Revolution*, a volume Charles edited in 1987 celebrating the bicentenary of the Constitution, he emphasized: "It is precisely the continued importance of republicanism that connects the political wisdom of *The Federalist* with that of the ancients, that connects the American Publius with the Roman Publius."[2] Charles's point here was that the modern improved science of politics set out in *Federalist* 9 – including such institutional innovations as separation of powers, checks and balances, an independent judiciary, and representative government – had to be understood as serving "the purposes of a prudent republicanism."[3] That republicanism tied honor to republican governance so as to vindicate "the honorable title of republic" (39:237).[4] As Charles concluded, this marriage of honor to republicanism "is the deeper reason why the new science of politics, the science of Machiavelli, Hobbes, and Montesquieu, is rejected in favor of the old science improved by prudence, experience, and new instrumentalities suited to modern conditions."[5]

Part of that old science, I contend, concerned how to reconcile republicanism with empire, a combination many of the greatest minds of antiquity and modernity thought was necessary for any kind of long-term freedom and political stability. Without something approaching empire, a nation will be subject to those impositions of "accident and force" that the opening paragraph of *The Federalist* admonishes Americans to avoid (1:27).

To suggest, however, that the Constitution was intended

to create an empire of any sort may seem strange, if not scandalous, to many Americans, not to mention constitutional scholars. Empire, we are told, is antithetical to republicanism and synonymous with imperialism and even despotism. Yet not only is empire a prominent theme in both Western and American political thought, it has not always been associated with imperialism or despotism. The very opening paragraph of *The Federalist* refers to the United States as "an empire in many respects the most interesting in the world" (1:27). Only a few paragraphs later Publius warns against the machinations of those who might benefit "from the subdivision of the empire into several partial confederacies" (1:28). If readers are suspicious of these passages because they were written by Alexander Hamilton, who may have been more inclined to defend America as a "republican empire,"[6] we would do well to remember that James Madison, like Hamilton, pleaded with his readers in *Federalist* 14 to reject that "unnatural voice" that told them that they "can no longer be fellow-citizens of one great, respectable, and flourishing empire" (14:98–99). Many other prominent founders such as Thomas Paine and early American statesmen such as John Quincy Adams referred to American empire with approbation, as did Thomas Jefferson, who famously demurred that America was "an empire for liberty."[7] King George III himself recognized that the American revolutionaries sought to create "an independent empire," as Michael Kochin and Michael Taylor have recently pointed out in their book by the same name.[8]

In this chapter I propose to examine the idea of empire in *The Federalist* and its relationship to two closely related concepts, enterprise and war. As Charles's comments above from *Saving the Revolution* suggest, contrary to much academic orthodoxy, the most important teachings of *The Federalist* did not have to do with the institutional structure of the federal government. Those teachings were certainly critical and consumed most of the latter half of the work (Nos. 47–83). However, the institutional teachings of *The Federalist* were proffered to serve the non-institutionalist ends of the Constitution set out in the first volume of the work, Numbers 1–36, and especially Numbers 2–14.[9]

The Ends of American Constitutionalism

What then are the ends of the Constitution? *Federalist* 10 provides us a succinct formulation: to "secure the public good and private rights," especially against majority faction (10:75). The Declaration of Independence had stipulated two principal self-evident truths: first, that all men were created equal; second, that they had inalienable rights. Among the latter were rights to life, liberty, and the pursuit of happiness. Promoting the Constitution's ends of the public good and the protection of private or individual rights, as *Federalist* 10 proposed, could be seen as extensions of these proclamations from the Declaration. The public good is an extension of the equality principle; the protection of private rights is an extension of those pre-political, inalienable rights the Declaration recognized, and also of that great document's further assertion that the very purpose of government – the very reason "Governments are Instituted among Men" – is "to secure these Rights."[10] The natural-rights constitutionalism that *The Federalist* defends thus implies limited government, i.e., government limited to protecting rights and promoting the public good.

But how exactly are rights to be protected and the public good promoted? As *Federalist* 2–14 emphasize, these would be achieved primarily through the provision of national security and the development of commercial prosperity that the new Constitution promised. The powers given the federal government – see, for instance, Article I, Section 8 – were split overwhelmingly between these two ends. And the two ends, national security and commercial prosperity, were connected by something that is almost always overlooked in *The Federalist*: the spiritedness of American enterprise. The "spirit of enterprise," which would assist both national security and commercial prosperity, is referred to for the first time in *Federalist* 7. But the manner in which it is introduced provides us a clue both as to why *The Federalist*'s republican theory is so revolutionary and why the idea of empire was connected to American constitutionalism. In *Federalist* 7 Publius remarks: "The spirit of enterprise, which characterizes the commercial part of America, has left no occasion of displaying itself unimproved." But then Publius immediately qualifies: "It is not at all probable that this unbridled spirit would pay much respect to those regulations of trade by which particular States might endeavor to secure exclusive benefits to their own citizens. The infractions of these regulations, on one side, the efforts to prevent and repel them, on the other, would naturally lead to outrages, and these to reprisals and wars" (7:57). *Federalist* 7 was written by Hamilton. *Federalist* 42, by Madison, says virtually the same thing. There Madison warns that the absence of a federal power under the Constitution to regulate commerce between the states would result in "future contrivances" by self-interested states to impose oppressive duties on those traders whose goods had to pass through their states, costs that would be borne by the traders and those consumers who bought their goods. All of this would "nourish unceasing animosities, and not improbably terminate in serious interruptions of the public tranquility" (42:264).

Publius's – both Hamilton's and Madison's – point here constitutes the first feature of his revolutionary republican theory. That consists of the rejection of the Enlightenment orthodoxy of the likes of Montesquieu, David Hume, and Thomas Paine that commercial republics were moderate or pacific in character rather than enterprising, spirited, and warlike. History had demonstrated the contrary of what those "visionary or designing men" thought, who proposed that the "genius of republics" was "pacific" or that "the spirit of commerce has a tendency to soften the manners of men, and to extinguish those inflammable humors which have so often kindled into wars." The "spirit of commerce" was quite opposed to moderation or pacificism. Although it could be pacific when tamed by the right constitutional instruments, absent those instruments it was too frequently a militant, warlike spirit that simply "administered *new* incentives to the appetite" for "territory or dominion" (6:50–51, emphasis added).[11] Like the spirit of commerce, the American spirit of enterprise was both expansionist and animated: an "unbridled," potentially warlike spirit. Acquisitive and aggressive, the spirit of enterprise could also, when appropriately harnessed by the Constitution, be a principal contributor to the general welfare if allowed to contribute through such constitutional vehicles as the Commerce Clause. *Federalist* 10 referred to "the first object of government" as the protection of the "diversity in the faculties of men, from which the rights of property originate" (10:73). *Federalist* 10 suggests that men enter political society not merely to protect their faculties of acquiring property – which the Constitution's promotion of commerce and enterprise would help – but more generally their faculties writ large. If we understand the concept of "enterprise" in its capacious, dictionary sense, as involving undertakings "requiring originality, boldness, or energy," or as an "adventurous spirit or ingenuity,"[12] we would be close to Publius's understanding of the term as it applies to the development of men's faculties. Protecting the diversity in the faculties of men means protecting the freedom to develop an individual's faculties as the individual sees fit. This is one way the Constitution will protect individual rights, by guaranteeing the right to equal opportunity, under which people are free to exercise their talents in increasingly innovative ways to improve their own welfare as well as the general welfare.

Federalists 7 and 42 recognize the spirit of enterprise as a dynamic force. Enabled by the appropriate instruments of the Constitution, it might serve to provide a significant *social* energy in American life in much the same way that the Constitution promises to provide *governmental* energy to institutions like the presidency. The spirit of enterprise would also assist in providing a new professional military instrument and military science that would be essential to the provision and expansion of America's national-security state – yet another critical end of the Constitution. In contrast to *Federalist* 10, *Federalist* 3 declared that "providing for their *safety* seems to be the first" object to which a "wise and free people find it necessary to direct their attention" (3:36, emphasis in original). *Federalist* 10 and *Federalist* 3 can be reconciled by understanding, as Publius suggests, that the people's safety is government's first object in the world of *necessity*, whereas the protection of the diverse faculties of men is the first object of government in the world of *freedom*, in which necessities have been provided for. But the two first objects of government here are connected insofar as the freedom to develop individual faculties through commerce and enterprise will be a key feature to improving America's national security. And this is where the spirit of enterprise joins republicanism and empire in providing against the threat of war in *The Federalist*'s constitutional theory.

Republicanism and Empire in Publius's Constitutional Theory

A second revolutionary aspect of Publius's republican theory is his rejection of the conventional wisdom that republics could only subsist in a "small extent" of territory. *Federalist* 9's attribution of "the ENLARGEMENT of the ORBIT" as the Constitution's contribution to the improved "science of politics" (9:67) and *Federalist* 10's famous multiplicity of interests argument, explained most fully by Martin Diamond, make it clear that not only is a large republic necessary to mitigate the problems of faction but only in a large *commercial* republic can this occur.[13] The reason a large *commercial* republic is necessary, according to Diamond, is that property interests must be sufficiently multiplied so that differences in *kinds* of property can prevail over differences in *amounts* of property. To speak anachronistically, the latter poses the Marxist danger of inevitable class conflict. The multiplicity of interests argument, as Diamond put it, is how "Madison gave a beforehand answer to Marx."[14] The Madisonian "scheme essentially comes down to this. The struggle of classes is to be replaced by a struggle of interests. The class struggle is domestic convulsion; the struggle of interests is a safe, even energizing, struggle which is compatible with, or even promotes, the safety and stability of society."[15]

The energizing struggle Diamond refers to here and its relationship to the safety and stability that the Constitution would provide can be further elaborated. While material progress is certainly not the equivalent of moral or political progress, *Federalist* 12 proposes that a "prosperous commerce" would "vivify and invigorate *all* the channels of industry" (12:70, emphasis added). Publius's strong suggestion here is that the enterprising activity that would derive from a "prosperous commerce" could have the salutary effect of bleeding over into the social, philosophical, and above all martial arts.[16] We know from Hamilton's post-*Federalist* writings – the Report on Manufactures, Report on Public Credit,[17] etc. – that facilitating large commercial enterprises through the new vehicle of the Constitution in the name of providing those instruments of war that America needed to protect itself against the imperial empires of the day was a critical task of the Washington administration. As much as this effort by Hamilton would lead to division between the Federalists and Jefferson and Madison, who had different ideas of constitutional development in the 1790s, this approach to improving America's military wherewithal was largely shared by Hamilton and Madison in *The Federalist*. Hamilton makes clear in *Federalist* 11, for instance, that the United States would need a blue-water navy to fight the leading empires of the day, above all the British, also the leading commercial empire of the late 1700s – Exhibit A, perhaps, that commercial nations were anything but pacific. Yet America might be able to emulate the island status of the British given its distance from Europe by having a relatively small standing army if the new constitutional union could muster a navy powerful enough to protect America's Atlantic shores from all comers.

Madison makes much the same argument in *Federalist* 41. He adds there that the Anti-Federalist insistence on small republics was, in the modern era of the nation-state and imperial empires, suicidal. The anachronistic character of small republics, like city-states, had been demonstrated during the fifteenth century by Charles VII of France who had introduced "military establishments in time of peace." All Europe was forced to follow Charles's example, failing which the continent would "long ago have worn the chains of a universal monarch" (41:253). A divided America would exemplify the same thing continental Europe exhibited before the nations there had equipped themselves with professional militaries. However, Madison's larger point, like Hamilton's, was that the expanded commercial republic the Constitution would facilitate might do more than bring about domestic peace by promoting free trade among the states, integrating the national economy while providing security and prosperity. The ultimate hope was that the constitutional reforms of 1787 would elevate American character, serving moral, political, and intellectual ends beyond those simply connected with generating wealth.[18] "A landed interest, a manufacturing interest, a mercantile interest, a moneyed interest, with many lesser interests, grow up *of necessity* in civilized nations," *Federalist* 10 observes (10:74, emphasis added). Civilized nations, Madison affirms, are *necessarily* commercial nations. The growth of civilization itself could be identified with the greater use of knowledge that a private economy with its multiplicity of interests would facilitate.

Federalist 10 is complemented by *Federalist* 11; there Hamilton proclaims that Americans must "aim at an ascendant in the system of American affairs" and "vindicate the honor of the human race" by disdaining "to be the instruments of European greatness" (11:85–86).

> Under a vigorous national government, the natural strength and resources of the country, directed to a common interest, would baffle all the combinations of European jealousy to restrain our growth. This situation would even take away the motive to such combinations by inducing an impracticability of success. An active commerce, an extensive navigation, a flourishing marine would then be the inevitable offspring of moral and physical necessity. We might defy the little arts of the little politicians to control or vary the irresistible and unchangeable course of nature. (11:82)

The irresistible and unchangeable course of nature Hamilton refers to here was to be found in the large commercial republican order the Constitution would create. That order would facilitate not just economic growth but *moral* and *political* growth as well. The little politicians – those who supported the feckless Articles of Confederation or who advocated for small, agrarian republics, fearing because of its alleged imperiousness the large commercial republic the Constitution would beget – failed to appreciate adequately just how much the faculties of men remained more or less idle absent the opportunities large-scale manufacturing and commerce provided to human development. The spirit of enterprise was just that – spirited. As *Federalist* 7 and 42 suggested, commerce and manufacturing seemed to appeal to human spiritedness as well as to human rationality because they provided those opportunities to individuals to acquire, advance the arts and sciences, develop specific aptitudes, and otherwise move toward greater individual excellence. Publius recognizes that the advancement of American wealth and military wherewithal would likely depend on the most talented and ambitious in society since these individuals were generally the driving force behind political, social, and technological progress. Yet such individuals could only succeed in the more advanced, complex, and technologically sophisticated economy the Constitution would provide.[19]

Hamilton's solicitation to Americans not to be "instruments of European greatness" is an invitation to promote a greatness of their own, one based on justice and political principle. *Federalist* 1 counsels Americans to choose the Constitution in order to demonstrate that men were capable "of establishing good government from reflection and choice" rather than being "forever destined to depend for their political constitutions on accident and force." Choosing the Constitution would be necessary to maintaining "an empire in many respects the most interesting in the world" (1:27). The United States was the most interesting empire in the world because it offered the world the most promising prospects of a secure, large republican government that would promote individual virtue, understood as daring, innovation, and industry, and liberty, understood as the choice to pursue the greatest variety of occupations or opportunities politically conceivable (this includes the intellectual and philosophical disciplines as well as all other pursuits of what academics consider a high-toned life). All of these endeavors by the ambitious and the thoughtful would contribute to national prosperity, security, and stability, providing for individual happiness and the general welfare while avoiding the prospect that the most talented and enterprising would languish and get bored, potentially becoming – as *Federalist* 7 and 42 intimated – quarrelsome and contentious.[20]

American Empire and Political Stability

If the national government and America more generally were to become (in the language of *Federalist* 11) so vigorous as to "baffle *all* the combinations of European jealousy," even taking "away the *motive* to such combinations, by inducing the impracticability of success," the size of the country and its military would have to grow significantly beyond what these were in 1787. The United States would have to be powerful enough to compete with the European empires of the day along the Atlantic seaboard. "A nation, despicable by its weakness, forfeits even the privilege of being neutral" (11:82). Even maintaining neutrality would require increased military wherewithal. We might speculate then that when *Federalist* 11 refers to an active commerce, extensive navigation, and a flourishing marine being a "physical necessity," Publius seems to contemplate what is necessary to promote international commerce and national security sufficient to protect that commerce as well as the United States more generally. When he refers to these features as a "moral" necessity, he seems to imply that they are what justice and honor require, since that is what individual and collective freedom necessitate and to lack the military wherewithal to protect the United States is not only unwise or imprudent but *despicable.*[21] A feeble and inept government is not simply incompetent; it is demoralizing.

If the political and military necessities mentioned above are to be provided for, the Constitution will not only have to create a republic but something approximating an empire. Multiple essays in *The Federalist* imply this, such as Number 1 and 14 cited above. Other *Federalist* entries as well as many provisions in the Constitution also foresee a growing and competitive America. These include not only provisions related to national security and war, such as Article I, Section 8, Clauses 10–16; they also include provisions such as Article IV, Section 3, which contemplates new states being "admitted by Congress into this Union" and the power of Congress to regulate and dispose of any "territory or other property belonging to the United States." Madison proclaims in *Federalist* 38 "that the Western territory is a mine of vast wealth to the United States," left underutilized by mismanagement under the Articles of Confederation. While Americans could rest assured "that a rich and fertile country of an area equal to the inhabited extent of the United States will soon become a national stock," that Congress had "assumed the administration of this stock," had "begun to render it productive," and had undertaken "to form new States, to erect temporary governments, to appoint officers for them, and to prescribe the conditions on which such States shall be admitted into the Confederacy," Congress had done all of this without the constitutional authority to do so. Yet Madison raises these matters not "to throw censure on the measures which have been pursued by Congress;"

he is "sensible they could not have done otherwise." As *Federalist* 38 concludes: "The public interest, the necessity of the case, imposed upon them the task of overleaping their constitutional limits" (38:235–36).

The enterprising and dynamic nature of the American people made it necessary for Congress to violate the express provisions of the Articles of Confederation to allow America to expand. Such expansion was necessary not only to accommodate the desires of the American people to settle the frontier; they were necessary as well to provide that security, stability, and social and political energy *The Federalist* maintains is essential to any good government. *Federalist* 37–39, which introduce the second volume of the work, are dedicated to demonstrating the "conformity of the proposed Constitution to the true principles of republican government" (1:30, emphases removed). It was necessary to demonstrate such conformity because of the size of the Constitution's proposed republic, a size that was going to expand for decades to come. "Energy in government," Madison wrote, is essential to "security against external and internal danger." Stability is necessary "to that repose and confidence in the minds of the people, which are among the chief blessings of civil society." Lack of energy and stability in government had plagued the United States under the Articles. Yet how to combine "the requisite stability and energy in government with the inviolable attention due to liberty and to the republican form" (37:222–23) was perhaps the most difficult question the Constitutional Convention faced.

It was a question that had confronted governments from time immemorial. As *Federalist* 1 suggests, the entire history of political philosophy might be described as a struggle to deal with the impositions of "accident and force" in politics.

Could any government, republican or otherwise, be established from "reflection and choice"? This was a much more complicated question than most political theory had been prepared to recognize. Yet the problem of force in politics was evident from the beginning of Western civilization in the histories of Herodotus and Thucydides. The former documented the Greeks' wars with the Persian empire; the latter recounted the twenty-year-long conflict between the Athenian and Spartan empires. Thucydides's history was an eight-book lamentation on the failure of Greek political union that the authors of *The Federalist* were all too familiar with – there are three direct references to the Peloponnesian War in *The Federalist* and many more references to the themes from Thucydides's history throughout Publius's work.

Empire is not a regime type one finds defended in the political thought of Plato or Aristotle. Plato's Socrates preferred the *kallipolis* in the *Republic*, a polis-like regime, and Aristotle's ideal polity was not that much bigger than a typical polis or ancient city-state. It was not until Xenophon's *Cyropaedia* (*The Education of Cyrus*), which appeared shortly after the *Republic* and before Aristotle's *Politics* (*ca.* 370 BC), that we first see empire introduced as a theoretically defensible regime type instituted to remedy the problem of political instability. Xenophon's Cyrus, a fictious character based loosely on Cyrus the Great, founder of the Persian empire, emerges from a Persia that looks more like ancient Sparta than the historical Persia of Herodotus's *Histories*. What is intriguing in Xenophon's portrayal of Cyrus's acquisition of empire is its rejection of the traditional understanding of virtue that ancient Sparta represented and that Socrates appears to defend, with some significant modifications, in the *Republic*. Cyrus openly mocks this understanding of virtue in Book

I of the *Cyropaedia*. The rest of Xenophon's "philosophical novel," as Wayne Ambler describes it,[22] recounts how Cyrus, frequently through deception and interpersonal rhetorical skill, creates an ever-expanding political regime favorable to acquisition, commerce, and a meritocratic spirit of enterprise. Through such enterprise, negotiation, war, and alliance-building, Cyrus forges an empire that treats his soldiers (both the aristocratic peers as well as the far more numerous commoners) and his allies as partners, not subjects. By the end of the *Cyropaedia*, the empire is so massive that it faces no challengers. Its only challenge is to maintain itself, which it ultimately fails to do. As Harvey C. Mansfield and Nathan Tarcov have highlighted, next to Livy himself, Xenophon is the ancient author most frequently referred to by Machiavelli in his *Discourses on Livy*.[23] There Machiavelli praises the Roman republic for its capacity to expand. Given the choice between a small republic, like Sparta or Venice, and a large republic, like Rome, Machiavelli advises that framers of constitutions opt for the larger republic because the things of men are forever in motion; since republics ordered to remain small are ruined the moment they have to expand, it is better to embrace a constitution that can accommodate such growth.[24]

Rome's republican empire has been said to have informed the emergent American empire.[25] Michael Kochin and Michael Taylor contend that America's growth from a simple collection of coastal settlements down the Atlantic seaboard "into one of the great powers of the world, is the most remarkable story in modern political history."[26] Whether it is the most remarkable story or not, it is clearly the case that America today is an empire. How much that empire was a product of constitutional design is open to discussion.

Robert Kaplan has suggested that empires emerge from necessity and are usually defined by ambiguous processes rather than formal structures. This is especially true of the United States and is a key to its strength across the world. Those such as Patrick Buchanan who contend "that America is a republic, not an empire," are simply wrong, Kaplan maintains, since "it is most certainly both."[27]

But America is not an imperial empire. Although it has all the trappings of an empire in terms of military power, sense of mission, and worldwide interests, the United States is perhaps best described as an "empire of ideas"; this is the real "Spirit of 1776."[28] The empire America has assembled through the twenty-first century is based above all on political principle. It is not, as its critics contend, an empire built upon force or coercion but is more a voluntary coalition of allies. Machiavelli, apparently following Xenophon's Cyrus in this regard, maintained that the key to the Roman empire was to make of its allies partners rather than subjects. But it was also important not to make of such partners "so much that the rank of command, the seat of empire, and the title of the enterprises do not remain with you."[29] It may be the case that all of these features, including the many "enterprises" the United States has undertaken internationally – both those conducted in trade and war – have largely remained "with" America; that is, they have largely been consistent with America's commercial and political interests as well as the principles of the Declaration of Independence and the Constitution. Patrick Garrity remarked in *Saving the Revolution* that if the United States could remove European influence ultimately from the Western hemisphere, being (in the language of *Federalist* 11) "able to dictate the terms between the old and the new world," the country would cease to be "the instrument of European greatness." Americans might "hope, erelong to become the arbiter of Europe in America, and to be able to incline the balance of European competitions in this part of the world as our interest may dictate" (11:65).[30] America succeeded in this strategic objective.

But why limit America's grand strategy to the West Indies or the Western Atlantic when, as *Federalist* 4 pointed out, even in 1787 America had commercial interests as far away as China and India that would have to be protected (4:41)? American grand strategy has accommodated this problem too, and the United States is now a world empire. Yet as Garrity noted, it is not enough simply to protect America's survival, interests, or prosperity, since monarchies or other non-republican regimes can do the same. As Publius emphasized, "the genius of the people of America" was consistent "with the fundamental principles of the Revolution; or with that honorable determination which animates every votary of freedom to rest all our political experiments on the capacity of mankind for self-government" (39:236).[31] Perhaps the ultimate test of American grand strategy and of America's "enterprises" in the fields of war and the maintenance of empire is the extent to which these enterprises are consistent with the principles of the Revolution. Whether the United States should assist other nations in their own experiments with self-government, and if so to what extent, are ongoing questions. But the key to guiding American grand strategy today begins, as it has always, with understanding the justice and morality of the Constitution and its animating principles; principles which originate in the Revolution. 1987 was a long way from 1787, but as Charles noted then, the goal of *The Federalist* was to educate Americans about how to govern themselves through reflection and choice. If "the bicentennial of the Constitution" was not to "be reduced to a mere pastime," Americans would have "to understand not only why the Constitution was adopted but why it is *good*, and therefore worthy of attention and devotion today."[32] This was a lesson Americans needed to take to heart in 1987. In their pursuit of both domestic and foreign policy today, it is a lesson Americans might again want to take to heart.

Defending American Natural-Rights Republicanism

Vincent Phillip Muñoz

How should the religiously orthodox be disposed toward America? A number of leading contemporary Catholic intellectuals contend that we should be suspicious of – if not hostile to – the liberal political project, including the American experiment in ordered liberty. In *Why Liberalism Failed*, my friend and Notre Dame colleague Patrick Deneen issues a full-blown indictment, charging that liberalism's deepest principles are hostile to traditional Christianity.[1] Harvard's Adrian Vermeule agrees. He concludes that "there is no reason to think that a stable, long-term rapprochement between Catholicism and the liberal state is realistically feasible" because "liberalism cannot ultimately tolerate the accommodation [with Catholicism] in principle while remaining true to itself."[2] Rod Dreher, who is Orthodox, recommends a "Benedict Option," implicitly rejecting an "American Option."[3] Even the former Philadelphia archbishop Charles Chaput, who has been friendlier to the idea that Catholics can find a home in America, recognizes that the faithful are now "strangers in a strange land."[4]

Is the "strangeness" now engulfing traditional religious

believers – their cultural persecution in elite circles and the increasing legal pressure on them in everyday life – a product of our liberal political principles working themselves out, as these critics contend? Is a political order based on rights necessarily and essentially hostile to traditional religious belief and practice?

I think not. Faithful Americans can and should be patriotic citizens and champions of American principles. The principles that animated the American Founding – human equality, natural rights, government by consent, religious freedom – do not stand opposed to orthodox religious beliefs and practices. While one might agree with the *First Things* editor Rusty Reno that "the American liberal tradition is in trouble,"[5] and with Carl Trueman that we live in a "Strange New World,"[6] our founding republican principles, rightly understood, remain the surest available means to help us restore a decent and just political order.

The "Radical" Catholic Critique of Liberalism

According to what Deneen originally labeled the "radical" Catholic critique, liberalism is a project of emancipation from traditional morality, natural necessity, and any limits on human willfulness.[7] After more than 200 years, liberalism has finally played itself out. Americans have become licentious in sex, consumerist in the market, and gluttonous in everything else, because they have been emancipated from all conventions except their own desires. The decadent and deplorable aspects of contemporary American life, this argument goes, reflect not a break from our principles but the fulfillment of them. In Deneen's catchy phrase, liberalism is failing because liberalism has succeeded.[8]

The "radical" Catholic critique is centered on three basic claims.

First, and most fundamentally, the critique asserts that America is animated by a political philosophy that denies the existence of transcendental truths and corresponding moral obligations. Liberalism – including, the "radical" Catholics say, American liberalism – rejects natural law and the related notion of teleology. Liberalism denies the idea of the human good, replacing it with "neutrality" toward competing conceptions of the good.

This purported neutrality gives rise to the critique's second point: that liberalism conceives of the human person as an unbounded autonomous individual. Liberal "neutrality" turns out to be anything but neutral because it smuggles in its own particular understanding of the human person. Liberalism, according to Deneen, is most fundamentally constituted by a pair of deeper anthropological assumptions that give liberal institutions a particular orientation and cast: 1) anthropological individualism and the voluntaristic conception of choice, and 2) human separation from and opposition to nature.[9]

In Deneen's view, liberalism teaches that the essence of man lies in his capacity to make willful choices and, more radically, it declares *a priori* that there are no wrong or bad choices. In rejecting moral grounds for judgement, liberalism thereby rejects classical natural right and Christian natural law, both of which hold that nature establishes moral standards for human behavior. Liberalism, its critics say, rejects morality grounded in nature and replaces it with a radical, modern conception of human autonomy. Man does not take his bearings from what he is or from his place in a created, ordered whole; rather, liberal man becomes somebody by creating himself. Or, in the more refined words of Alasdair MacIntyre, "The individual moral agent, freed from hierarchy and teleology, conceives of himself and is conceived of by moral philosophers as sovereign in his moral authority."[10]

Liberalism can't assert a notion of intrinsic moral obligation, according to the late Catholic theologian David L. Schindler, because liberal freedom "is not originally-intrinsically conditioned by anything beyond the self; it consists in an act of choice that is, *a priori*, unbounded."[11]

Liberalism, according to the "radical" Catholics, replaces duties with rights, reason with preferences, and nature with "lifestyle." Liberalism's denial of an objective moral order and its understanding of man as an autonomous, choosing, willful being leads to the third point of the "radical" Catholics' criticism: America's decline into decadence, relativism, and materialism is the inevitable outcome of liberalism's principles.

Every political regime fosters a certain type of citizen; therefore, liberalism fosters liberal citizens. Liberal individuals become relativists because they hold no objective standards of right and wrong. "Who is to say what is right or wrong?" and "You have your values, I have mine" are the quintessential ways Americans now think about moral questions. Liberals become technocratic materialists because they understand nature, including human nature, as something to be controlled and manipulated for our own purposes and desires. They become hedonistic and consumerist because they see the purpose of life as the fulfillment – or, at least, the temporary satiation – of desire. Put these traits together, the critics say, and you can understand how American culture ushered in (and was then easily overtaken by) capitalism, nihilism, and the sexual revolution.

If this were not bad enough, liberalism, like every totalizing "ism," is intolerant of those who reject its principles. At the core of the liberal project, the critics maintain, lies a deep and ineradicable animus toward everything liberals perceive to be illiberal. Therefore, it's not enough for abortion rights or homosexual marriage to be secured; pro-lifers must advertise abortion services, and Christian bakers must bake cakes for same-sex weddings. Thus is liberalism's professed "relativism" belied in practice by an intolerant totalitarianism.

The critics conclude that our current situation reigns because of America's liberal founding principles, not despite them. If you want to understand the true character of America, the "radical" Catholics contend, just look to the Supreme Court's plurality opinion in the abortion-rights case *Planned Parenthood vs. Casey* (1992): "At the heart of liberty is the right to define one's own concept of existence, of meaning, of the universe, and of the mystery of human life."[12]

America's Founding Principles, Rightly Understood

Casey was a moral and legal abomination, in no small part because its holdings in no way follow from the principles of the American Founding. Nor do the other ills the "radical Catholics" lament. To understand this, one must have a proper understanding of the true principles of American liberalism, or rather natural-rights republicanism, to use the founders' idiom.

Liberalism's critics contend that the political philosophy of the American Founding rejects the existence of objective truth, but this is simply untrue. The founders' principles are discernable from many documents, but nowhere more authoritatively than in the Declaration of Independence, which boldly and unambiguously proclaims a statement of *truth*: "We hold these truths to be self-evident, that all men are created equal, that they are endowed by the Creator with certain unalienable rights."

"Self-evident" does not mean obvious or necessarily known by all. Rather, in the Declaration, the term is employed in the same manner Thomas Aquinas uses a similar phrase (*per se notum*): a self-evident proposition is one in which the predicate is contained within the subject. In other words, the Declaration teaches that if we properly understand the nature of men, we will understand that they are created equal.

But in what sense are men created equal? Thomas Jefferson offered a clear explanation at the very end of his life. In June 1826, as the nation was preparing to celebrate the Declaration's fiftieth anniversary, he offered the following commentary on the meaning of equality:

> All eyes are opened, or opening, to the rights of man. The general spread of the light of science has already laid open to every view the palpable truth, that the mass of mankind has not been born with saddles on their backs, nor a favored few booted and spurred, ready to ride them legitimately, by the grace of God.[13]

Horses are not born with saddles on their backs, but it is legitimate that men break horses, saddle them, and ride them for their own purposes. A good owner should treat his steed humanely, of course; but men may own horses and expropriate their labor because of the natural species inequality between man and animals. No similar natural inequality exists among human beings. Jefferson's point is that no man may legitimately rule another man as a man may rule an animal, because all men, by nature, have an equal title to exercise dominion over their own lives and liberty. "All men are created equal" means that no man is, by nature, the rightful ruler or owner of any other man.[14]

Jefferson, in both the Declaration and in his later commentary, grounds the truth of human equality in the created order of nature. The founders do not say, "We are declaring the truth of human equality because that is what we have decided. We choose to make men equal." Willful choice is not their starting point; rather, they begin with the laws of nature and nature's God.

Yet Jefferson and many other founders were slave-owners. The Constitution they wrote included explicit protections for slavery. But whatever the founders' deficiencies in practice, the principles they articulated recognize a truth about man that is established by God and discernable by reflection on human nature and mankind's place within God's creation. In creating man with a common human nature of reason and freedom, God made all men equal. The Declaration recognizes this truth and, in that sense, lies within the natural-law tradition. Indeed, the Declaration's natural-law principles provide the very basis of our just criticisms of the founders' practice of slavery.

Now, to say that the Declaration of Independence is a natural-law document is not to say that it is a Thomistic document. The natural-law truth that the Declaration recognizes is a claim about human freedom – that God created all individuals equal in their natural rights to life, liberty, and property. Aristotle and Thomas Aquinas might not concur, but this is a debate among natural-law thinkers about the nature of human freedom.[15]

The founders' embrace of liberty does not mean that they conceived of the human person as an autonomous individual or that they rejected the Aristotelian idea that man is a political animal. Far from it. Our natural independence, or self-dominion, is part of the founders' argument about natural authority and how human beings can rightly institute political authority among themselves. The founders do not deny that human beings are relational creatures or that they flourish in political communities; they simply contend that legitimate political relations require consent. Because all men are created equal – which is to say, that by nature no men have been "born with saddles on their backs, nor a favored few booted and spurred ... by the grace of God" – consent is a necessary (though not sufficient) condition of *legitimate* rule of man over man.

Consent follows from natural human equality. As stated in Article 1 of Virginia's Declaration of Rights (1776), "All men are born equally free and independent; therefore, all government of right originates from the people, is founded in consent, and instituted for the general good." To reject the necessity of consent, which some "common good" Catholics seem to do, is to reject natural equality.

The founders' understanding of the natural right of liberty also does not mean that our choices are "unbounded" by substantive moral norms. The founders distinguished liberty from license. They understood liberty to be the exercise of freedom consistent with the precepts of the natural law; license was understood to be the exercise of freedom contrary to the natural law's precepts.[16]

Even as they drew on Locke, the founders rejected

Hobbes precisely on the grounds that he failed to recognize a morally authoritative natural law. This is an involved argument, of course, but we can start by simply stating what the young Alexander Hamilton said about Hobbes. In responding to a Loyalist critique that associated the revolutionaries' arguments with Hobbes, Hamilton wrote that:

> [G]ood and wise men, in all ages, have embraced a very dissimilar theory [from that of Hobbes]. They have supposed, that the deity, from the relations, we stand in, to himself and to each other, has constituted an eternal and immutable law, which is, indispensably, obligatory upon all mankind, prior to any human institution whatever. This is what is called the law of nature.

On this morally obligatory law of nature, Hamilton continues, "depend the rights of mankind." "Hence, in a state of nature," he concludes, "no man had any *moral* power to deprive another of his life, limbs, property or liberty" (Hamilton's emphasis).[17]

Hamilton scorned Hobbes because, like the founders more generally, he understood natural rights as correlative to natural duties, both of which were part of the natural law. As Hadley Arkes likes to say, the founders did not believe in a "right to do a wrong," meaning that our natural rights themselves lie within the natural law's moral prescriptions.[18] James Wilson, perhaps the founding generation's leading jurist, put the matter thus in his *Lectures on Law*: "In a state of natural liberty [i.e., the state of nature], every one is allowed to act according to his own inclination, provided he transgress not those limits, which are assigned to him by the law of nature." Elsewhere in his *Lectures*, Wilson says that "the laws of nature are the measure and the rule; they ascertain the limits and extent of natural liberty."[19]

Because natural rights are not opposed to the idea of binding moral obligations, the founders did not conceive of the rights-bearing individual as an unencumbered, autonomous self.[20] The founders understood the human person to have rights on account of God-given reason and freedom. These essential attributes of human nature establish both the grounds of our rights and the limits to them.[21] The human person as a rights- and duty-bearing individual was understood to be a part of the Creator's moral order and therefore morally subject to the natural law that governs that order.

Indeed, the nature of our duties to God is the underlying purpose for creating a liberal political order. "We hold it for a fundamental and undeniable truth," Madison writes in his "Memorial and Remonstrance" (quoting Jefferson's Virginia Statute for Religious Liberty), "'that religion or the duty which we owe to our Creator, and the manner of discharging it, can be directed only by reason and conviction, not by force or violence.'"

Because we are made to worship God freely – because we are called to love God and because love can only be given freely – we have a right to do so. Our rights follow from our duties, and our duties imply rights. Our duty to worship the Creator according to conviction and conscience demands that religion be free from legal coercion. Liberalism, accordingly, recognizes that religious authority and the teaching of religious truth properly fall under the domain of churches alone. The liberal state is limited to safeguarding liberty because religious truth lies beyond its authority. In disparaging liberalism, the "radical" Catholics, perhaps unwittingly, raise doubts about the propriety of the separation of church and state and about the legitimacy of religious freedom.

One might accept this defense of our founding principles yet still press an aspect of the "radical" Catholics' third criticism – that American liberalism, whatever its original character, has produced a decadent and deplorable legal and moral culture. One might contend that even if the founders accepted natural law, moral duties, and limits on rights, their account of freedom has proved to be too thin. It provides too much freedom for bourgeois, comfortable self-preservation, what the moral theologian Servais Pinckaers calls "freedom for indifference," and insufficient cultivation of "freedom for excellence."[22]

An honest assessment of America and our history must acknowledge that there is something to this criticism. The founders held that the primary purpose of government is to secure natural rights. They believed that a just political order would preserve political freedom and nurture personal responsibility and, at the same time, not lord over citizens and command all the moral virtues.

Critics home in on this point in their identification of America as part of the modern philosophical "project" of emancipation. But "project" assumes that some mastermind stands at the helm (Hobbes, according to the "radical" Catholics) or that, once set forth, history necessarily moves in a certain direction. The criticism fails to recognize the reality and implications of human freedom.

America is better characterized as an "experiment." The founders well understood that every generation would need to be taught to use its freedom well, which is why they sought to cultivate virtue through education and religion. They did not embrace Aristotle's teachings that the purpose of politics is to make men virtuous and that law should be used coercively to habituate moral virtue, but they did understand that their constitutional republic would depend on virtue for its success. "Our Constitution was made only for a moral and religious People," John Adams stated. "It is wholly inadequate to the government of any other."[23] This is why America is an experiment: can a free people remain sufficiently virtuous to maintain, and deserve to maintain, their freedom?

Restoring American Classical Liberalism and Constitutional Republicanism

If we Americans are no longer sufficiently virtuous, the fault lies primarily with us, not our founding principles. Our political and economic institutions have never been perfect, but (aside from slavery and its legacies) they have never been so corrupt that they have made virtuous living impossible. Original sin may make corruption probable, and political liberty may make it possible, but the causes of America's problems lie primarily in the poor choices Americans have made.[24]

That means the solution to our problem lies, to a large extent, in our own choices. To choose well, we must regain both political wisdom and the character that befits a constitutional people. Reacquaintance with our actual liberal principles and a return to belief in the existence of an obligatory moral law are essential.

The latter may require a reemergence of religious belief, especially among the cultural elite where such belief has precipitously declined. The necessity of morality for liberal democracy, and of religion for morality, cannot be understated. As Tocqueville recognized, religion is the first of America's political institutions. It teaches us to respect the equality of all individuals and provides the grounds for moderation and self-restraint, both individually and communally.

Morality, it must be recalled, is a precondition of political freedom. Take as a simple example freedom of association. The idea that, for the most part, individuals should be free to associate or not in matters of friendship or commerce makes intuitive sense to most Americans. Yet once people believe that individuals will use their freedom badly – that they will refuse to associate with others for irrational and bigoted reasons – the commitment to freedom of association begins to evaporate. Very few will remain partisans of liberty when it produces widespread injustice in practice. A free people must be a moral people to exercise and maintain their freedom.

Our political well-being, accordingly, has always depended on the health of the non-governmental institutions that cultivate virtue and morality, especially the family and churches. America's cultural decline, unsurprisingly, has corresponded with the weakening of the family and of religious faith. The rise of fatherless homes and the decimation of mainline Protestantism (as Jody Bottum ably documents in *An Anxious Age*)[25] have been terrible for America. Politics affects culture, of course, but culture shapes, limits, and sometimes directs politics. Cultural renewal, including a revival of traditional religion, is an essential facet of political renewal.

A free people must also be a constitutional people. They must govern through law and be governed by the rule of law. Recovering our constitutional character also requires that those who govern respect the Constitution and understand that it authorizes their own authority. That the Constitution no longer governs us in practice or only partially governs us is not a new story.[26] When Congress evades accountability by improperly delegating its legislative authority to administrative agencies, or when the president casts off his obligation to take care that duly enacted laws are enforced, it teaches the American people that there are no rules that govern us and that the only limitations on power are what you can't get away with. This is doubly true of the Supreme Court, which seems to admit no restraint in transforming the Constitution to decree the justices' own moral and social preferences. We cannot expect the people themselves to act responsibly or to remain moderate and self-restrained when those who govern fail to abide by the Constitution.

A revival of constitutionalism will also require a revival of limited government. The Constitution imposes limits on how power may be exercised; it also limits what government may legitimately do. The role of the state is not to make us pious or pure. Attempts to do so – especially in a country as divided and diverse as contemporary America – will lead to oppression. It is particularly important to remember that political liberty requires moderation and tolerance: moderation in what we demand from our political life, and tolerance of our fellow citizens who choose to live differently from us. Reclaiming the private sphere as private and therefore beyond state regulation would lower the stakes of our disagreements. Our politics would be much better if, on matters about which people can reasonably disagree, we left one another alone.

* * *

On matters that must be decided politically, our founding principles should be our first guide. Nowhere is this truer than the issue of abortion, and it remains especially true after *Dobbs v. Jackson* (2022). America's foundational commitments to human equality and to the natural rights of life and liberty extend to all human beings, including the unborn.

The pro-life movement could and should adopt the reasoning that Abraham Lincoln applied to Stephen Douglas's pro-choice position on slavery. The following is a modification of a passage from Lincoln's Peoria Address (1854). I have substituted "liberty" for "self-government," "fetus" for "negro," and "person" for "man":

> The doctrine of liberty is right – absolutely and eternally right – but it has no just application, as here attempted. Or perhaps I should rather say that whether it has such just application depends upon whether a fetus is not or is a person. If the fetus is not a person, why in that case, he who is a person may, as a matter of liberty, do just as he pleases with him. But if the fetus is a person, is it not to that extent, a total destruction of liberty, to say that he too shall not [have the chance to] govern himself? . . . If the fetus is a person, why then my ancient faith teaches me that "all men are created equal"; and that there can be no moral right in connection with one man's making a slave of [or aborting] another. (Lincoln's emphases)

A tragic irony of the "radical" critique of America is that, among other things, it undermines the pro-life cause. They hold that *Roe* and *Casey* follow from a proper understanding of American liberalism. If they are consistent, they must concede that the Princeton professor Peter Singer, who advocates infanticide,[27] is a more faithful interpreter of our constitutional principles than Clarence Thomas or Samuel Alito.

The "radical" Catholics' misinterpretation of America is thus no mere academic matter. Their mistakes blind us to how our republican principles offer a moral framework by which to support life. They are unable to appreciate the greatness of Lincoln or discern his moral wisdom and constitutional statesmanship. They preach local community and relationship to the past, but fail to understand their own community and eschew America's own traditions and what is most noble about them.

In doing so, "radical" Catholicism alienates from the American experiment those who should be America's most faithful friends, dispiriting young conservatives in particular. If liberalism was never attractive to begin with – if abortion is consistent with the Constitution – why fight for America? Why run for office or give one's time or treasure to those who do? Why even vote and implicate oneself in an inevitably failing and corrupt political regime? The political alienation the "radical" Catholics foster cannot help but engender disdain for engaged citizenship and responsible patriotism among the young, religiously orthodox citizens that America most needs right now.

Our current politics illustrates that decent, democratic self-government should not be taken for granted. Our experiment in republican constitutionalism is just that – an experiment that can fail if not properly sustained. Insofar as America is a set of principles and ideals, she must be understood if she is to be fully appreciated. It is only by coming to understand the actual principles of our liberal regime that one can see how lovable she truly is and why she remains worthy of our devotion.

This chapter is adapted from an essay that originally appeared on National Review Online *on June 11, 2018.*

How Natural Right Fell Out of Favor in American Thought

Preparing the Ground for Progressivism in the Post–Civil War Era

STEVEN F. HAYWARD

We have wrongly taught that "social Darwinism" is inherently conservative, just as "rights talk" is inherently liberal. Progressives, from the most scientific-technocratic to the most radical-socialist, conceived of their projects as having coherence and meaning because they were located within a social evolutionary framework.

ELDON EISENACH[1]

Political liberalism began with a rejection of the Constitution and the morality underpinning it.

CHARLES R. KESLER[2]

CHARLES KESLER is pre-eminent among the small circle of contrarian scholars who have generated a wholesale revision of our understanding of Progressivism and its decisive role in the gradual transformation of our constitutional republic into an administrative state.[3] For a long time the modern conservative intellectual movement that coalesced starting in the 1950s laid the blame for modern American liberalism at the feet of Franklin Roosevelt and the New Deal, and largely ignored or downplayed Woodrow Wilson and Progressivism. In part, this neglect stemmed from the historical contingency that the Progressive movement appeared evanescent, and because the changes the Progressives wrought were opaque in many ways. The most popular court historians of Progressivism such as Charles Beard, J. Allen Smith, and Vernon Parrington obscured or deflected attention from the profound philosophical break with the principles of the American Founding, while the work of political scientists and legal thinkers of the era such as John Burgess and Roscoe Pound remained out of focus.

This scene has changed decisively over the last two or three decades. It is now understood that the dramatic and enduring political realignment of the New Deal rested upon Progressive foundations. Likewise, "administrative state" – the name for the new regime the Progressives set in motion – has become a commonplace term, after languishing in obscurity as the specialized jargon of a subset of political scientists for decades.

At a century's remove it is possible to view the Progressivism of Woodrow Wilson and his cohort with fresh eyes, and appreciate more fully how thorough was their attack on the American Founding. And yet a closer look will also reveal one more important piece of the story: the Progressives were pushing on an open door, so to speak. Much of the work to discredit the American Founding had already taken place in the late nineteenth century, such that Progressives didn't need to construct their attack *de novo*. The larger irony is that much of the prepatory work was done in part by so-called conservatives, though the standard historical accounts have always gotten this story badly wrong. Central to this story line is the gradual replacement of natural rights by capital-H History during the nineteenth century. This philosophical shift is usually regarded primarily as a European-driven change, but American thinkers played an important role not wholly derivative of European thought.

The outcome of the Civil War could be said to represent the vindication and amplification of the centrality of the idea of natural right in American political discourse. Yet within a generation after war's end the idea of natural right had fallen into desuetude. By the Progressive Era, the idea of natural right had been nearly erased from American political thought entirely, replaced by the idea of Darwinian evolution – the key informing insight to the general historicism that underlay the idea of a "living" or adaptable Constitution. Darwinian evolution not only supplied the scientific veneer for the philosophic historicism that had been imported from German thought; it also supplied the essential ammunition for the subsequent Progressive attack on the Constitution. The linchpin of the Progressive criticism of the Constitution was that it was undemocratic, because its mechanisms did not live up to the egalitarian principles of the Declaration of Independence.[4]

It was ironically the anti-reform "Social Darwinists" who most forcefully opened the wedge between the Declaration of Independence (the lodestar of the idea of natural right in American thought) and the Constitution, hence preparing the way for the Progressive critique. The Social Darwinist attack on natural right could be compared to an artillery barrage that precedes an infantry attack; it was the Darwinian attack on natural right that more than anything led conservatives, as Eric Goldman observed, "to dismiss the Declaration [of Independence] as a collection of windy generalities."[5]

There are several aspects of this ironic transition that have been ill-explored in the historiography of America, again in large part because of the sympathy writers have felt for the fundamental ideas of the reformers. Perhaps the best way to unravel this story is to work backwards from the apogee of Progressivism itself, starting with Woodrow Wilson. Woodrow Wilson, as Harvey C. Mansfield Jr. noted, "was the first American president to criticize the Constitution."[6] In his most famous and significant formulation, Wilson wrote:

> The government of the United States was constructed upon the Whig theory of political dynamics, which was a sort of unconscious copy of the Newtonian theory of the universe. In our own day, whenever we discuss the structure or development of anything, whether in nature or in society, we consciously or unconsciously follow Mr. Darwin .... The trouble with the [Newtonian] theory is that government is not a machine, but a living thing .... Living political constitutions must be Darwinian in structure and in practice.[7]

Perhaps the most revealing phrasing in this passage is not the references to Darwin or Newton and all that this comparison implies, but rather the way Wilson refers to the "conscious" and "unconscious" following of ideas. When Wilson suggests that the Framers' embrace of the idea of the separation of powers is "a sort of unconscious copy" of Newton, he does not mean that they were unwitting or ignorant of any deeper meaning of Newtonian teaching. To the contrary, Wilson credits the framers with following Montesquieu's new doctrine "with genuine scientific enthusiasm."[8] The vital clue comes from Wilson's equivocation about whether his own generation of leaders "consciously or unconsciously" follows Mr. Darwin.

Recent scholarship exploring Wilson's own writings has revealed just how enamored he was of Hegelian historicism: "The philosophy of any time is, as Hegel says, 'nothing but the spirit of that time expressed in abstract thought'; and political philosophy, like philosophy of every other kind, has only held up the mirror to contemporary affairs."[9] In doubting whether he and his generation "consciously or unconsciously" come to their thoughts and ideas, Wilson is conscious – so to speak – of the obvious consequence of this simple kind of historicism, namely, that not reason and ideas, but sub-rational forces and ideology determine the thought of any given moment.

Equally revealing is Wilson's conflation of nature and society: "whenever we discuss the structure or development of anything, *whether in nature or in society*, we . . . follow Mr. Darwin" (emphasis added). This conflation of the fundamental classical distinction between *physis* (nature) and *nomos* (law or convention, i.e., human contrivance) is of course the logical consequence of the denial of natural right, which Wilson implicitly accepts.

The key to understanding why Wilson was never compelled to make his rejection of natural right more explicit lies in answering the following seemingly superficial question: how is it possible for Wilson to appeal to a "Darwinian constitution" as a hallmark of progressive politics when just a few years before such a phrase was thought to imply *reactionary* politics? The essential theoretical or philosophical continuity between Social Darwinism and Progressivism has been obscured by conventional historiography. That account emphasizes the superficial link between Social Darwinism of the Spencerian variety and the rise of "robber baron" capitalism, the protection of which became the central concern of economic conservatism. But the standard narratives seldom delve deeply into the significance of the Social Darwinist attack on natural right.[10] The Progressive critique of uncontrolled capitalism makes it seem like the polar opposite of Social Darwinism, but insofar as the rejection of natural right is even more central to Progressive ideology, and its "living" constitutionalism, the Social Darwinists did the dirty work for the Progressives. The success of the Social Darwinists' early attack on natural right is one reason why the later Progressive rejection of natural right is not more obvious, and hence one reason why the outlines of Progressive ideology are difficult to make out.

In his career-launching book *Social Darwinism in American Thought*, Richard Hofstadter noted that although Social Darwinism "lacked many of the signal characteristics of conservatism as it is usually found," it was nonetheless "one of the great informing insights in this long phase in the history of the conservative mind in America."[11] Subsequent historians have criticized and superseded Hofstadter's (and also Sidney Fine's)[12] account, downplaying the significance of Social Darwinism in American thought. Once again, Hofstadter has taken it on the chin from these corrections, making him increasingly the George Bancroft of our century – a figure widely revered in his time, but widely dismissed after.[13] Donald Bellomy concludes that recent scholarship on Social Darwinism "has left no consensus on its scope, implications, or relevance." Bellomy notes that the term "Social

Darwinsim" probably didn't come into currency until 1903, when it was used by Edward Ross. Hence, Bellomy argues, "'Social Darwinism' was not a broad cultural phenomenon at all, at least not in Gilded Age America."[14] Robert Bannister similarly argues that not only were very few Americans actually Social Darwinists in the Gilded Age, but indeed that it is largely a myth "usually unsubstantiated or quite out of proportion to the evidence, that Darwinism was widely and wantonly used by forces of reaction."[15]

Still, even as we acknowledge the fresh insights of revisionists who downplay the significance of Social Darwinism, there remains in the popular mind a vital linkage between the idea of Social Darwinism and conservatism. More than just an epithet for partisan journalists, Social Darwinism seems to have some real staying power as an established category of American thought. "A resurgence of Social Darwinism," Hofstadter wrote, "is always a possibility," so it is not surprising to find one of the old liberal lions of American history, Arthur M. Schlesinger Jr., claiming that the conservatism of the 1980s "repeats conservative themes not just of the 1950s and 1920s but of the 1890s and before: the exaltation of *laissez faire* and the unfettered market (Herbert Spencer's *Social Statics*, 1850.)"[16] Schlesinger exaggerates for effect, of course; there are no conservative intellectuals of any note in recent times who have explicitly embraced Herbert Spencer or William Graham Sumner as exemplars of their ideas. Indeed, most contemporary theorists of *laissez faire* take great pains to differentiate the basis of their belief in free markets from Social Darwinism, especially when offering organic analogies for market activity.[17] Whether this dissociation from Social Darwinism has been entirely successful will be considered in due course.

How Natural Right Fell Out of Favor

Critics of what might be called the "old standard account" of Social Darwinism are right in pointing out that the term "Social Darwinism" has rarely been clearly defined. Subsequent interest in Darwinism has bolstered the important distinction between Darwinism (or natural selection) and simple "social organicism," i.e., biological metaphors for the natural and social world that in fact predate the appearance of Darwin's *Origin of the Species*.[18] But the revisionists who have carefully sharpened and corrected our view of Darwinism have nonetheless missed a key aspect of the story just as much as Hofstadter did. To the extent that Darwinism of any variety (whether scientifically understood or whether adapted as a social myth) influenced social thought, it changed radically the idea of nature and hence the idea of natural law. As such, this change from an understanding of nature that was fixed and eternal to an understanding of nature that was endlessly adapting through evolutionary progress, was crucial to undermining the idea of natural right – "the Laws of Nature and of Nature's God" – at the heart of American political thought. To the extent that the general idea of Darwinian evolution – whether understood and applied accurately or not – became an element of conservative thought in the Gilded Age, it undermined the ancient basis of American political thought. Even if the extent of the influence of Social Darwinism has been overstated, this is nonetheless significant, for it meant that conservative resistance to Progressive reform would not be based on a defense of the founding principles of the American regime. In other words, to the extent that Darwinian thought was assimilated into the attitudes of the Right, conservatives no longer sought to "conserve" what is specifically American in the American political tradition.

Although the essential mutability of nature had been proclaimed as far back as Democritus, and the possibility that nature could be conquered by science for "the relief of man's estate" dated to Machiavelli and Bacon, the advent of Darwinism represented a significant breakthrough. Nature as permanent "flux" moved from the speculative to the practical realm, and greatly enhanced Darwinism's political importance. At the same time it further undermined the already shaky philosophical foundation of the idea of natural right.

Once nature is abandoned as the standard for thinking about political life, then so-called Social Darwinism and other more reform-minded varieties are really contesting a very narrow ground. Although the Social Darwinists, especially Herbert Spencer and William Graham Sumner, explicitly opposed government intervention in social life, Hofstadter's account is basically correct: their philosophical and scientific premises elide almost imperceptibly into Progressivism through a lineage that includes Lester Ward, Edward Bellamy, and pragmatists such as John Dewey.

Although Herbert Spencer seems to endorse the traditional Lockean understanding of natural right (especially with regard to property), he nevertheless points the way toward the Social Darwinist rejection of natural right as "the unchanging ground of changing experience" for political life. "Let us, then," Spencer wrote in *The Man Versus the State*, "transfer this question of natural rights from the court of politics to the court of science – the science of life."[19] This modified approach to natural right is explained most clearly in Spencer's discussion of "The Social Organism," in which he considers the traditional political analogies, especially in

Plato's *Republic* and Hobbes's *Leviathan,* between the composition and health of the human body, and the composition and health of political constitutions. While admitting that "these speculations have considerable significance," they are ultimately in error because they are "lacking the great generalizations of biology." Lacking the knowledge of the spontaneous process by which nature orders and transforms itself, Plato, Hobbes, and other political theorists err in thinking political constitutions are matters of human artifice. Nature provides no guidance for choosing our political institutions, because these are not matters of choice. According to Spencer, "constitutions are not made, but grow."[20]

The task of completing the explicit rejection of natural right was left to William Graham Sumner. Hofstadter notes that "Sumner concluded that these principles of social evolution negated the traditional American ideology of equality and natural rights."[21] Sumner put his rejection of natural right in terms that nearly matched Bentham's famously pungent line that natural rights were "nonsense on stilts." "Before the tribunal of nature," Sumner wrote in his most memorable formulation, "a man has no more rights than a rattlesnake; he has no more right to liberty than any wild beast."[22] "There can be no rights against nature or against God," because rights "are not absolute. They are not antecedent to civilization. They are a product of civilization."[23] Condemning "the complete and ruinous absurdity of this view," Sumner wrote: "The notion of natural rights is destitute of sense, but it is captivating, and it is the more available on account of its vagueness. It lends itself to the most vicious kind of social dogmatism . . . "[24]

Hofstadter also notes that Sumner even anticipates

J. Allen Smith's and Charles Beard's critiques of the founding.[25] Indeed, Sumner anticipates well the kind of rhetoric that would become central to Progressivism:

> The public men of the Revolutionary period were not democrats – they feared democracy. The Constitution-makers were under an especial dread of democracy, which they identified with the anarchism of the period of 1783–1787. They therefore established by the Constitution a set of institutions which are restrictions of democracy. They did not invent any of these institutions, for all of them were already familiar in the colonies, being of English origin and developed and adapted to the circumstances here. Their general character is that while they ensure the rule of the majority of legal voters, they yet insist upon it that the will of that majority shall be constitutionally expressed and that it shall be a sober, mature, and well-considered will. This constitutes a guarantee against jacobinism. Now the whole genius of this country has been democratic. I have tried to show that its inherited dogmas and its environment made it so inevitably. Down through history, therefore, the democratic temper of the people has been at war with the Constitutional institutions.[26]

This passage is less ironic that it seems. Sumner obviously approved of the procedural limitations on pure majoritarian democracy that the founders incorporated into the Constitution. But by rejecting natural rights he abandons the purpose and substantive ends of these limitations on pure democratic rule, namely the protection of the natural rights of the individual against unjust acts of willful majorities. By attributing the American form of government merely to "inherited dogmas," Sumner betrays a casual attention to the thought of the founding. "It does not appear," Sumner wrote in the same essay, "that anybody payed any attention to the first paragraph of the Declaration of Independence when it was written or that anybody except Thomas Paine then held to the dogmas of democracy."[27] This is blithely to ignore not only the narrow issue of the close attention paid by the Continental Congress to the wording and terms of the Declaration's prologue, but also the many parallel passages found in the state constitutions of the time (such as, for example, the Virginia Declaration of Rights).[28] Having rejected the substantive end of natural right spelled out in the Declaration, Sumner goes on to make the now-familiar argument that the Constitution is a mere instrumentality:

> The Constitution of 1787 is also remarkable, considering the time at which it was framed, for containing no dogmatic utterances about liberty and equality and no enunciation of great principles. Indeed this was made a ground of complaint against it by the leaders of the popular party; they missed the dogmatic utterances to which they had become accustomed during the war and they forced the passage of the first ten amendments. Even then, however, the Constitution contained no declaration of rights, but was simply a working system of government.[29]

What Lincoln identified as the central "proposition" of the American regime – "an abstract truth applicable to all men at all times" – Sumner dismisses as a "dogmatic utterance." To the contrary, Sumner makes a claim that could nearly be attributed to Oliver Wendell Holmes or Roscoe Pound or another Progressive positivist:

> There are no dogmatic propositions of political philosophy which are universally and always true; there are views which prevail, at a time, for a while, and then fade away and give place to other views. . . . The eighteenth century notions about equality, natural rights, classes, etc., produced nineteenth century states and legislation, and strongly humanitarian in faith and temper; at the present time the eighteenth century notions are disappearing, and the mores of the twentieth century will not be tinged by humanitarianism as those of the last 100 years have been. If the State should act on ideas of every man's duty, instead of on notions of natural rights, evidently institutions and usages would undergo a great transformation.[30]

Sumner also implicitly endorses the Roger Taney view of the Declaration in the *Dred Scott* case:

> But no man ever yet asserted that "all men are equal," meaning what he said. Although he said, "all men," he had in mind some limitation of the group he was talking about. Thus, if you asked Thomas Jefferson, when he was writing the first paragraph [he actually means the second paragraph] of the Declaration of Independence, whether in "all men" he meant to include negroes, he would have said that he was not talking about negroes. Ask anybody who says it now

> whether he means to include foreigners – Russian Jews, Hungarians, Italians – and he will draw his line somewhere ... Now, if we draw the line at all, the dogma is ruined.[31]

The rejection of natural right becomes even more pronounced in the works of the "transitional" figures who pointed the way toward reform Darwinism. Lester Ward is the preeminent figure in this process of rejection. In *Dynamic Sociology*, Ward writes:

> Not until we have succeeded in banishing the metaphysical conception of abstract right, and taken down the unrealizable standards of an imaginary disinterestedness in action, shall we be prepared to discuss intelligently the conditions of man's progress conceived as capable of accomplishment by his own efforts.[32]

Ward argues that the primary law of nature is force, and to deploy force in pursuit of progress means that there must be an organized source of power in human society. "It is here," Ward wrote, "that the new science is destined to be strongly antagonized by the growth of erroneous ideas respecting liberty. The so-called 'abstract rights' of mankind must be denied if society is ever to become the arbiter of its own destiny ... "[33] Ward's turn from Spencer and Sumner's *laissez faire* is accomplished by the simple extension of man's dominion over nature to include *human* nature. Ward rightly notes that Spencerian and Sumnerian Social Darwinism is applied selectively. Spencer and Sumner object only to *government* meddling in social life, not private meddling.

> This *laissez faire* school has entrenched itself behind the fortification of science, and while declaring with truth that social phenomena are, like physical phenomena, uniform and governed by laws, they have accompanied this by the false declaration and *non sequitur* that neither physical nor social phenomena are capable of human control; the fact being that all the practical benefits of science are the result of man's control of natural forces and phenomena which would otherwise have run to waste or operated as enemies to human progress.[34]

Why then, Ward asks in many times and in many ways, cannot science be applied to the conquest of human nature and human society as well? His most memorable statement of this creed appears in *Dynamic Sociology*:

> Objectively viewed, society is a natural object, presenting a variety of complicated movements produced by a particular class of natural forces. The question, therefore, simply is, Can man ever control these forces to his advantage as he controls other, and some very complicated, natural forces? *Is it true that man shall ultimately obtain the dominion of the whole world except himself?*[35] (Emphasis added.)

If "abstract right," as Ward calls it, is abandoned as the ground of liberty and as the end of civil government, one might expect an indifference to the kind of "regime analysis" that informed classical as well as early modern political authors, such as the American Founders. Ward is forthright enough to recognize this implication. He describes a new universal form of government, "Sociocracy," which he admits is "quite distinct from democracy," and distinct from socialism as well.

> Sociocracy stands opposed only to the absence of a regulative system .... *It recognizes all forms of government as legitimate,* and, ignoring *form,* goes to the *substance,* and denotes that, in whatever manner organized, it is the duty of society to act consciously and intelligently, as becomes an enlightened age, in the direction of guarding its own interests and working out its own destiny.[36] (Emphasis added.)

Gone are individual rights, consent of the governed, the classical understanding of the relationship between the form of a government, the substance of its rule, and any rational test of the moral legitimacy of regimes.

* * *

Today, Social Darwinism (like Darwinism generally) retains currency as a powerful idiom in American political and social discourse. The term still conjures up a stigma against the idea of free markets. Social Darwinism might be said to stand in relation to free-market ideology as McCarthyism stands in relation to anti-Communism. To extend the comparison, just as McCarthyism compelled anti-Communism to turn away from frothy conspiracy theories to a more intellectual and principled opposition, so too the popular revulsion against the enduring stigma of Social Darwinism has caused modern advocates of free markets to rearticulate the ancient Smithian faith on new grounds. These grounds do not, for the most part, include a revival of the idea of natural right on which previous versions of free-market ideology were based. This may be considered the permanent triumph of Darwinism and Progressivism. The most sophisticated version of modern free-market ideology can be said to rest on epistemological rather than teleological grounds. It often includes strong evolutionary overtones.

Whereas the Progressive idea of the administrative state was based on confidence in scientific "expertise" to guide the further evolution of society, the new *laissez faire* came along to say to the putative experts: you can't know enough to do it right. This, in crude form, is the core of the teaching of the twentieth century's preeminent free-market theorist, Friedrich Hayek. Hayek can be credited with launching the counter-revolution in economics against the idea of the administrative state. The "new" *laissez faire* in fact shares some of the essential aspects of the decayed *laissez faire* that Progressivism replaced. This is an important consideration because contemporary free-market ideology – especially the "public choice" variety – frequently represents itself as a restoration of the political economy of the American Founding. But the political economy of the founding was for the most part Lockean, and rested on the centrality of politics and statesmanship directed toward an appreciation of the classical idea of human excellence. Locke is missing from Hayekian political economy (which explains the almost complete absence of any discussion of individual rights in Hayek), and his allies in other varieties of free-market ideology share his anti-political bent. To the extent that Progressivism attacked *laissez faire* as a means of completing the rejection of the idea of natural right, the new *laissez faire* cannot be said to represent a restoration or revival of pre-Progressive thought. The "new" *laissez faire* is in many ways entirely harmonious with certain aspects of Progressive ideology. All of which means that the project of vindicating the American Founding does not run primarily through the economics department.

Progressivism, Conservatism, and the Work of Charles R. Kesler

Ronald J. Pestritto

Scholarly work on America's original Progressives has been fairly robust over the last decade or two, with political theorists and political scientists adding their contributions to an area of study previously occupied almost entirely by historians. Treatments of progressivism and the most important figures of the Progressive Era have even, with some regularity, appeared in the popular press during this time and been the subject of argument among public intellectuals. The emergence of Progressivism from its previous obscurity is owing in large measure to a recent intensification of long-simmering trends in American politics and the crisis in which the regime now finds itself.

While it is difficult to fix too precisely the moment of this change, the 2008 presidential election cycle was clearly a major catalyst. It was during that cycle that the Left embraced its Progressive Era roots. In part, this change in the public articulation of its political principles came from a desire to avoid the term "liberal," which the Right had succeeded over the preceding decades in turning into a dirty word. Instead, the Left's public figures began connecting themselves to their Progressive Era forebears, in search not only of a more palatable way of saying "liberal," but also as a result of some more serious reflection on the roots of their public philosophy. On the campaign trail in 2008, Democrats began citing the likes of Woodrow Wilson and Theodore Roosevelt. Much more significantly, when President Obama was elected he began to *govern* as a progressive, serving notice that his campaign pledge to "transform America" was more than mere rhetoric.

If progressivism represented – for Obama and his fellow Leftists – an expression of their philosophy of transformation, it was also a motivation for the Right to reconsider how the regime had been torn from its roots. This ushered in a renewed interest in the principles and political science of the American Founding. It also gave rise to a search, by conservative scholars, for a better understanding of where things had gone off the rails – a search that led many of them to America's original Progressives. Unlike these latecomers to the party (or the funeral, depending upon one's point of view), scholars in the Claremont orbit had been on the case long before 2008, and it was this pre-existing scholarship – preeminently the work of Charles Kesler – to which the conservative intellectual world was able to turn to understand the damage wrought by the Progressives and their progeny.

For most of the twentieth century, almost all of work on the Progressives had been done by historians, who as a rule did not see anything radical in Progressivism. Instead, from the historians' perspective, Progressive Era statesmen like Wilson and Teddy Roosevelt were men of great practical vision, responding to unprecedented circumstances that the nation's founders could not have envisioned, and adjusting the nature of American government in order to deal with those new challenges. The work done by Claremont scholars took a different view; we saw (and still see) in the Progressive changes to American government a more fundamental departure from the regime's core principles, and thus came to understand the Progressives as central figures in the story of America's decline.

Not all of this kind of work came out of the Claremont orbit. Paul Eidelberg's *Discourse on Statesmanship* made an early case for Progressivism's pivotal role, and the "modern presidency" school – exemplified by James Ceaser's *Presidential Selection* – looked to the influence of Progressivism on American institutions and rhetoric.[1] But these works shared a common ancestry with those coming out of Claremont: they were influenced to one degree or another by Leo Strauss and his approach to the study of politics, which understood the American regime through the natural-law principles of its founders. Progressives launched their own project with a self-conscious rejection of those natural-law principles, and thus many scholars influenced by Strauss came to see the story of America as represented in the clash between founding principles and their rejection by the Progressive fathers of modern liberalism.

In this vein, my own work on Wilson and other Progressives, and Bradley Watson's on progressive jurisprudence, was preceded by the work of John Marini on the administrative state and Dennis Mahoney on Progressivism and the discipline of political science.[2] But most influential on my generation of scholars was the work of Kesler, who not only taught multiple classes dealing with Progressivism but also authored two landmark essays on Progressivism and early liberalism whose core arguments find their way into many subsequent pieces of scholarship on the Progressives, and into two important books by Kesler himself.

The first of the essays, "Woodrow Wilson and the Statesmanship of Progress," was published in 1984 in the festschrift for Harry Jaffa, who was one of Strauss's chief students and the godfather of the Claremont school of Straussianism.[3] The second essay, on "The Public Philosophy of The New Freedom and The New Deal," came in 1989, in a collection on the New Deal and its legacy.[4] Animated by these two earlier essays, Kesler's more recent book, *Crisis of the Two Constitutions,* is organized around two poles, the founders' constitution and the modern-day progressives' constitution, and is premised on the contrast between their two opposing public philosophies.[5]

With respect to the second pole, Kesler's other recent book provides a fuller account of the story. In *I Am the Change: Barack Obama and the Crisis of Liberalism,* the Progressive and post-Progressive constitution is cast as a series of liberal waves, the first coming with Wilson and original progressivism, the second with FDR and the New Deal, the third with the Great Society of LBJ, and the final wave crashing down with Barack Obama, who saw himself as a transformative figure on the order of FDR.[6] Kesler's thesis on these successive waves of modern liberalism rests on his assessment of the Progressives; this is an assessment which is foundational not only to his own later work, but also to much of what the Claremont school has contributed to the study of progressivism and modern liberalism. We turn now to these landmark essays.

The combined effect of the essays is to trace the modern American welfare state not just to the practical transformation in government that was consummated in the New Deal, but to the rejection of the founders' core principles – a rejection that animated the rise of modern liberalism in the early part of the twentieth century. America since the mid-twentieth century constitutes, for all intents and purposes, a fundamentally new regime, built on a repudiation of the founders' philosophy and a dismantling of their constitutional arrangements. This sharp contrast between the original and the new America is exemplified in Kesler's contrast of Wilson and Abraham Lincoln – between the latter's "New Birth of Freedom" and the former's "New Freedom." Lincoln's "new birth," Kesler contends, was a "reawakening" to old, timeless principles – a "rededication to the principles that our forefathers had brought forth in 1776. Wilson's New Freedom, by contrast, was the dictate of a completely new age, the declaration of a break with the past."[7] The seeds of what would later become Kesler's "two constitutions" thesis are found here in the context of the Civil War and its aftermath. One kind of newness was really a return to, or perfection of, the original regime's liberty principles, now strengthened by the demise of slavery; but the other kind of newness was genuinely novel. Put differently, the old contradiction in America – a dedication to equal natural rights in principle while slavery was still legal in the South – was resolved under Lincoln, only to give rise to the new, fundamental contradiction between natural-rights constitutionalism and the progressive modern state.[8]

For Kesler, it was Wilson's New Freedom that marked

the first departure from the original freedom, even though most observers would presumably point to the New Deal, which is when, after all, American government really began to *look* different. But one of Kesler's achievements in his essays is to show the connection of the New Deal to the New Freedom – to show how they were animated by the same public philosophy, and thus to credit Wilson as the real father of modern American liberalism.

The tie between the New Freedom and the New Deal is the rejection, by both, of the nation's original political philosophy. Kesler enlists FDR himself in making this case, documenting FDR's many direct attributions of Wilson as the real founder of his project.[9] As Kesler explains, "the incompleteness of the New Freedom was the starting point, indeed the *raison d'etre*, of the New Deal." Wilson's "theoretical and practical achievements made the New Deal thinkable."[10] What FDR did not share with Wilson, at least entirely, was his methods. FDR knew better than Wilson that the practical achievement of the aims they shared depended on supplying a veneer of continuity with the past, and so FDR was not nearly as explicit about breaking with the founders as Wilson had been. And while Wilson had emphasized, in the New Freedom, the need to break up the big economic combinations, FDR accepted their existence and sought, instead, to regulate and channel them for progressive ends.[11] Kesler follows a similar mode when assessing the underlying political philosophies of the New Freedom and the New Deal. He explains that, like Hegel and Marx, both Wilson and FDR subscribed to the philosophy of historicism. Yet Wilson reflected more of Hegel's idealism, while FDR's economic assumptions made him more of a neo-Marxist.[12]

The historicism of the New Freedom and the New Deal ushered in a new regime based upon a claim to a new kind of insight: knowledge of the outcome of history, which theretofore had been considered to be beyond the grasp of the human mind. The founders' governing philosophy, by contrast, had always maintained a healthy sobriety about the limits of human reason: confident enough in it to embrace popular government, but cautious enough to require the refinement of that consent through the Constitution's political science. The Progressive critique of the founders spurned this caution about human reason, as well as the Constitution's many mechanisms for filtering direct popular rule. Kesler's analogy to explain this new progressive assumption about the capacity of human reason is the Fall of Man in the Garden of Eden. As a consequence of the Progressives' utopianism, he writes,

> Hope-filled experiments in American politics began to be conducted, whose character was not altogether unlike that epochal experiment dared by our ancestors in the Garden, while God was not looking. The same pretension that found its temptation, and purpose, in the liberation of the passions reached out for knowledge of a new kind – for the wisdom of history that was at once a completion and nullification of the knowledge of good and evil.[13]

Thus the Progressives ushered in an understanding of the nature of man different from that which had informed the framing of the Constitution. This observation is likely why many of Kesler's students write and teach about *The Federalist*, as this work perhaps more than any other exemplifies the connection between the institutional arrangements of the Constitution and the founders' philosophic assumptions about human nature.[14] It is also why the Progressive transformation of American government is not primarily about institutions or policies; while the Progressive substitutions *are* different from the founders' institutions, the founders clearly envisioned that new policies and even new institutional arrangements would inevitably arise in response to exigencies that they knew they could not foresee. The transformation is, more fundamentally, about ends of government – about what the founders considered to be the core, timeless truths of human nature.

Both Wilson and FDR took direct aim at this claim, and insisted, instead, that there could be no permanent ends of government. This critique comes out most clearly in Kesler's treatment of FDR's 1932 Commonwealth Club Address as the centerpiece of the New Deal's public philosophy. He shows that FDR, for all of his optimism about man's capacity to employ the *science* of government, was skeptical of any claim to a "final word" on the *principles* of government. It is out of this skepticism that FDR rejected natural rights as a foundation for politics, replacing them with "a quest, a never-ending seeking for better things."[15] His aim here, as Kesler points out, was practical as well as principled; he employed this rhetoric both to argue that the country could free itself from the Depression and to urge that we free ourselves from our own first principles.

For Wilson's part, "freedom" meant liberating ourselves from the spell of Thomas Hobbes, whose hyper-individualistic philosophy Wilson put at the center of the founding. But unlike the "Eastern" Straussian critics of the founding, Wilson's aim was not to reject Hobbes's base account of human nature for a more noble one from the past, but to reject human nature altogether as a guide for moral and political life.[16] Government, instead, must be contingent upon history, and thus evolutionary as opposed to fixed. The core of Wilson's New Freedom campaign in 1912 was to reject the precise, mechanistic, "Newtonian" philosophy of the founders, and to replace it with the Darwinian principle of evolution.[17] Wilson thus made frequent criticisms of what the Federalists had called the great "improvements" to the science of politics: separation of powers, checks and balances, and the competition of interests in the extended sphere.[18] Nevertheless, Wilson's pervasive and undisguised criticisms of the Constitution and the bedrock ideas of American government were either ignored by the conventional historical scholarship or casually explained away. Kesler's writings are significant for highlighting the radicalism of the Progressives, and putting Wilson at the center of their bold, new conception of American government.

In laying out Wilson's critique of both the Constitution and its underlying philosophy of natural rights, Kesler thus illuminates the necessarily tight reliance of the founders' institutional arrangements on the philosophy of the Declaration of Independence. In showing this connection, Kesler is too polite to explain how it cuts against the argument of his teacher, Harvey C. Mansfield Jr., who had contended that the forms of the Constitution were an important corrective to the philosophic exuberance of the Declaration.[19] For Kesler, the continuity between the Declaration and Constitution is of the greatest importance, as is Wilson's attempt to "sever" that connection. Kesler shows that Wilson's often lengthy dives into the political theory of the Declaration included twisting its words out of any recognizable or coherent meaning.[20] Subsequent Claremont scholarship on the Progressives has emphasized the vitality of the tie between the Declaration and Constitution – a tie that had, of course, been highlighted by Harry Jaffa.[21]

FDR also knew that, in order to weaken the Constitution, he had to undermine the Declaration. Kesler's explanation of how this was accomplished in the Commonwealth Club Address is highly original, showing that FDR claimed to be abiding by the terms of the Declaration's social contract while he actually altered their meaning in fundamental ways. FDR's social contract was no longer between individuals but rather between the rulers and their subjects. As Kesler demonstrates, this new "deal" granted more power to the rulers in exchange for more rights to their subjects.[22] And of course these were not natural rights (which don't come, after all, from government) but entitlement rights. FDR was prudent enough to know that this could only be sold by making it appear to align with America's origins. This rhetorical prudence was mostly absent from FDR's Progressive predecessors, who emphasized rupture with the past, yet only their tactics differed. In terms of the new principles, Kesler explains, "Roosevelt adopts Wilson's theory of the Constitution wholesale.... The terms of the agreement, far from resting on unchanging and unalienable rights, are offered up as negotiable and renegotiable."[23] Roosevelt even telegraphed what he was up to, telling us in the same space that he was embracing the rights tradition of the founding, but also that "the task of statesmanship has always been the redefinition of these rights."[24]

Statesmanship and Leadership

If rights are up for redefinition from one epoch to the next and if government is all about evolution, what is it that actually determines the course of our politics? The New Freedom and the New Deal tell us that the answer is supplied by history, which replaces the role previously assigned by the founders to nature. But what does that mean? Perhaps the most important of the contributions made by Kesler's landmark essays is to focus on Wilson's radically new understanding of statesmanship in laying out an answer to this question. This new, anti-philosophic understanding is most clearly seen in Wilson's 1889 essay "Leaders of Men";[25] Kesler draws on that text as well as Wilson's unfinished draft of *The Philosophy of Politics* to uncover the term "statesmanship of progress" and give fuller meaning to the novelty of Wilson's account of statesmanship and leadership.[26] When the people decide for themselves, from one generation to the next, what form their liberty will take, Wilson explained that they need guidance – and they are guided not by nature or by God, but by leaders with vision, whose role Wilson described as the "statesmanship of progress."[27]

Kesler begins his explanation of this concept by looking first to the traditional understanding of statesmanship, locating it in Aristotle's definition of prudence. Aristotelian prudence rests on two kinds of knowledge: the first is knowledge of what is good and just by nature and is grounded in moral virtue; the second is knowledge of the particulars of one's own regime, and of what is possible given the limitations of prevailing laws, customs, mores, and external circumstances, e.g., actually or potentially hostile neighbors. The exercise of prudence requires both kinds of knowledge, which form the statesman's effort to effectuate natural justice as far as conventional circumstances allow.[28] The practice of statesmanship will thus vary from one circumstance to the next, but the guide for statesmanship will always be the timeless principles that nature supplies as a lodestar for moral and political life. As Kesler explains, "Prudence is the ability to deliberate well concerning the best means to the ends supplied by moral virtue. But moral virtue ... presumes that [the] human being is articulated in a fixed and permanent way."[29] On this point, Kesler puts his finger on the great significance of Wilson, who contended that the older account of statesmanship, which rests on a fixed account of nature, is made obsolete by the new knowledge of historical progress. "Wilson," he elaborates, "believed that the historical school of philosophy in England and Germany had succeeded in anachronizing – and so disproving – the idea of nature as a standard for moral and political life, opening the way for the introduction of a new kind of statesmanship into American politics."[30] Instead of the prudent applications of the same, consistent understanding of human nature, Wilson believed in a new and ever-evolving account of what it means to be a human being.

Put another way, Wilson's concept of statesmanship does not rest on a distinction between the theoretical and the practical. His statesman doesn't look beyond the particulars of his own circumstances in order to apprehend universals. He doesn't see the good apart from history; he sees it only *in* history. The reforming leader is an embodiment of the historical *Geist*, not someone who gains a statesmanlike perspective by detaching himself from it. As Kesler explains, "However great [the leader] may be, in the final analysis his greatness has very little to do with himself. He is produced by the occasion.... Great reformers are 'early vehicles of the Spirit of the Age,' but nothing more."[31] The likes of Washington or Lincoln were great because they were the best expressions of their times, not because they could see something higher or better in spite of their times.[32] Though Kesler doesn't quite put it this way, these leaders were closer to Hegel's world-historical individual than they were to Aristotle's statesman. The only thing that truly matters for Wilson's leaders is to embody and to see the direction of history, to follow it, and to impel the people to follow it. The analogy that Kesler uses is the steamboat captain on a foggy river: he cannot navigate by looking to the sky or the stars, because those things cannot be seen; instead, there is a flow or a current to the river that the captain must follow.[33]

The account of the statesman that sees him as a man of his times does not mean that Wilson's statesman is simply a slave to public sentiment – far from it, as Wilson had no great regard for the sentiments of the average man. The statesman, as a man of his times, has keen insight into the path of history, and he becomes the means of reconciling majority sentiment to the historical cause. "The rallying point for reform ... is a vision of the future – an understanding of the direction that history is about to take. ... The highest kind of statesmanship [is] quickening the conscience of society and freeing it from the sluggishness of all self-interest and partial attachments."[34] So the statesmanship of progress is about the superiority of the statesman's vision of history's path and the ability to bring the public around to that vision. This is where Kesler's analysis leans heavily on Wilson's "Leaders of Men," where Wilson was candid about the power of the leader to move men – to mold them as clay in his hands. The most effective way to mold and to move men, Wilson believed, is to make them receptive to the general idea of progress itself, to "foster a confidence in the beneficence of change," as Kesler explains.[35] So the people must become attached to the broad notion of progress, while the details are left deliberately vague; the people will move if the leader keeps them focused on the necessity of progress itself. And such a popular focus can best be achieved by attaching the people to the person of the leader, whom they see as the embodiment of their own future, as the "imagination-capturing avatar of the dawning spirit of the age."[36]

Kesler's 1989 essay "The Public Philosophy of the New Freedom and New Deal" brings further precision to the distinction between the "statesman" and the "leader." *Statesmanship*, in this context, refers to the more traditional, Aristotelian understanding. *Leadership*, by contrast, reflects Wilson's historicized visionary. Kesler explains that "leadership" was a "new word in American politics that Wilson helped to define and popularize," so that the leader becomes "the herald of the overcoming of his own times."[37] Modern leadership also relies on a certain kind of political structure: in order for the people to see and feel in the leader an embodiment of themselves and their future, a direct connection is required and mediating institutions must be diminished or removed. The popular arts of leadership must be given opportunity to work their influence on the public mind. As Kesler explains, this necessity is what accounts for Wilson's preference for direct government over political parties and traditional political institutions.[38]

FDR's political reforms were, like Wilson's, predicated on historical progress, which is how Kesler connects their public philosophies. FDR argued in the Commonwealth

Club Address that the time was ripe for a new order or "deal." But reaching this point of liberation had required the nation to undergo a prior period of unchecked greed and individualism. This was particularly true of the "financial Titans" of the nineteenth century, whose methods were nasty, but whom FDR does not really criticize because their nastiness had been historically necessary.[39] Readers of Hegel's *Philosophy of History*, or even of Marx's *Communist Manifesto*, will recognize this argument, and Kesler explains that, to FDR, "it is as if morality were impossible in those days."[40] Morality is only possible at the culmination of history, and past "crimes" are minimized due to their historical utility. This historicism translated to FDR's economic principles as well, which rested on the assumption that production had now been maximized, and that it was time for a new epoch of regulation and redistribution. In connecting this assumption to German historical economics – running backward from Adolfe Berle and Rexford Tugwell to Simon Paten and Richard T. Ely – Kesler shows how mistaken these historical assumptions proved to be in light of what was to come next, especially the massively ramped-up production necessitated by the Second World War.[41] This assumption that economic necessity had been overcome by history justified the argument that it was time to move beyond questions of individual interest and concerns for providing for oneself. These interests could now be managed by the government, freeing the citizen for something higher. The argument of the Commonwealth Club Address was that "the search for a good existence, for the good life, can now be conducted without reference to the constraints of nature."[42] The practical consequences of this novel public philosophy become obvious in the new direction of American politics in the twentieth century: nationalization of commerce, major public works, independent regulatory commissions, progressive income taxation, welfare-state benefits coupled with the redistribution of income, federal financial assistance to – and thus control over – states and localities, and federal involvement in both lower and higher education.[43]

Progress and Conservative Intellectuals

In addition to its impact on American government, Kesler's account of Progressivism's public philosophy also helps to illuminate some important arguments among the conservative intellectuals who were, in various ways, critics of modern liberalism. One of the more interesting and original parts of the "Statesmanship of Progress" essay is the manner in which Kesler targets the Eastern Straussians by tying them to a key element of Wilson's Progressivism. Like Wilson, Kesler explains, the Eastern Straussians are also critics of the founding, seeing it – as do the Progressives – as base and hyper-individualistic.[44] Unlike the Progressives, the Eastern Straussians look, instead, to a dreamy vision of the common good as exemplified in the ancient polis. Yet Kesler contends that they – like the Progressives – are too ready to see the founding through the eyes of modern political philosophers, making them susceptible to overly romanticized notions of politics. "Since those who hold a vision of the past wish to see it reborn as a vision of the future, they have common ground with those who specialize in such visions: The road to radical modernity is paved with well-intentioned longings for antiquity." The proper study of American politics, by contrast, requires the citizen to resist utopian notions.

As Kesler contends, "This manner of study begins and ends with the perspective of a good citizen in the highest sense of the term, not with the perspective of an ungrateful dreamer who wishes he had been born elsewhere and in another time."[45]

Given the Progressives' utopianism about historical progress, it may seem strange that Wilson expressed considerable admiration for Edmund Burke and fashioned himself a Burkean of sorts. Wilson championed Burke's antipathy for theoretical or abstract principles like natural rights, and it was on the basis of this Burkean position that Wilson diminished the theory of the Declaration of Independence as mere rhetorical flourish.[46] While Kesler allows that there was much about Burke that Wilson did not know or get right, he follows Leo Strauss's critique of Burke from *Natural Right and History*[47] in pointing out that Burke's radical focus on the concrete and his antipathy to abstract right make him vulnerable to abuse from the likes of Wilson. After all, if one cannot understand political justice outside of history or tradition, what is to prevent progressives like Wilson from arguing that the principles of government are merely the products of any given historical age? Making precisely this point, Kesler makes sure to cite Wilson's quotation of Burke where the latter defines "free government" as "what the people think."[48] Liberty is not, for Burke or Wilson, a timeless concept tethered to the law of nature, but is something to be "conservatively" redefined from one age to the next. Kesler also quotes Wilson on the connection between Burkean conservatism and the idea of progress: "You have the law of conservatism disclosed: it is a law of progress."[49] Some historians claim that there are two irreconcilable Wilsons: the Burkean and the progressive nationalist. Kesler wants to show that there is more continuity between these two positions than is commonly understood. And this argument also brings out a second purpose, which is to suggest that Burkean traditionalism may not be the strongest or most coherent defense against modern liberalism.

Kesler's account of Progressivism, in fact, is pretty clearly aimed at the misconceptions of American political thought by various elements of the intellectual Right. He rejects the libertarian depiction of nineteenth-century America, and concedes that some of the federal expansion during that century was not inconsistent with the founders' or Lincoln's principles. The nineteenth century in America was not, in other words, a libertarian utopia that was ruined by the rise of Progressivism, and thus Kesler would reject the facile narrative of a clear-cut distinction between twentieth-century statism and a nineteenth-century Wild West. But Kesler's critique applies even more to today's post-liberals, who do not see in Progressive liberalism anything all that different from the founders' original liberalism. His account of the Progressives' public philosophy, which FDR carried forward into the New Deal, rests on the Progressives' rejection, both in principle and in practice, of the founders' enterprise.

Kesler's work on the Progressives and the rise of modern liberalism is thus important on two levels. On the level of scholarship, the 1980s essays were a key part of a very small number of works on the Progressives by political theorists, at a time when almost no one in the discipline paid much attention to them. These works helped form a foundation for subsequent scholarship by Kesler's students and others in the Claremont orbit – work that ended up garnering considerable attention both in academia and the public press when interest in the Progressive Era intensified after 2008.

On the level of politics, Kesler's framework for understanding the role of Progressivism provides a persuasive and compelling alternative to two powerful intellectual camps on the Right today. One camp, loosely termed post-liberalism, sees the entire American project as poisoned from the start by its Enlightenment origins. For this group, the distinction made by Kesler between early and later American liberalism is a small matter, since liberalism itself is the problem. The critical break for them was not between twentieth-century liberalism and the founders' liberalism, but between American liberalism generally and the pre-liberal order that preceded it. The argument is most famously exemplified today by Patrick Deneen, though it is widespread on the Right and was a significant element of the conservative intellectual movement in America for many decades prior to Deneen.[50] On the other end of the Right, there is the neoconservative camp that is largely at peace with all of American liberalism. Like the post-liberals, this camp does not buy into what Kesler calls the "two constitutions" framework; the differences between contemporary liberalism and the founders' liberalism do not, in their view, amount to any kind of regime change. This view is also widespread on the Right, though one of the best expressions of it can be found in Shep Melnick's critical review of *Crisis of the Two Constitutions*.[51] Kesler's framework, according to this camp, is politically dangerous, because in depicting the founding as the ideal, and in arguing that today's regime is a radical departure from the founding, Kesler allegedly stokes a revolutionary temper, alienating those under his influence from their own regime – forcing them to choose, in other words, between fidelity to the founding or fidelity to America today.

Kesler's work, fortunately, provides a more palatable alternative to both of these problematic positions on the

Right. Against the post-liberals, he shows why conservatives ought to be patriotic Americans. What post-liberals detest about modern America comes not from the regime's original principles but from a self-conscious repudiation of those principles by the Progressives and their progeny. In this way, conservatives can save themselves from the despair not only of the post-liberal Right, but also of its often nihilistic cousin – those elements of the online or "alt" Right that reject all notions of a principled foundation for the American regime. And against the neoconservatives, Kesler's framework offers an alternative to blind acceptance of the regime's decline and potential demise. The position of Melnick and others, after all, is remarkably unphilosophic – it wants to suggest that any detachment from the present, any criticism of it from the perspective of the regime's first principles, is inherently revolutionary and dangerous. But if that's true, then what are we left with besides a fatalistic historicism? Kesler shows, instead, that true reform must begin with understanding our first principles and recognizing how radically separated from them we have become; this is the only way that the work of recovery can begin.

About the Authors

MICHAEL ANTON is the Claremont Institute's Jack Roth Senior Fellow in American Politics and a lecturer at Hillsdale College. He is the author of *After the Flight 93 Election: The Vote that Saved America and What We Still Have to Lose* and most recently *The Stakes: America at the Point of No Return.*

MURRAY S. Y. BESSETTE is vice president of education at Common Sense Society and was previously an associate professor of government at Morehead State University and director of academic programs at the Victims of Communism Memorial Foundation.

TIMOTHY W. CASPAR is associate vice president for external affairs, deputy editor of *Imprimis,* and lecturer in politics at Hillsdale College. He is the author of *Recovering the Ancient View of Founding: A Commentary on Cicero's* De Legibus.

GLENN ELLMERS is the Claremont Institute's Salvatori Research Fellow in the American Founding. He is the author of *The Soul of Politics: Harry V. Jaffa and the Fight for America* and most recently *The Narrow Passage: Plato, Foucault, and the Possibility of Political Philosophy.*

STEVEN F. HAYWARD is a fellow of the Public Law and Policy Program at Berkeley Law, and the Gaylord Distinguished Visiting Professor at Pepperdine University's School of Public Policy.

VINCENT PHILLIP MUÑOZ is the Tocqueville Professor of Political Science, Concurrent Professor of Law, and founding director of the Center for Citizenship & Constitutional Government at the University of Notre Dame, and a Distinguished Fellow of the Civitas Institute at the University of Texas at Austin. His most recent book is *Religious Liberty and the American Founding: Natural Rights and the Original Meanings of the First Amendment Religion Clauses.*

ANTHONY A. PEACOCK is a professor in the Political Science Department at Utah State University, and the director of USU's Center for the Study of American Constitutionalism. His most recent book is *Vindicating the Commercial Republic:* The Federalist *on Union, Enterprise, and War.*

RONALD J. PESTRITTO is graduate dean and Shipley Professor of the American Constitution at Hillsdale College, and a senior fellow of the Claremont Institute. His most recent book is *America Transformed: The Rise and Legacy of American Progressivism.*

MATTHEW SPALDING is the Kirby Professor in Constitutional Government at Hillsdale College, the dean of the Van Andel Graduate School of Government at Hillsdale College's Washington, DC, campus, and is a senior fellow of the Claremont Institute.

BRADLEY C. S. WATSON teaches at the Van Andel Graduate School of Government at Hillsdale College in Washington, DC. He is a senior fellow of the Claremont Institute and has authored or edited many books, including *Living Constitution, Dying Faith: Progressivism and the New Science of Jurisprudence* and most recently *Progressivism: The Strange History of a Radical Idea.*

Notes

ON FIRST LOOKING INTO PLATO'S *LAWS*

1. Plato, *Laws*, 853c. All quotations are from *The Laws of Plato*, trans. Thomas L. Pangle (New York: Basic Books, 1980).
2. Ibid., 854b.
3. Ibid., 853b.
4. Ibid., 854a, 854c.
5. Ibid., 853b.
6. Ibid., 863b–c.
7. Leo Strauss, *The Argument and the Action of Plato's Laws* (Chicago: University of Chicago Press, 1975), 133.
8. *Laws*, 867a.
9. Ibid., 804b.
10. Ibid., 875c–d.
11. The Stranger sets forth these goals for the penal law at 854d, 855a, and 862d. But as we shall see, he ends deviating from them.
12. Ibid., 859e-860c.
13. Pangle, Interpretive Essay, in *The Laws of Plato*, 498.
14. *Laws*, Bk. IV.
15. Ibid., 862e.
16. Ibid., 862d–e.
17. Ibid., 862e.
18. Ibid., 862d–863a.
19. Ibid., 873e.
20. Ibid., 872d-873a.
21. Plato, *Protagoras*, 324b.
22. Plato, *Gorgias*, trans. Walter Hamilton (Harmondsworth, UK: Penguin, 1983), 525b.
23. Ibid., 507d.
24. *Laws*, 645a–b.
25. *Politics*, trans. Carnes Lord (Chicago: University of Chicago, 1984), 1321b40.

Notes

26. Aristotle, *Politics*, 1322a1.
27. Aristotle, *Nicomachean Ethics*, 1179b–1180b and 1131b–1132b.
28. *NE*, trans. Martin Ostwald (New York: Macmillan, 1962), 1113b.
29. Ibid., 1113b.
30. Thucydides, *Peloponnesian War*, trans. Richard Crawley, rev. R. Feetham, Bk. III, chap. 40.
31. Roger Scruton, *A Dictionary of Political Thought* (London: Pan Books, 1983), 388. This definition is but one example of the near-universal distinction that is drawn in contemporary discussions of punishment. But Scruton is more perspicacious than most, for he includes an aspect of forward-looking (utilitarian) justifications that is frequently missed: "There is the 'expressive' theory, which justifies punishment in terms of its ability to express and relieve the feelings of public outrage at crime and to reaffirm the common moral sentiments of the community."
32. Thomas Hobbes, *Leviathan*, chap. 30.
33. *Leviathan*, chap. 30.
34. *Leviathan*, chap. 28.
35. *Leviathan*, chap. 27.
36. *Leviathan*, chap. 30.
37. See generally Rousseau, *Second Discourse, On the Origin and Foundations of Inequality Among Men.*
38. Rousseau, *The Social Contract*, in *On the Social Contract with Geneva Manuscript and Political Economy*, ed. Roger D. Masters, trans. Judith R. Masters (New York: St. Martin's Press, 1978), Bk. II, chap. v, p. 65.
39. Rousseau, *Discourse on Political Economy*, trans. Masters, 215.
40. Kant, *The Science of Right*, trans. W. Hastie, 49E.
41. Kant, *Critique of Pure Reason*, trans. J.M.D. Meiklejohn and Vasilis Politis (London: J.M. Dent, 1993), 376–79.
42. Hegel, *Elements of the Philosophy of Right*, ed. Allen W. Wood, trans. H.B. Nisbet (Cambridge: Cambridge University Press, 1991), s. 220.
43. *Philosophy of Right*, s. 100.
44. James Q. Wilson and Richard Hernnstein, *Crime and Human Nature* (New York: Simon and Schuster, 1985), 519.
45. Clarence Darrow, *Resist Not Evil* (Montclair, NJ: Patterson Smith, 1972), 94–95.
46. Robert Nisbet, *Prejudices: A Philosophical Dictionary* (Cambridge, MA: Harvard University Press, 1982), 72–74.
47. *Laws*, 853c.

Notes

CICERO: STATESMAN AND TEACHER OF STATESMEN

1. Anthony Everitt, *Cicero: The Life and Times of Rome's Greatest Politician* (New York: Random House, 2001), 140–45. Everitt offers a sympathetic, if at times overly psychoanalytic, account of Cicero's life and a general introduction to his times, though he does not see Cicero as an original thinker.
2. A.E.Douglas, "Cicero the Philosopher," in *Cicero*, ed. Thomas Dorey (London: Routledge, 1965), 162.
3. Cicero, *Letters to Atticus*, vol. 1, ed. and trans. D. R. Shackleton Bailey (Cambridge: Harvard University Press, 1999), 11.
4. For a list of several of "the seminal contributions to this now-booming trend," see the introduction to *The Cambridge Companion to Cicero's Philosophy*, ed. Jed W. Atkins and Thomas Bénatouïl (Cambridge: Cambridge University Press, 2022), 1n1. Two other recent works are James E.G. Zetzel, *The Lost Republic: Cicero's* De oratore *and* De re publica (New York: Oxford University Press, 2022), and Moryam VanOpstal, *An Ancient Guide to Good Politics: A Literary and Ethical Reading of Cicero's* De Re publica (Lanham: Lexington Books, 2023).
5. Marcus Tullius Cicero, *On the Republic* and *On the Laws*, Translated with Introduction, Notes, and Indexes by David Fott, (Ithaca: Cornell University Press, 2014), I.45, II.45. References will be abbreviated as DRP for *De re publica* (*On the Republic*) and DL for *De legibus* (*On the Laws*).
6. Everitt 2001, 161-164.
7. Cicero, *On the Ideal Orator*, trans. and ed. James M. May and Jakob Wisse (New York: Oxford University Press, 2001); see, e.g., I.59, II.33–34, III.60–61, 80–81. References will be abbreviated as DO for *De oratore*.
8. Marcus Tullius Cicero, *On Duties*, trans. and ed. Benjamin Patrick Newton (Ithaca: Cornell University Press, 2016).
9. Cicero, *Letters to Friends*, vol. 1, trans. and ed. D.R.Shackleton Bailey (Cambridge: Harvard University Press, 2001), 3.
10. *Letters to Friends*, Letter 20, 145.
11. Cicero, Ibid., 129.
12. Plato, *Republic*, trans. and ed. Allan Bloom (Basic Books, 1991), 488a–489d.
13. Julia Mebane, "Cicero's Ideal Statesman as the Helmsman of the Ship of State," *Classical Philology*, vol. 117, No. 1, January 2022: 120–38; 123: "In almost every speech that he delivered between his return from exile in 57 and departure for Cilicia in 51, he compares politics to a tumultuous sea voyage." In addition to *De re publica* and *De legibus*, which are the focus of this essay, see also DO I.8, 38, 46, and 214, III.131, and *De officiis*, I.77.
14. Cicero, *De senectute. De amicitia. De divinatione.*, Translated by William Armi-

stead Falconer (Cambridge: Harvard University Press, 1996), II.1–4. Further references to *De divinatione* will be abbreviated as DD.

15. DRP, I.2.
16. DL, I.14.
17. DRP, I.12.
18. Ibid., I.34.
19. DL, I.39, III.13–14; Cicero, *On Moral Ends*, ed. Julia Annas, trans. Raphael Woolf (New York: Cambridge University Press, 2001), II.74, 76–77.
20. See, e.g., Cicero, *Tusculan Disputations*, trans. J. E. King (Cambridge: Harvard University Press, 1996), V.11. Further references will be abbreviated as TD. See also *DD*, II.1. For additional references to Cicero's Academic skepticism, see *On Duties*, 201.
21. DRP, I.13; cf. TD, I.6, and Cicero, *On Academic Scepticism*, trans. and ed. Charles Brittain, (Indianapolis: Hackett, 2006), I.11.
22. Ibid., I.45.
23. Ibid., I.45.
24. Ibid., I.69; cf. I.54.
25. Ibid., I.52.
26. Ibid., I.69; cf. I.45, 54.
27. Ibid., I.70.
28. Walter Nicgorski, "Cicero's Focus: From the Best Regime to the Model Statesman," *Political Theory*, vol. 19, No. 2 (May 1991): 241.
29. DRP, I.65.
30. Ibid., II.44-51; quote is at 47.
31. Ibid., II.45.
32. Ibid., I.45.
33. Ibid., I.44.
34. Ibid., II.51.
35. For praise of Plato, see, e.g., DRP, I.16, 29, 65 and II.3, 21; DL, I.15, II.14, 39, and III.1, 5. For Cicero's independence, see, e.g., DRP, II.51–52; DL, II.17 and III.32; DF, I.6–7.
36. Ibid., II.51.
37. Ibid., I.2, 11.
38. Ibid., II.51 and n63: For further treatment of this "type," Fott points the reader to 2.67, 69; 3.3; 5.2–5; 6.1; 6.17. For further discussion, see Mebane 2022 (esp. 130 ff.), who argues, contrary to the view of some Cicero scholars past and present, that the title of helmsman is not restricted to one person at any given time but is rather descriptive of a certain virtuous human type; see also J. G. F. Powell,

"The *rector rei publicae* of Cicero's *De Republica*," *Scripta Classica Israelica* 13 (1994): 19–29.

39. DL, III.28.
40. Ibid., III.29.
41. Ibid., III.30.
42. Ibid., III.31.
43. Ibid., III.1, 32.
44. In his letter to Spinther, Cicero notes "the tendency for the members of a political society (*re publica*) to resemble its leaders (*principes*)." See Cicero, *Letters to Friends*, 129.
45. DRP, II.51.
46. Ibid., II.69.
47. Ibid., V.2.
48. E.g., DF, III.14–15, 55.
49. DRP, V.2.
50. Ibid., I.12.
51. Ibid., I.39.
52. Cf. Nicgorski 1991.
53. DRP, I.27–28; cf. Plato, *Republic*, 331c–d, 428b–429a, 473c–e, 475b–c, 479e–480a, 484b–d and DO, I.31, III.95.
54. DRP, I.31–34.
55. Ibid., III.27.
56. DL, I.20, II.23, III.4.
57. Ibid., I.18.
58. DRP, III.27.
59. DL, I.19.
60. Ibid., III.2.
61. DRP, II.57.
62. Ibid., II.56.
63. Ibid., II.57.
64. Ibid., II.59.
65. Ibid., II.45.
66. Ibid., II.59.
67. Ibid., II.69.
68. DL, III.19.
69. Ibid., III.23.
70. DRP, II.45, 51, 59.
71. DL, III.24, DRP, II.69.

72. One important theme of *De officiis* is the role circumstances often play in determining whether an action is honorable or disgraceful: see I.31, II.55–60, III.18–19, 29–32, 95.
73. DD, II.3.
74. Cicero, *Letters to Atticus*, Letter 21, 133.
75. Cicero, "Letters to Friends," 147; cf. Everitt 2001, 161-64.

THE MESSIAH OF THE MACHIAVELLIAN MOMENT

1. John Langton and Mary G. Deitz, "Machiavelli's Paradox: Trapping or Teaching the Prince," *American Political Science Review* 81, No. 4 (1987): 1277.
2. Rafael Major, "A New Argument for Morality: Machiavelli and the Ancients," *Political Research Quarterly* 60, No. 2 (2007): 172. And yet one might ask, what other than the end sought could justify the means selected? Moreover, to say "the end justifies the means" is not to say that the end justifies any and every means. The statement is compatible with the rational limitation that the selected means not undermine the end pursued in either the short or the long term (in this regard consider the American Founders' concern with the means of the popular demagogue – rhetoric – as evidenced in the first and last essay of *The Federalist Papers*).
3. Leo Strauss, *Thoughts on Machiavelli* (Glencoe, IL: Free Press, 1958), 9.
4. Paul A. Rahe, ed., *Machiavelli's Liberal Republican Legacy* (New York: Cambridge University Press, 2005), xxii; cf. Strauss, *Thoughts on Machiavelli*; Harvey C. Mansfield, *Machiavelli's Virtue* (Chicago: University of Chicago, 1966); Harvey C. Mansfield, *Machiavelli's New Modes and Orders: A Study of the* Discourses on Livy (Chicago: University of Chicago Press, 1979); Leo Paul S. Alvarez, *The Machiavellian Enterprise* (DeKalb, IL: Northern Illinois University Press, 1999); Paul A. Rahe, *Against Throne and Altar: Machiavelli and Political Theory in the English Republic* (Cambridge: Cambridge University Press, 2008). Waller R. Newell, in *Tyranny: A New Interpretation* (New York: Cambridge University Press, 2013), argues that Machiavelli "waffles between endorsing republican self-government in which citizens are responsible for their actions and an absolute monarchy that rules according to reason and leaves no scope whatever for citizen participation" (278).
5. John G. A. Pocock, *The Machiavellian Moment: Florentine Political Thought and the Atlantic Republican Tradition* (Princeton: Princeton University Press, 1975); Quentin Skinner, *The Foundations of Modern Political Thought: Volume One, The Renaissance* (New York: Cambridge University Press, 1978); Maurizo Viroli, "Machiavelli and the Republican Idea of Politics," in *Machiavelli and Republicanism*, eds. Gisela Bock, Quentin Skinner, and Maurizo Viroli (New York: Cambridge University Press, 1990): 143–72; Maurizio Viroli, *Machiavelli* (New

York: Oxford University Press, 1998); Philip Pettit, *Republicanism: A Theory of Freedom and Government* (Oxford: Oxford University Press, 1999).

6. Pocock, Viroli, and Pettit emphasize Machiavelli's partisanship of virtue, while Skinner and Irving Ribner ("Machiavelli and Sidney: The 'Arcadia' of 1590," *Studies in Philology* 47, No. 2 [1950]: 152–72) emphasize his dedication to liberty. Related to the emphasis on liberty is the interpretation of Machiavelli as a proponent of the rule of law and limited government put forth by Michelle T. Clarke ("The Virtues of Republican Citizenship in Machiavelli's *Discourses on Livy*," *Journal of Politics* 75, No. 2 [2013]: 317–29) and James Hankins ("Exclusivist Republicanism and the Non-Monarchical Republic," *Political Theory* 38, No. 4 [2010]: 452–82). For interpretations that emphasize Machiavelli's dedication to glory and empire as opposed to liberty and individual rights, see Mikael Hörnqvist, *Machiavelli and Empire* (Cambridge: Cambridge University Press, 2004) and Vickie B. Sullivan, *Machiavelli, Hobbes, and the Formation of a Liberal Republicanism in England* (New York: Cambridge University Press, 2004).
7. Miguel Vatter, "Machiavelli and the Republican Conception of Providence," *Review of Politics* 75, No. 4 (2013): 608.
8. John P. McCormick, "Addressing the Political Exception: Machiavelli's 'Accidents' and the Mixed Regime," *American Political Science Review* 87, No. 4 (1993): 888–900; John P. McCormick, "Machiavellian Democracy: Controlling Elites with Ferocious Populism," *American Political Science Review* 95, No. 2 (2001): 297–314; John P. McCormick, "Machiavelli Against Republicanism: On the Cambridge School's 'Guicciardinian Moments,'" *Political Theory* 31, No. 5 (2003): 615–43; John P. McCormick, Machiavelli's Political Trials and 'The Free Way of Life,'" *Political Theory* 35 No. 4 (2007): 385–411; John P. McCormick, *Machiavellian Democracy* (Cambridge: Cambridge University Press, 2011); John P. McCormick, "Subdue the Senate: Machiavelli's 'Way of Freedom' or Path to Tyranny?," *Political Theory* 40, No. 6 (2012): 714–35.
9. "The Many and the Few: On Machiavelli's 'Democratic Moment,'" *Review of Politics* 74, No. 4 (2012): 561. See Miguel E. Vatter, *Between Form and Event: Machiavelli's Theory of Political Freedom* (Dordrecht: Kluwer Academic, 2000). In "The Many and Few," Balot and Trochimchuk have articulated an interpretation that better accounts for Machiavelli's understanding of the necessity of individual statesmanship and elite intervention than does the populist reading proposed by McCormick or Vatter. For a related discussion of Machiavelli's preference for the "palazzo" mode of thought over the "piazza," see Timothy J. Lukes, "Descending to the Particulars: The Palazzo, the Piazza, and Machiavelli's Republican Modes and Orders," *Journal of Politics* 71, No. 2 (2009): 520–32.
10. One possible answer, an answer provided by Alexandre Kojève in "Tyranny and

Wisdom" (in Leo Strauss, *On Tyranny* [Chicago: University of Chicago Press, 2013], 135–76), is that to foreswear tyranny in any and every circumstance may to be forego any chance of progress (138). There are political circumstances in which the only two choices are between tyranny and anarchy, and as Thomas Hobbes argues in *Leviathan*, in such circumstances there really is no choice at all.

11. *Machiavelli, Leonardo, and the Science of Power* (Notre Dame, IN: University of Notre Dame Press, 1996), 49.
12. *The Machiavellian Moment*, viii.
13. Vatter, "Machiavelli and the Republican Conception of Providence," 620.
14. Parenthetical citations refer to Niccolò Machiavelli, *Discourses on Livy*, trans. Marvey C. Mansfield and Nathan Tarcov (Chicago: University of Chicago Press, 1996). Cited by book, chapter, and paragraph.
15. Leo Strauss, *Thoughts on Machiavelli*, 21.
16. These good men are not philosophers; they could not write this work, but had to ask for it to be written. In "Subdue the Senate," McCormick suggests the addressees of the *Discourses* are the oligarchically inclined "sons of Brutus" (735 n. 16). If McCormick is correct in this characterization and Machiavelli was truthful in his, there would appear to be a difficulty in identifying the philosopher as a straightforward advocate of popular rule. For a deeper discussion of the role of elite intervention in Machiavellian republics, see Balot and Trochimchuk, "The Many and the Few."'
17. Government can be expelled with a fork, but nevertheless always returns.
18. Cf. Plato, *Republic*, 489c and 520a.
19. Insofar as Machiavelli is proposing a new way of acting, one can understand this proposal as "a new morality" (Major, "A New Argument for Morality"; cf. Strauss, *Thoughts on Machiavelli*, and Clifford Orwin, "Machiavelli's Unchristian Charity," *American Political Science Review* 72, No. 2 [1978]: 1217–28).
20. Cf. Plato, *Republic*, 347d; and Plato, *Apology of Socrates*, 32e.
21. Cf. Aristotle, *Nicomachean Ethics*, 1156b9–25.
22. Cf. Plato, *Republic*, 369dff. In founding the first "true" or "healthy" iteration of the "city in speech," Socrates is silent regarding this most important need, mentioning only food, housing, and clothing. Only with the emergence of the "feverish" or luxurious city does the need for a warrior class emerge.
23. Cf. Machiavelli, *The Prince*, chap. 6.
24. Cf. ibid.; Plato, *Laws*, 709a–d.
25. A similar and related point is made by Peter Breiner who, in examining *The Prince*, argues it is impossible to get beyond "the primordial moment of acquisition," and that this moment "is constantly replayed in maintaining states and

beneath established institutions" ("Machiavelli's 'New Prince' and the Primordial Moment of Acquisition," *Political Theory* 36, No. 1 [2008]: 66). For an interesting discussion of the *Discourses* that treats each of its three parts as focused upon founding, maintenance, and re-founding respectively, see Jacqueline R. Hunsicker, "From Machiavellian Foundings to Republican Law," *The Good Society* 15, No. 2 (2006): 47–52.

26. Cf. Plato, *Laws*, 708c–d.
27. Cf. ibid., 708b–c.
28. Obviously Machiavelli's "state of nature" could be compared with those of Hobbes, Locke, and Rousseau, but undertaking such a comparison would exceed the scope of the current paper.
29. Machiavelli's selection of security as *the* origin of cities can be contrasted with the silence of Socrates in the *Republic* regarding this need. The emphasis on security seems to lead to the selection of one as head (principality), whereas the emphasis on material wellbeing seems to lead to greater equality (republic). Since security is the necessary condition of the enjoyment of property, and prosperity is the primary good, those who provide this good might merit a greater role in the city than those who provide the goods security allows to be enjoyed. The initial silence of Socrates regarding security, which allows him to defer the introduction of the warrior class, thereby allows for the subsequent division of labor to admit of equality. Socrates indicates that security is necessary (and highlights his previous silence regarding it) by the inclusion of war at the end of the account of the city of utmost necessity (*Republic* 372c); it is not by accident that the guardian class comes to rule in the city.
30. Murray S. Y. Bessette, "Theories of Regime Development Across the Millennia and Their Application to Modern Liberal Democracies," in *Advances in Cross-Cultural Decision Making*, eds. Dylan Schmorrow and Denise Nicholson (Boca Raton, FL: CRC Press, 2011), 109. Cf. *Discourses*, I.16.1. The corrupt people who need a prince may find the rule of the few who despise them to be more arduous than the rule of one whose interests are best served by founding his rule upon them (*Discourses*, I.40.5; cf. *Prince* 9).
31. Cf. Norman Wilde, "Machiavelli," *International Journal of Ethics* 38, No. 2 (1928): 212–25, where Wilde argues that the Europe of Machiavelli's day was characterized by these conditions.
32. Machiavelli later says what a good man must do when faced with a wicked prince: "For a licentious and tumultuous people can be spoken to by a good man, and it can easily be returned to the good way; there is no one who can speak to a wicked prince, nor is there any remedy other than steel" (*Discourses*, I.58.4).
33. For a more detailed discussion of Machiavelli's understanding of corruption

which connects it to American politics, see S. M. Shumer, "Machiavelli: Republican Politics and Its Corruption," *Political Theory* 7, No. 1 (1979): 5–34.

34. For a more detailed discussion of the desires of a free people that may be harmful to freedom, see Lukes, "Descending to the Particulars." For a detailed discussion of how the civic-minded statesman might check these desires and preserve the republican regime, see McCormick, "Subdue the Senate."

35. See the discussion below of virtue as the foundation of religious authority. For a recent discussion of the place of religion in Machiavelli's thought, see Vatter, "Machiavelli and the Republican Conception of Providence." For an overview of debate on the subject within the Machiavelli literature, see Marcia L. Colish, "Republicanism, Religion, and Machiavelli's Savonarolan Moment," *Journal of the History of Ideas* 60, No. 4 (1999): 597–616, especially the notes. Finally, for a discussion of elite intervention through civic religion, see Balot and Trochinchuk, "The Many and the Few."

36. Cf. Plato, *Laws*, 710d.

37. Of course this presupposes that there are two or more good men inhabiting the same city at the same time. That may or may not be the case in reality. It is certainly possible that good men could collaborate on an enterprise over time, each in turn taking up where the other left off, moving it ahead in the appropriate manner – the Enlightenment's struggle against the Kingdom of Darkness could be characterized as such an enterprise.

38. Whether or not we should excuse Machiavelli for publicly teaching the "maxims of gangsterism" then would depend on his intention (Strauss, *Thoughts on Machiavelli*, 9).

39. Cf. Plato, *Laws*, 714d. See Langton and Deitz, "Machiavelli's Paradox: Trapping or Teaching the Prince."

40. An important question is whether founding one's princely rule upon the people is a necessary precursor to popular rule upon the death of the prince (cf. *Discourses*, I.40.5; I.16.4–5).

41. Note Machiavelli here speaks directly to his addressees: "It is impossible for those who live in a private state in a republic or who either by fortune or by virtue become princes of it, if they read the histories and make capital of the memories of ancient things [cf. *Discourses*, I.Preface], not to wish to live in their fatherlands rather as Scipios than Caesars if they are private individuals and rather as Agesilauses, Timoleons, and Dions than Nabises, Phalarises, and Dionysiuses if they are princes" (*Discourses*, I.10.2). As Machiavelli's almost immediate repetition of the central examples indicates, the contrast is truly between Timoleon and Phalaris (*i.a.*, Timoleon died in old age; Phalaris died in the bra-

zen bull – a torture instrument he is said to have invented). Timoleon is named four times in the *Discourses* (I.10.2 twice; I.17.1; III.5.1).

42. Cf. Plato, *Laws*, 709e–710c.
43. Cf. Thomas Hobbes, *Leviathan*, chap. 7. "When a man's discourse beginneth not at definitions, it beginneth either at some other contemplation of his own, and then it is still called opinion, or it beginneth at some saying of another, of whose ability to know the truth, and of whose honesty in not deceiving, he doubteth not; and then the discourse is not so much concerning the thing, as the person; and the resolution is called belief, and faith: faith, in the man; belief, both of the man, and of the truth of what he says. So that in belief are two opinions; one of the saying of the man, the other of his virtue."
44. Strauss, *Thoughts on Machiavelli*, 167.
45. Cf. Friedrich Nietzsche, *Beyond Good and Evil*, Aphorism 51.
46. For a discussion of Machiavelli's use of the term "accident," see McCormick, "Addressing the Political Exception: Machiavelli's 'Accidents' and the Mixed Regime."
47. In a sense, then, the freedom of Rome could be said to originate out of the virtue of a man (Brutus) and a woman (Lucretia).
48. Cf. Livy, *The History of Rome*, I.57–60.
49. Cf. McCormick, "Addressing the Political Exception: Machiavelli's 'Accidents' and the Mixed Regime."
50. Livy, *The History of Rome*, I.59. For an extensive discussion of the accumulation of symbolic capital through honorable deeds, see Clarke, "The Virtues of Republican Citizenship in Machiavelli's *Discourses on Livy*." In *Julius Caesar*, Shakespeare demonstrates some of the political problems associated with such accumulated symbolic capital through the character of Brutus.
51. Livy, *The History of Rome*, I.59.
52. Cf. Machiavelli, *The Prince*, chap. 9.
53. For a discussion of how this satisfaction gives rise again to the "primordial situation" of founding, see Breiner, "Machiavelli's 'New Prince' and the Primordial Moment of Acquisition," 72.
54. His mention of "two virtuous" individuals at the end of the chapter (*Discourses*, I.17.3) is intended to point the reader back to the example of Dion and Timoleon, highlighting this fact.
55. Plutarch, *The Parallel Lives*, "The Life of Timoleon," 39.7 (end).
56. Cf. Machiavelli, *The Prince*, chap. 3.
57. In a previous chapter Machiavelli sought to moderate the actions of the tyrannical type by showing him that the security of his rule depends upon the security

of the people, that is, in their being secure against his wickedness (cf. *Discourses*, I.16.5). For an extensive and insightful discussion of Machiavelli's counsel to tyrants within the context of *The Prince*, especially chapter 19 thereof, see Hörnqvist, *Machiavelli and Empire*.

58. Friedrich Nietzsche, *Twilight of the Idols*, "Forays of an Untimely Man," 43.
59. Plato, *Republic*, 347c.
60. Ibid., 520d.
61. Publius, *The Federalist Papers*, No. 44. Cf. Nos. 23, 31, and 71.
62. Precedent, of course, is only a problem after the fact. If the good man is successful, he might be able to cover over the extraordinary origins of the city, thereby erasing the precedent (cf. Plato, *Republic*, 414cff.).
63. Cf. *Discourses*, III.35. In comparing these sections it is important to note the following differences: he who is the head of an innovation in a province is in command thereof, whereas he who counsels a prince must depend upon the actions of the prince; the head of innovations treats something new, whereas the counselor treats a grave and important decision; the head will receive the benefit of success, whereas the counselor may receive the ingratitude of the prince or people (cf. *Discourses*, I.30); finally, the head will be one alone, whereas the counselor will be one of few.
64. Cf. Nietzsche, *Twilight of the Idols*, "Forays of an Untimely Man," Aphorism 39; Plato, *Republic*, 563d. Any order for a corrupt people will feel like oppression, despite the fact that order is necessary to freedom – corrupt people mistake license for liberty. This is nicely demonstrated by Shakespeare's *Measure for Measure*. See also Wilde, "Machiavelli," 214. For a discussion of the importance of the rule of law to liberty and in distinguishing between oppression and government within Machiavelli's thought, see McCormick, "Subdue the Senate," especially 721–25.
65. This conclusion is implied in the analysis provided by McCormick, "Addressing the Political Exception: Machiavelli's 'Accidents' and the Mixed Regime," 889 and 896.
66. On the necessity of action for "moral regeneration" and "a revival of civic virtue," see Wilde, "Machiavelli."
67. In a free city, a "good and worthy man" may be sufficient (*Discourses*, III.25.1).

"WIND UP THE UNTUNED AND JARRING SENSES"

1. Harry Jaffa, "Macbeth and the Moral Universe," *Claremont Review of Books* (Winter 2007/08), 36.
2. Harry Jaffa, "The Limits of Politics: An Interpretation Act I scene i of *King Lear*," in *Shakespeare's Politics*, by Allan Bloom, with Harry V. Jaffa (Chicago: University of Chicago Press, 1964), 138.

Notes

3. Paul Cantor, "*King Lear*: The Tragic Disjunction of Wisdom and Power," in *Shakespeare's Political Pageant*, ed. Joseph Alulis (Lanham, MD: Rowman & Littlefield, 1996), 190.
4. A.C. Bradley, *Shakespearean Tragedy* (New York: Penguin, 1991), 228–29.
5. Ibid., 242–43.
6. Travis Williams, "*King Lear* Without the Mathematics: From Reading Mathematics to Reading Mathematically," in *The Palgrave Handbook of Literature and Mathematics*, ed. Robert Tubbs, Alice Jenkins, and Nina Engelhardt (London: Palgrave, 2021), 400.
7. Sylvia Bigliazzi, "Oedipus at Colonus and King Lear: Classical and Early Modern Intersections," *Skenè Journal of Theatre and Drama Studies* (2019): 292.
8. References to Shakespeare use the Arden editions.
9. Yves Bonnefoy, *Shakespeare and the French Poet* (Chicago: University of Chicago Press, 2004), 281.
10. John Alvis, "Shakespeare's *Hamlet* and Machiavelli: How Not to Kill a Despot," in *Shakespeare as a Political Thinker*, ed. Alvis and Thomas G. West (Wilmington, DE: ISI Books, 2000), 290.
11. Friederich Nietzsche, *The Antichrist*, in *The Portable Nietzsche*, trans. Walter Kaufmann (New York: Penguin, 1982), 572.
12. Alvis, "Shakespeare's *Hamlet* and Machiavelli," 311.
13. Harry Jaffa, "The Unity of Comedy, Tragedy, and History: An Interpretation of the Shakespearean Universe," in *Shakespeare as a Political Thinker*, 31.
14. Ibid.
15. Leo Strauss, *What is Political Philosophy?* (Chicago: University of Chicago Press, 1988), 299.
16. Leo Strauss, *On Tyranny* (Chicago: University of Chicago Press, 2013), 207.
17. Leo Strauss, *City and Man* (Chicago: University of Chicago Press, 1964), 241.
18. *Republic* course, 1957, session 13, https://leostrausstranscripts.uchicago.edu/philologic4/strauss/navigate/2/14/.
19. *Laws* course, 1959, session 7, https://leostrausstranscripts.uchicago.edu/philologic4/strauss/navigate/3/8/.
20. Leo Strauss, "The Origins of Political Science and The Problem of Socrates: Six Public Lectures," *Interpretation* (Winter 1996): 196.
21. Ibid., 138.
22. David Janssens, "The Problem of Place in Greek Tragedy," *The Locus of Tragedy: Studies in Contemporary Phenomenology*, vol. 1 (2008): 14.
23. Harry Jaffa, introduction to *Shakespeare's Understanding of Honor*, by John Alvis (Durham, NC: Carolina Academic Press, 1990), ix.
24. Michael Davis, "Seth Benardete's Second Sailing: On the Spirit of Ideas," *The*

Political Science Reviewer, vol. 32 (2003): 28.

25. Strauss, "The Origins of Political Science," 137.
26. Leo Strauss, *Thoughts on Machiavelli* (Chicago: University of Chicago Press, 1984), 292.
27. Ibid., 129; see also 11, 60, 91, 233.
28. Aristotle, *On Poetics*, trans. Seth Benardete and Michael Davis (South Bend, IN: St. Augustine Press, 2002), 1451b, 1450a34.
29. Alvis, introduction to *Shakespeare as a Political Thinker*, 4.
30. Strauss, *Thoughts on Machiavelli*, 296.
31. Harry Jaffa, "Macbeth and the Moral Universe," *Claremont Review of Books* (Winter 2007/08), https://claremontreviewofbooks.com/macbeth-and-the-moral-universe/.
32. George Anastaplo, *The Constitution of 1787: A Commentary* (Baltimore: Johns Hopkins University Press, 1989), 75–76.
33. Leo Strauss, *Rebirth of Classical Political Rationalism* (Chicago: University of Chicago Press, 1989), 269.
34. Strauss, *Thoughts on Machiavelli*, 13.
35. Bonnefoy, *Shakespeare and the French Poet*, 485, 489.

THE FOUNDERS AND CLASSICAL PRUDENCE

1. Thomas Jefferson to Walter Jones, January 2, 1814, in *Memoirs, Correspondence, and Private Papers of Thomas Jefferson*, ed. Thomas Jefferson Randolph (London: Henry Colburn and Richard Bentley, 1829), vol. IV, 241–42.
2. Aristotle's *Politics*, trans. and ed. Carnes Lord (Chicago: The University of Chicago Press, 1984), 1252b30–1253a15.
3. *Nicomachean Ethics*, trans. and ed. Joe Sachs (Newbury Port: Focus Publishing, 2002), 1094a.
4. *Ethics*, 1141b8–10.
5. Ibid., 1140a25–28.
6. Ibid., 1144a28–29.
7. Ibid., 1098a9–18.
8. Ibid., 1144a36–37.
9. Ibid., 1141b33–34.
10. Niccolò Machiavelli, *The Prince*, trans. and ed. Harvey C. Mansfield (Chicago: The University of Chicago Press, 1985), 61.
11. In general, see Harvey C. Mansfield, *Machiavelli's Virtue* (Chicago: The University of Chicago Press, 1996), 13–16 and 36–45.
12. *The Prince*, 69.
13. Ibid., 61.

14. Ibid., 62.
15. Ibid., 71.
16. Ibid., 91.
17. Ibid., 98.
18. Ibid., 100–1.
19. Thomas Hobbes, *Leviathan*, ed. C. B. MacPherson (New York: Penguin Books, 1985) part I, chap. 8, 139.
20. Ibid., 186.
21. Ibid., 227.
22. Ibid., 183.
23. Ibid., 682.
24. Immanuel Kant, *Foundations of the Metaphysics of Morals*, trans. and ed. Lewis White Beck (Indianapolis: Bobbs-Merrill Company, 1959), 33.
25. George Washington to Catherine Macaulay Graham, January 19, 1790, in *George Washington: A Collection*, ed. W. B. Allen (Indianapolis: Liberty Classics, 1988), pp. 537–39.
26. Ibid.
27. See Leo Strauss, *Natural Right and History* (Chicago: The University of Chicago Press, 1950), 162.
28. George Washington, First Inaugural Speech, April 30, 1789, in *George Washington: A Collection*, 462.
29. *Ethics*, VI, 1145a6–11.
30. In general, see Charles R. Kesler, "The Founders and the Classics," in *The American Founding: Essays on the Formation of the Constitution*, ed. J. Jackson Barlow et. al. (New York: Greenwood Press, 1988).
31. Alexander Hamilton, James Madison, and John Jay, *The Federalist Papers*, ed. Clinton Rossiter and Charles R. Kesler (New York: Signet Classics, 2003), 236, 276.
32. Ibid., 73, 226.
33. Ibid., 317–22, 67.
34. Ibid., 319.
35. See Harry V. Jaffa, *Crisis of the Strauss Divided: Essays on Leo Strauss and Straussianism, East and West* (Lanham: Rowman & Littlefield, 2012),21.
36. *The Laws of Plato*, trans. and ed. Thomas L. Pangle (Chicago: The University of Chicago Press, 1980), 708d, 712a.
37. *Ethics*, 1144a29–30.

Notes

THE FEDERALIST AND THE ANCIENTS

1. Stanley Rosen, "Kojève's Paris: A Memoir," in *Metaphysics in Ordinary Language* (New Haven and London: Yale University Press, 1999), 258.
2. I find no reference in Nietzsche to such a duty. He does say that "one repays a teacher badly if one always remains nothing but a pupil," which, taking praeceptticide to be a metaphor, would seem to mean more or less the same thing. See *Thus Spoke Zarathustra: A Book for All and None*, trans. Walter Kauffman (New York: Viking Penguin, 1954; German original published in four volumes, 1883–85), I 22.3.
3. Directed by George Stevens (Burbank, CA: Warner Bros. Pictures, 1956).
4. Kesler, *Crisis of the Two Constitutions: The Rise, Decline, and Recovery of American Greatness* (New York: Encounter Books, 2021), xvi.
5. Quoted most famously in Allan Bloom, *The Closing of the American Mind: How Higher Education Has Failed Democracy and Impoverished the Souls of Today's Students* (New York: Simon & Schuster, 1987), 167, where Bloom attributes the phrase to Leo Strauss. But as Harry Jaffa and George Anastaplo both pointed out, Strauss himself attributed the phrase to Winston Churchill, whom he (Strauss) merely quoted. See Jaffa, "Humanizing Certitudes and Impoverishing Doubts: A Critique of *The Closing of the American Mind*," *Interpretation* 16, No. 1 (Fall 1988): 111–38; and Anastaplo, "Allan Bloom and Race Relations in the United States" (presented to the Institute of Human Values, Canadian Learned Societies Conference, Windsor, Ontario, June 10, 1988). Both were republished in *Essays on* The Closing of the American Mind, ed. Robert L. Stone (Chicago: Chicago Review Press, 1989), 129–53 and 225–34, respectively.
6. Joseph Cropsey, "The United States as Regime and the Sources of the American Way of Life," *Political Philosophy and the Issues of Politics* (Chicago: University of Chicago Press, 1977), 1–15. One might also cite Bloom: "America is actually nothing but a great stage on which theories have been played as tragedy and comedy. This is a regime founded by philosophers and their students. All the recalcitrant matter of the historical *is* gave way here before the practical and philosophical *ought to be*, as the raw natural givens of this wild continent meekly submitted to the yoke of theoretical science" (emphases in original); and "Our Nation, a great stage for the acting out of great thoughts, presents the classic confrontation between Locke's views of the state of nature and Rousseau's criticism of them" (*Closing of the American Mind*, 97, 172). For perhaps the most complete statement of this view, see Thomas L. Pangle, *The Spirit of Modern Republicanism: The Moral Vision of the American Founders and the Philosophy of Locke* (Chicago: University of Chicago Press, 1988).
7. Adair taught at the Claremont Graduate School (now University) until his sui-

cide in 1968. Diamond taught at Claremont Men's College (the name was changed to Claremont McKenna in 1981) and the Claremont Graduate School from 1958 to 1977, when he left for the American Enterprise Institute in Washington, DC. Diamond famously testified before the Senate Judiciary Committee's Subcommittee on the Constitution the morning of the day he died. Kesler became a professor at Claremont McKenna in 1983.

8. Kesler, ed., *Saving the Revolution*: The Federalist Papers *and the American Founding* (New York: The Free Press, 1987).
9. Clinton Rossiter and Charles R. Kesler, eds., *The Federalist Papers* (New York: Mentor, 1999).
10. "Extended sphere" is the "Play it again, Sam" of *The Federalist*: everyone who's the least familiar with the work knows the phrase, but it nowhere appears in exactly those words. The nearest approximations are "extending the sphere" (*Federalist* 9), "extend the sphere" (No. 10), and "extension of the sphere" (No. 27). Yet "extended sphere" may be said to encapsulate both the founders' justification for a large republic and the argument of *Federalist* 10, the book's most famous and influential essay.
11. "[I]t was Diamond's great achievement to expound the central importance of [this] principle to the republicanism of *The Federalist*"; Kesler, "*Federalist* 10 and American Republicanism," in *Saving the Revolution*, 14; republished as Chapter 3 of *Crisis of the Two Constitutions*.
12. "*Federalist* 10 and American Republicanism," 18.
13. *Crisis of the Two Constitutions*, xiv.
14. Kesler, "Is Conservatism Un-American?" *National Review*, March 22, 1985, 28–37; referring to *The History of Political Philosophy*, ed. Leo Strauss and Joseph Cropsey (Chicago: University of Chicago Press, 1987, third edition).
15. Strauss, *Natural Right and History* (Chicago: University of Chicago Press, 1953), 251.
16. Kesler, "The Founders and the Classics," in *The Revival of Constitutionalism*, ed. James W. Mueller (Lincoln: University of Nebraska Press, 1988; republished as Chapter 1 of *Crisis of the Two Constitutions*), 16–17.
17. That seminar is perhaps Charles's most-oft taught and highly regarded graduate course, during which he explains the structure and purpose of the whole of *The Federalist* while going into detail on the parts. It remains a point of great good fortune that I was able to take that class in 1996 and a source of shame that I never finished my intended paper (en route to abandoning my PhD altogether). I hope that Charles will consider this chapter to be, finally, the fulfillment of that lingering disgraceful incomplete.
18. On the significance of "Publius," see Kesler's introduction to *The Federalist*

Papers, x–xi; "*Federalist* 10 and American Republicanism," 19; and "The Founders and the Classics," 21–22.

19. "The Founders and the Classics," 8.
20. Nos. 4–6, 8–10, 14, 16, 18, 22, 25, 34, 38, 41, 43, 45, 49, 52, 55, 58, 63, 70 and 75. The ancients are mentioned in No. 19, but only to refer back to the discussion in the previous paper. The word "ancient" is also used as a synonym for "old" and/or "firmly established" in Nos. 17, 18, 25, 38, 40, 49, 71, 81, 83 and 84. "Antiquity" appears in the text seven times, always in one of the twenty-three papers containing a thematic discussion of the ancients. ("Classic" or a variant does not appear at all.) Publius also mentions Greece (including "Greek" and "Grecian") twenty-four times (plus numerous other mentions of specific Greek cities, confederacies, peoples, and individuals), Rome and the Romans twenty-six times, and Carthage seven times – again, always in one of the twenty-three papers containing a thematic discussion of the ancients.
21. Some might cite, as contrary evidence, the phrase "empire of liberty," coined and popularized by Thomas Jefferson. But leaving aside the facts that Jefferson was not Publius, wrote none of *The Federalist Papers* (he wasn't even in the country at the time), and was, broadly speaking, to the "left" of the founding consensus on the desirability of spreading liberty as an aim of American foreign policy (i.e., he was sympathetic while most were against it), what Jefferson meant by "empire of liberty" was the peaceful settlement of more or less empty western lands by Americans and, at most, the incorporation of Canada into the American union should the opportunity arise via war with Britain. See Jefferson's letter to James Madison of April 27, 1809. Needless to say, three years later, there was a war with Britain, Madison was still president, and Canada was not incorporated.
22. On the plan of *The Federalist*, see Diamond, "*The Federalist*," in *The History of Political Philosophy*, 662; Kesler gives a more detailed rendering in his introduction to *The Federalist Papers*, xv–xvi.
23. "It is very probable," Publius approvingly quotes Montesquieu in *Federalist* 9, "that mankind would have been obliged at length to live constantly under the government of a single person, had they not contrived a kind of constitution that has all the internal advantages of a republican, together with the external force of a monarchical government." In the context of No. 9, this passage (only the first part of a six-paragraph quotation) is cited to marshal Montesquieu in support of the efficacy of the large republic (cf. note 29, below). But the statement could just as equally be cited to justify or vindicate the presidency's broad Article II powers over the military and foreign affairs, as well as shared federal and state sovereignty, with the federal government handling all external matters.
24. Cf. Diamond, "*The Federalist*," 667.

25. Above all in "*Federalist* 10 and American Republicanism."
26. Cf. No. 6: "Rome was never sated of carnage and conquest"; the reference in No. 18 to "the vast projects of Rome," i.e., its lust for conquest; the observation (also in No. 18) that "the arms of Rome found little difficulty in completing the ruin which their arts had commenced"; and the reference in No. 70 to those who "menaced" (i.e., threatened to stop) "the conquest and destruction of Rome."
27. Twelve times, in Nos. 9 (four times), 43 (twice), 47 (five times), and 78. Publius praises Montesquieu as "that great man" and "this enlightened civilian" (No. 9) and famously calls him "the celebrated Montesquieu" (Nos. 47 and 78).
28. Emphasis in *Federalist* 9, though not in Montesquieu's text (*Spirit of the Laws* IX 1). The authors of *The Federalist* relied on Thomas Nugent's 1750 translation of *The Spirit of the Laws*. Cohler et al. (Montesquieu, *The Spirit of the Laws*, trans. Anne M. Cohler, Basia Carolyn Miller, and Harold Samuel Stone [Cambridge: Cambridge University Press, 1989; French original published 1748]) render Montesquieu's "*la répubilque fédérative*" as "the federal republic."
29. Publius is slightly disingenuous on this point. He implies, but is too careful explicitly to claim, that Montesquieu argues in favor of the large republic and/or denies that republics must be small – assertions he must know Montesquieu's text cannot support. The soundness of Publius's argument stands or falls by the accuracy of his equation of Montesquieu's recommended confederacy with Publius's proposed federal government. But as Publius's argument tacitly admits, the "constituent parts" of Montesquieu's confederacy are much smaller than even the smallest American states; hence the confederacy of American states under the proposed constitution cannot really be compared to Montesquieu's confederacy. Publius seems willing to stretch a point in order to claim the authority of Montesquieu, who was widely admired by the Constitution's advocates and opponents alike. Cf. note 23, above.
30. See *The Spirit of the Laws*, bk. VIII, chaps. 16, 17, and 20, and bk. IX, Chaps. 1, 3, 4, and 6.
31. Cf. No. 52: "The scheme of representation, as a substitute for a meeting of the citizens in person, being at most but *very imperfectly known to ancient polity*, it is *in more modern times only that we are to expect instructive examples*" (emphases added).
32. Thomas Hobbes, *Elements of Law, Natural and Politic* (1640), dedicatory letter.
33. Cf. Machiavelli, *Discourses on the First Decade of Titus Livy*, bk. I, chap. 9, "That It Is Necessary to Be Alone If One Wishes to Order a Republic Anew or to Reform It Altogether outside Its Ancient Orders," in *Discourses on Livy*, trans. Harvey C. Mansfield and Nathan Tarcov (Chicago: University of Chicago Press, 1996; Italian original published 1531). I vividly recall Charles's dramatic reading of this chapter in the first session of his *Federalist* course.

34. As Kesler also notes, the phrase is Tocqueville's: see *Democracy in America*, introduction. Diamond also uses the phrase and seemingly attributes it to Publius, but carefully avoids extending his quote marks around the word "new," thus – accurately – attributing to Publius only the phrase "science of politics." Still, the impression left (and, I believe, meant to be left) is that Publius sees himself as inventing a "new science of politics." Diamond, "*The Federalist*," 678.
35. "*Federalist* 10 and American Republicanism," 18–19.
36. The only possible candidate would be the reference to Plato in No. 49, but interpreting that as a criticism requires assuming that Publius thinks Plato actually expected the rule of philosopher-kings.
37. The phrase "human nature" appears in *The Federalist* eighteen times (in Nos. 4, 6, 15, 17, 24, 36 twice, 51 twice, 55, 57, 65, 66, 71, 76 twice, 78, and 79); "the nature of man" once (in No. 10). In addition to these, and leaving aside references to impermanent things and colloquial usage (e.g., "naturally tends" or "of a similar nature" and the like), we also find references to "a state of nature" (No. 51), "natural rights" (No. 2), "the greatest natural abilities" (No. 35), the "natural and unsophisticated dictates of common-sense" (No. 31), "the natural conceptions which the mind, without the aid of philosophy, would be led to entertain upon the subject" (No. 31), the "natural and experienced course of human affairs" (No. 25), "the natural and tried course of human affairs" (No. 34), the "nature of war" (No. 8), the "nature of popular government" (No. 12), the "nature of [democracy]" and the "natural limit of a democracy" versus a republic (No. 14), the "NATURE OF A FREE GOVERNMENT" (No. 47; emphasis in original), the "nature of sovereign power" (No. 15) and "of sovereignty" (Nos. 19 and 81), the "nature of the judicial power" (No. 81) and "of judiciary power" (No. 82), the "nature of just and constitutional laws" (No. 57), man's entitlement "by nature and compact" to free travel (No. 15), the "tempting advantages which nature has kindly placed within our reach" (No. 11), "an advantage which nature holds out to us" (i.e., America's distance from Europe; No. 12), "the beneficence of nature" (No. 14), "the great kingdom of nature" and "the works of nature" (No. 37), the "nature of the thing" (Nos. 23 and 83), "the nature and reason of the thing" (No. 78, twice), the "nature of things" (Nos. 21 and 46), the "natural course of things" (Nos. 8 and 60), "the irresistible and unchangeable course of nature" (No. 11), and above all "the transcendent law of nature and of nature's God" (No. 43), which mirrors the language of the Declaration of Independence. I note for my fellow Straussians that this last phrase appears in precisely the central essay of *The Federalist*. That might be a coincidence, but if so, it's a *curious* coincidence; on curious coincidences, see Kesler's teacher Harvey C. Mansfield, *Machiavelli's Virtue* (Chicago: University of Chicago Press, 1996), 227.

38. Cf. Leo Strauss, *What Is Political Philosophy?* (Glencoe: The Free Press, 1959), 40–43.
39. Hobbes, *Leviathan* (1651), chaps. VIII and XV; cf. "On the Basis of Hobbes's Political Philosophy," in *What Is Political Philosophy?* 176n2.
40. John Locke, *Second Treatise of Government* (1690), chap. VIII, § 95.
41. Strauss, *What Is Political Philosophy?* 50.
42. *The Spirit of the Laws*, bk XX, chaps. 1 and 2. Cf. bks XX–XXII, *passim*.
43. E.g., "the fiery and destructive passions of war reign in the human breast with much more powerful sway than the mild and beneficent sentiments of peace; and that to model our political systems upon speculations of lasting tranquility, is to calculate on the weaker springs of the human character" (No. 34); and "[t]he history of human conduct does not warrant that exalted opinion of human virtue which would make it wise in a nation to commit interests of so delicate and momentous a kind, as those which concern its intercourse with the rest of the world, to the sole disposal of a magistrate created and circumstanced as would be a President of the United States" (No. 75).
44. Strauss, *What Is Political Philosophy?* 43.
45. While Publius may at first glance appear to leave this last designation open to question – "*if* we mean to be a commercial people" he says twice (Nos. 24 and 34; emphasis added) – the context leaves no doubt that he thinks Americans already believe themselves to be a commercial people and advises them that if they wish to remain so, they must adopt policies to protect their commerce.
46. Here I follow Kesler (introduction to *The Federalist Papers*, xviii–xix), who follows Publius, in borrowing from the Declaration of Independence, which identifies effecting the people's "safety and happiness" as the purpose and end of government. The phrase "safety and happiness" appears in *The Federalist* five times: in Nos. 2, 15, 40 (twice), and 43 – this last being the only place in the work where the Declaration is explicitly cited (cf. note 37 above). In addition, Publius implicitly refers to the Declaration in Nos. 22, 38, 43, 81, and 85 (consent legitimizes government) and in Nos. 39, 40, 43, and 78 (the right of revolution).
47. On the plan of *The Federalist*, see note 22, above.
48. Kesler, introduction to *The Federalist Papers*, xvii–xix.
49. "It is safer to try to understand the low in the light of the high than the high in the light of the low. In doing the latter one necessarily distorts the high, whereas in doing the former one does not deprive the low of the freedom to reveal itself fully as what it is." Strauss, preface to *Spinoza's Critique of Religion*, trans. E. M. Sinclair (New York: Schocken Books, 1965; German original published 1930), 2.
50. Contrast Machiavelli, *Discourses* I.3: "It is necessary to whoever disposes a republic and orders laws in it to presuppose that all men are bad, and that they

always have to use the malignity of their spirit whenever they have a free opportunity for it."

51. For a different take on gratitude, see Machiavelli, *Discourses* I.28–32.
52. Excluding three instances of "by virtue of," Publius speaks of human virtue twenty-one times: in Nos. 2, 6, 22, 36, 49, 53, 55 (twice), 57, 64, 66, 68, 72, 73 (three times), 75 (twice), 76 (twice), and 83.
53. Kesler, "Responsibility in *The Federalist*," in *Educating the Prince: Essays in Honor of Harvey Mansfield* (Lanham, MD: Rowman & Littlefield, 2000), 219–32.
54. One could go on, e.g., passages that describe, and ascribe to Americans, "wisdom and virtue" (No. 36), "humanity" (No. 42), "MODERATION" and "PRUDENCE" (No. 43; emphases in original), noble refusal to tolerate corruption (Nos. 66 and 76), and the sagacity of the common people (No. 41).
55. "The Founders and the Classics," 14. Aristotle actually says "oligarchic," not "aristocratic" (*Politics* V.9, 1294b9). Still, Kesler is surely correct that election is intended to produce a better class of officeholder: wiser, more moderate, and more capable than the common man, who while certainly his leaders' equal in God-given natural rights, is not necessarily their equal in talent or virtue.
56. Cf. Kesler, introduction to *The Federalist Papers*, xx.
57. See, e.g., the discussion in *Federalist* 52 of the flaws of the British House of Commons, which the proposed House of Representatives is intended to correct.
58. Charles is not much given to criticism (or praise, for that matter) but more than once has described me as "gloomy," a charge I do not deny and which he does not mean as a compliment. My original idea for this chapter, nearly completed, was to consider the question "Why Did the American Founding Fail?" But on refection, it seemed a poor gesture to honor Charles with an argument he abhors. Hence, for this reason (and also to save space), I here merely assert that things have turned out badly without any attempt to substantiate that judgement. I may eventually publish my attempt at substantiation – though I doubt Charles will want it for the *Claremont Review of Books*!
59. Kesler, *I Am the Change: Barack Obama and the Crisis of Liberalism* (New York: Bombardier Books, 2012).

THE FEDERALIST ON ENTERPRISE, WAR, AND EMPIRE

1. See Leo Strauss, *Liberalism Ancient and Modern* (Chicago: The University of Chicago Press, 1995), 16.
2. Charles R. Kesler, "*Federalist* 10 and American Republicanism," in *Saving the Revolution: The Federalist Papers and The American Founding*, ed. Kesler (New York: The Free Press, 1987), 22.
3. Ibid.

4. The text of *The Federalist* used in this book is Alexander Hamilton, James Madison, and John Jay, *The Federalist Papers*, ed. Clinton Rossiter and Charles R. Kesler (New York: Signet Classic, 2003). The current reference and all subsequent references to *The Federalist* are to this edition. Citations from *The Federalist* are provided in brackets within the text of the chapter. For example, the reference here cited (39:237) refers to *Federalist* 39 at page 237.
5. Kesler, "*Federalist* 10," 23.
6. Karl-Friedrich Walling, *Republican Empire: Alexander Hamilton on War and Free Government* (Lawrence: University Press of Kansas, 1999).
7. Quoted in Bradley A. Thayer, "The Case for the American Empire," in *American Empire: A Debate*, by Thayer and Christopher Layne (New York: Routledge, 2007), 8. Thayer discusses support for the idea of American empire in early American political development as well as by non-American observers at 5–12.
8. See Michael S. Kochin and Michael Taylor, *An Independent Empire: Diplomacy and War in the Making of the United States* (Ann Arbor: University of Michigan Press, 2020), 22.
9. I develop many of the themes in this chapter in greater detail in *Vindicating the Commercial Republic: The Federalist on Union, Enterprise, and War* (Lanham: Lexington Books, 2018).
10. David F. Epstein has noted: "*Federalist* 10's formulation, 'the public good and private rights,' appears to be a comprehensive statement of the political prosperity which good government should secure. The 'public good and private rights' are the central concerns of, respectively, republican and liberal political thought" (Epstein, *The Political Theory of The Federalist* [Chicago: University of Chicago Press, 1984], 9).
11. See Kesler, "*Federalist* 10," 30.
12. *Random House Webster's Concise Dictionary*, second ed. (New York: Random House, 1998), 218.
13. Martin Diamond, *As Far as Republican Principles Will Admit*, ed. William A. Schambra (Washington, DC: AEI Press, 1992), 55–56.
14. Ibid., 32. See, also, Kesler, "*Federalist* 10," 17, and W. B. Allen with Kevin A. Cloonan, *The Federalist Papers: A Commentary* (New York: Peter Lang, 2000), 111.
15. Diamond, *As Far as Republican Principles Will Admit*, 33.
16. See Michael D. Chan, *Aristotle and Hamilton on Commerce and Statesmanship* (Columbia: University of Missouri Press, 2006), 152–53; Walling, *Republican Empire*, 193; and Allen, *A Commentary*, 73.
17. Alexander Hamilton, "Report on the Subject of Manufactures," in *The Papers of Alexander Hamilton*, ed. Harold C. Syrett (New York: Columbia University

Press, 1961–79), vol. 10, 230; and "Report on a Plan for the Further Support of Public Credit," ibid., vol. 18, 46.

18. See Walling, *Republican Empire*, 180–81 and Jerry Z. Muller, *The Mind and the Market: Capitalism in Western Thought* (New York: Anchor Books, 2003), 52.
19. See Chan, *Aristotle and Hamilton*, 152–53.
20. Ibid.
21. *Federalist* 25 reiterates this theme when demurring that "the rights of a feeble government are [unlikely] to be respected, even by its own constituents" (25:156).
22. Wayne Ambler, introduction to *The Education of Cyrus*, by Xenophon, trans. and ed. Wayne Ambler (Ithaca: Cornell University Press, 2001), 13.
23. Harvey C. Mansfield and Nathan Tarcov, introduction to *Discourses on Livy*, by Niccolò Machiavelli, trans. Harvey C. Mansfield and Nathan Tarcov (Chicago: University of Chicago Press, 1996), xxxvi. Mansfield and Tarcov appear to follow Leo Strauss here. Strauss maintained that throughout all of Machiavelli's works, not just the *Discourses*, Xenophon represented classical political philosophy and was referred to more than any other ancient political writer save for Livy. See Leo Strauss, *Thoughts on Machiavelli* (Chicago: University of Chicago Press, 1958), 59, 161–62, 291, and 293.
24. Machiavelli, *Discourses on Livy*, I.7.4 (22–23).
25. Kochin and Taylor, *An Independent Empire*, 98.
26. Ibid., 5.
27. Robert D. Kaplan, *Warrior Politics: Why Leadership Demands a Pagan Ethos* (New York: Random House, 2002), 148. See, also Kaplan, *Imperial Grunts: The American Military on the Ground* (New York: Random House, 2005), 3–15.
28. Thayer, "The Case for the American Empire," 7. See also ibid., 3.
29. Machiavelli, *Discourses on Livy*, II.4.1 (136).
30. Patrick J. Garrity, "Foreign Policy and *The Federalist*," in Kesler, *Saving the Revolution*, 92.
31. Ibid., 95.
32. Kesler, introduction to *Saving the Revolution*, 3; emphasis in original.

DEFENDING AMERICAN NATURAL-RIGHTS REPUBLICANISM

1. Patrick J. Deenen, *Why Liberalism Failed* (New Haven: Yale University Press, 2018).
2. Adrian Vermeule, "As Secular Liberalism Attacks the Church, Catholic's Can't Afford to be Nostalgic," *Catholic Herald*, January 5, 2018 (https://catholicherald.co.uk/as-secular-liberalism-attacks-the-church-catholics-cant-afford-to-be-nostalgic/ accessed on January 30, 2023).

Notes

3. Rod Dreher, *The Benedict Option: A Strategy for Christians in a Post-Christian Nation* (New York: Sentinel, 2017).
4. Charles J. Chaput, *Strangers in a Strange Land: Living the Faith in a Post-Christian World* (New York: Henry Hold and Company, 2017).
5. R. R. Reno, "America and Liberalism," *First Things* (May 2018).
6. Carl R. Trueman, *Strange New Word: How Thinkers and Activists Redefined Identity and Sparked the Sexual Revolution* (Wheaton, IL: Crossway, 2022).
7. Patrick J. Deneen, "A Catholic Showdown Worth Watching," *The American Conservative*, February 6, 2014 (https://www.theamericanconservative.com/a-catholic-showdown-worth-watching/, accessed January 30, 2023). Deneen's "radical" critique has now become part of the "common good" Catholicism intellectual movement. It lies beyond this essay to explore the differences between Deneen's "radicalism" and "Common Goodism" as both positions are continually evolving. It is safe to say, however, that significant overlap exists. For "Common Goodism," see Adrian Vermeule, *Common Good Constitutionalism* (Medford, MA: Polity, 2022). See also Michael Hanby, "The Birth of the Liberal Order and the Death of God," *Newpolity* 2 (February 2021).
8. Deneen, *Why Liberalism Failed*, 3.
9. Deneen, *Why Liberalism Failed*, 31–42.
10. Alasdair MacIntyre, *After Virtue* (Notre Dame, IN: University of Notre Dame Press, 1981), 75.
11. David L. Schindler, "The Repressive Logic of Liberal Rights: Religious Freedom, Contraceptives and the 'Phony' Argument of the *New York Times*," *Communio* 38 (2011): 526.
12. *Planned Parenthood of Southeastern Pennsylvania v. Casey* 505 U.S. 833, 851 (1992).
13. Thomas Jefferson to Roger Weightman, June 24, 1826, Thomas Jefferson Papers, Series 1: General Correspondence, 1651–1827, Library of Congress, http://hdl.loc.gov/loc.mss/mtj.mtjbib024904.
14. For a more complete elaboration of this point, see: Charles R. Kesler, "The Special Meaning of the Declaration of Independence," which serves as the introduction to *American Conservatism and the American Founding*, by Harry V. Jaffa (Durham, NC: Carolina Academic Press, 1984), 1–17; Harry V. Jaffa, "Equality as a Conservative Principle," in *How to Think About the American Revolution* (Durham, NC: Carolina Academic Press, 1978), 13–48; Thomas G. West, *The Political Theory of the American Founding: Natural Rights, Public Policy, and the Moral Conditions of Freedom* (New York: Cambridge University Press, 2017), part I; Glenn Ellmers, *The Soul of Politics: Harry V. Jaffa and the Fight for America* (New York: Encounter Books, 2021), chap. 5; Vincent Phillip Muñoz, *Religious Liberty and the American Founding: Natural Rights and the Original Meaning of*

the First Amendment Religion Clauses (Chicago: University of Chicago Press, 2022), 42–46. For a discussion of the place of the family and paternal power in relationship to the principle of natural equality, see Thomas G. West, "Locke's Neglected Teaching on Morality and the Family," *Society* 50 (2013): 472–76.

15. See Harry V. Jaffa, "Thomas Aquinas Meets Thomas Jefferson," *Interpretation* 22 (2006): 177–84; Dominic Legge, O.P., "Do Thomists Have Rights?" *Nova et Vetera* 17 (2019): 127–47; Kody W. Cooper and Justin Bucley Dyer, *The Classical and Christian Origins of American Politics: Political Theology, Natural Law, and the American Founding* (New York: Cambridge University Press, 2022).
16. For an extended discussion of the various ways the Founders' public policy fostered liberty and discouraged license, see West, *The Political Theory of the American Founding*.
17. Emphasis in the original. Alexander Hamilton, "The Farmer Refuted," February 23, 1775, in *The Papers of Alexander Hamilton*, ed. Harold C. Cyrett (New York and London: Columbia University Press, 1961–79).
18. Hadley P. Arkes, "A Natural Law Manifesto or an Appeal from the Old Jurisprudence to the New," *Notre Dame Law Review* 87 (2012): 1246.
19. James Wilson, *Lectures on Law*, in *Collected Works of James Wilson*, eds. Kermit L. Hall and Mark David Hall (Indianapolis: Liberty Fund, 2007), 2:1056, 1:639.
20. For an excellent account of the invention of the modern self, see Carl Trueman, *The Rise and Triumph of the Modern Self: Cultural Amnesia, Expressive Individualism, and the Road to Sexual Revolution* (Wheaton, IL: Crossway, 2020).
21. In this light, consider the following from James Wilson:

> Nature has implanted in man the desire of his own happiness; she has inspired him with many tender affections towards others, especially in the near relations of life; she has endowed him with intellectual and with active powers; she has furnished him with a natural impulse to exercise his powers for his own happiness, and the happiness of those, for whom he entertains such tender affections. If all this be true, the undeniable consequence is, that he has a right to exert those powers for the accomplishment of those purposes, in such a manner, and upon such objects, as his inclination and judgment shall direct; provided he does no injury to others; and provided some publick interests do not demand his labours. This right is natural liberty. Every man has a sense of this right. Every man has a sense of the impropriety of restraining or interrupting it. Those who judge wisely, will use this liberty virtuously and honourably: those, who are less wise, will employ it in meaner pursuits: others, again, may, perhaps, indulge it in what may be justly censured as vicious and dishonourable. Yet, with regard even to these last, while they are not injurious to

others; and while no human institution has placed them under the control of magistrates or laws, the sense of liberty is so strong, and its loss is so deeply resented, that, upon the whole, more unhappiness would result from depriving them of their liberty on account of their imprudence, than could be reasonably apprehended from the imprudent use of their liberty. (Wilson, *Lectures on Law*, 1:638–39)

22. Servais Pinckaers, O.P., *The Sources of Christian Ethics*, third ed. (Washington, DC: Catholic University of America Press, 1995), Chaps. 14 and 15.
23. John Adams to Massachusetts Militia, October 11, 1798, the Adams Papers, "Founders Online," National Archives, https://founders.archives.gov/documents/Adams/99-02-02-3102 (early access document).
24. For accounts that emphasize the abandonment of natural rights philosophical principles by leading American elites, see: Charles R. Kesler, *I Am the Change: Barack Obama and the Future of Liberalism* (New York: Broadside Books, 2012); Michael Anton, *After the Flight 93 Election: The Vote that Saved America and What We Still Have to Lose* (New York: Encounter Books, 2019), 40–59; Bradley C. S. Watson, *Progressivism: The Strange History of a Radical Idea* (Notre Dame, IN: University of Notre Dame Press, 2020); Ronald J. Pestritto, *America Transformed: The Rise and Legacy of American Progressivism* (New York: Encounter Books, 2021).
25. Joseph Bottum, *An Anxious Age: The Post-Protestant Ethic and the Spirit of America* (New York: Image, 2014).
26. For an especially perceptive account of this point see Charles R. Kesler's introductory essay in his volume *Crisis of the Two Constitutions* (New York: Encounter, 2021).
27. For a discussion of Singer's advocacy of infanticide, see Nat Henthoff, "A Professor Who Advocates for Infanticide," *The Washington Post*, September 11, 1999.

HOW NATURAL RIGHT FELL OUT OF FAVOR IN AMERICAN THOUGHT

1. Eldon J. Eisenach, *The Lost Promise of Progressivism* (Lawrence: University Press of Kansas, 1994), 6.
2. Charles R. Kesler, *Crisis of the Two Constitutions: The Rise, Decline, and Recovery of American Greatness* (New York: Encounter Books, 2021), 147.
3. The extended list of scholars working in a related vein should at least include Harvey C. Mansfield Jr., Paul Eidelberg, James Ceaser, Jean Yarbrough, and John Marini.
4. As Martin Diamond wrote, "the dispute about the founding has in a sense always revolved around the understanding of the Declaration and the Constitution, and

how they stand toward each other." ("The Declaration and the Constitution: Liberty, Democracy, and the Founders," in *As Far As Republican Principles Will Admit: Essays by Martin Diamond*, ed. William A Schambra (Washington, DC: American Enterprise Institute, 1992; originally published in *The Public Interest*, Summer 1975), 230.

5. Eric Goldman, *Rendezvous With Destiny: A History of Modern American Reform* (New York: Alfred A. Knopf, 1953), 87.
6. Harvey C. Mansfield Jr., *America's Constitutional Soul* (Baltimore: The Johns Hopkins University Press, 1991), 5.
7. Woodrow Wilson, *Constitutional Government in the United States* (New York: Columbia University Press, 1908), 54–55, 56, 57.
8. Ibid., 56.
9. Wilson, "The Study of Administration," *Political Science Quarterly* 2 (June 1887); reprinted in *Classics of Public Administration*, ed. Albert Hyde and Jay M. Shafritz, second ed. (Chicago: The Dorsey Press, 1987), 11.
10. Eric Goldman offered a more direct and succinct narrative than Hofstadter of the continuity between Social Darwinism and reform Darwinism in *Rendezvous With Destiny*, 85–104. But Goldman only mentions the idea of natural right once in the entire book.
11. Richard Hofstadter, *Social Darwinism in American Thought* (Boston: Beacon Press, 1955; originally published by University of Pennsylvania Press, 1944), 7, 5.
12. Sidney Fine, *Laissez Faire and the General Welfare State* (Ann Arbor: University of Michigan Press, 1956).
13. The leading works in this revision are Irvin G. Wyllie's *The Self-Made Man in America* (Rutgers University Press, 1954); Joseph Wall, *Andrew Carnegie* (New York, 1970); and especially Robert C. Bannister, *Social Darwinism: Science and Myth in Anglo-American Social Thought* (Philadelphia: Temple University Press, 1979).
14. Donald C. Bellomy, "'Social Darwinism' Revisited," *Perspectives in American History*, New Series, No. 1 (1984): 2.
15. Bannister, *Social Darwinism*, 9. Bannister can be criticized for overplaying a good hand. This can be seen in his acknowledgement of some difficulty in accounting for the widespread use of the idea of Social Darwinism as an epithet against the opponents of Progressive reform, and also in his near exoneration of both Herbert Spencer and William Graham Sumner from the charge of Social Darwinism.
16. Hofstadter, *Social Darwinism in American Thought*, 203; Arthur M. Schlesinger Jr., *The Cycles of American History* (Boston: Houghton-Mifflin, 1986), 38.
17. The most popular recent organic analogy for free-market capitalism is Michael

Rothschild's *Bionomics: The Inevitability of Capitalism* (New York: Henry Holt & Company, 1990). Rothschild includes a postscript to the book explaining why "it is important to distinguish bionomics from Social Darwinism."

18. In addition to Bannister, other recent general works that attest to the continuing interest in Darwinism include Michael Ruse, *Taking Darwin Seriously* (Oxford: Basil Blackwell, 1986), and Carl N. Degler, *In Search of Human Nature: The Decline and Revival of Darwinism in American Social Thought* (Oxford University Press, 1991).
19. Herbert Spencer, *The Man Versus the State* (Indianapolis: Liberty Classics, 1981; originally published, London: Williams and Norgate, 1884), 149.
20. Spencer, "The Social Organism," in *The Man Versus the State* (originally published in The Westminster Review, January 1860), pp. 383-434. This phrase is of course reminiscent of Edmund Burke, whose view of the organic or natural growth of constitutions can be argued to have been among the forerunners of historicism, and therefore a forerunner of Darwinian constitutionalism.
21. Hofstadter, *Social Darwinism in American Thought*, 59.
22. Sumner, "The Boon of Nature," in *War and Other Essays*, ed. Albert Galloway Keller (New Haven: Yale University Press, 1911), 320.
23. Sumner, "Rights," in *Selected Essays of William Graham Sumner*, ed. Albert Galloway (Yale University Press, 1924), p. 178.
24. William Graham Sumner, "Socialism," in *On Liberty, Society, and Politics: The Essential Essays of William Graham Sumner*, ed. Robert Bannister (Indianapolis: Liberty Fund, 1992; originally published in *The Challenge of Facts*, ed. Albert G. Keller [New Haven: Yale University Press, 1914]), 170. Sumner's discussion of natural rights, both here and especially in the tenth chapter of *What Social Classes Owe to Each Other*, is limited to the most extreme modern understanding of natural rights, in which the link to nature as the "unchanging ground of changing experience" nearly disappears completely. In this respect, Sumner's account of natural rights is almost indistinguishable from the willful character of positive right, i.e., claims asserted against government or society. For example, in *What Social Classes Owe to Each Other*, Sumner writes: "natural rights are claims which certain persons have by prerogative against some other persons." In his essay "Socialism," Sumner explains: "for if a man has natural rights, then the reasoning is clear up to the finished socialistic doctrine that a man has a natural right to whatever he needs, and that the measure of his claims is the wishes he wants fulfilled. If, then, he has a need, who is bound to satisfy it for him? Who holds the obligation corresponding to his right?" (170). This is certainly not the understanding of natural rights in the Declaration of Independence, but Sumner ironically anticipates the way rights have become claims against government in

recent times – a development that stems in part from the Progressive severance of constitutionalism from the Founding idea of natural right.

25. "In a brilliant essay which he never published, but which was written some time before the studies of J. Allen Smith and Charles A. Beard, Sumner divined the intentions of the Founding Fathers in the making of the American Constitution. They feared democracy, Sumner pointed out, and attempted to set limits upon it in the federal structure ..." (Hofstadter, *Social Darwinism in American Thought*, 60).
26. Sumner, "Advancing Social and Political Organization in the United States," in *Essays of William Graham Sumner*, ed. Albert Galloway Keller and Maurice R. Davie, vol. II (New Haven: Yale University Press, 1911), 349–50.
27. Ibid., 321.
28. See Carl Becker, *The Declaration of Independence* (New York: Alfred A. Knopf, 1922), especially 24–79; 135–92.
29. Sumner, *Essays*, 321–22.
30. Sumner, "The Mores of the Present and the Future," in *On Liberty, Society, and Politics*, 402.
31. Ibid., 317–18. This assessment should be contrasted with Lincoln's famous repudiation of the *Dred Scott* decision. In condemning "this obvious violence to the plain unmistakeable language of the Declaration," Lincoln expounded:

    > I think the authors of that notable instrument intended to include *all* men, but they did not intend to declare all men equal *in all respects*. They did not mean to say all were equal in color, size, intellect, moral developments, or social capacity. They defined with tolerable distinctness, in what respects they did consider all men created equal – equal in "certain inalienable rights, among which are life, liberty, and the pursuit of happiness." This they said, and this they meant. They did not mean to assert the obvious untruth, that all were actually enjoying that equality, nor yet, that they were about to confer it immediately upon them. In fact they had no power to confer such a boon. They meant simply to declare the *right*, so that the *enforcement* of it might follow as fast as circumstances should permit. They meant to set up a standard maxim for free society, which should be familiar to all, and revered by all; constantly looked to, constantly labored for, and even though never perfectly attained, constantly approximated, and thereby constantly spreading and deepening its influence ... (Speech at Springfield, Illinois, June 26, 1857, in *The Collected Works of Abraham Lincoln*, ed. Roy Basler, vol. II [New Brunswick: Rutgers University Press, 1953], 405–6.)

32. Lester Ward, *Dynamic Sociology*, in *Lester Ward and the Welfare State*, ed. Henry Steele Commager (Indianapolis: Bobbs-Merrill, 1967), 48.

33. Ibid., p. 33.
34. Ward, "Theory and Practice Are at War," in *Lester Ward and the Welfare State* (originally published in *The Penn Monthly*, May 1881), 35.
35. Ward, *Dynamic Sociology*, op. cit., 36. Following hard on this premise, Ward also helps lay the groundwork for the confidence that scientific administration can successfully promote the progress of society, in words that would become practically the Progressive creed of public administration. In a section of *Dynamic Sociology* entitled "The Superiority of Government Over Private Administration of Public Concerns," Ward argued:

> Nearly every present acknowledged function of government has once been intrusted to private enterprise ... Now, of all the enterprises which the state has thus appropriated to itself, there is not one which it has not managed better and more wisely than it had been managed before by private parties... The superiority of governmental administration over private management, in large enterprises of a general public character, has been clearly seen and frequently pointed out ... It might similarly be shown that all the functions of government are usually performed with far greater thoroughness and fidelity than similar functions intrusted to private individuals.

36. Ward, "Theory and Practice Are at War," op. cit., 36.

PROGRESSIVISM, CONSERVATISM, AND THE WORK OF CHARLES R. KESLER

1. Paul Eidelberg, *Discourse on Statesmanship: The Design and Transformation of the American Polity* (Urbana: University of Illinois Press, 1974); James W. Ceaser, *Presidential Selection: Theory and Development* (Princeton: Princeton University Press, 1979). See also Ceaser, Glen E. Thurow, Jeffrey K. Tulis, and Joseph M. Bessette, "The Rise of the Rhetorical Presidency," *Presidential Studies Quarterly* 11, No. 2 (Spring 1981): 158–71.
2. Ronald J. Pestritto, *America Transformed: The Rise and Legacy of American Progressivism* (New York: Encounter Books, 2021); Pestritto, *Woodrow Wilson and the Roots of Modern Liberalism* (Lanham, MD: Rowman & Littlefield, 2005); Bradley C. S. Watson, *Living Constitution, Dying Faith: Progressivism and the New Science of Jurisprudence* (Wilmington: ISI Books, 2009); Dennis Mahoney, *Politics and Progress: The Emergence of American Political Science* (Lanham, MD: Lexington Books, 2004). John Marini's recent book, *Unmasking the Administrative State* (New York: Encounter Books, 2019), incorporates several earlier pieces on the Progressives and the administrative state.
3. Charles R. Kesler, "Woodrow Wilson and the Statesmanship of Progress," in

Natural Right and Political Right, ed. Thomas B. Silver and Peter W. Schramm (Durham, NC: Carolina Academic Press, 1984), 103–27.

4. Kesler, "The Public Philosophy of the New Freedom and the New Deal," in *The New Deal and Its Legacy*, ed. Robert Eden (New York: Greenwood Press, 1989), 155–66.
5. Kesler, *Crisis of the Two Constitutions: The Rise, Decline, and Recovery of American Greatness* (New York: Encounter Books, 2021).
6. Kesler, *I Am the Change: Barack Obama and the Crisis of Liberalism* (New York: Broadside Books, 2012).
7. Kesler, "Public Philosophy," 155.
8. Kesler, "Woodrow Wilson and the Statesmanship of Progress," 103.
9. Franklin Delano Roosevelt, "Campaign Address on Progressive Government at the Commonwealth Club," in *The Public Papers and Addresses of Franklin D. Roosevelt*, ed. Samuel I. Rosenman (New York: Russell & Russell, 1969), vol. 1, 749–50.
10. Kesler, "Public Philosophy," 159–60.
11. Ibid., 162.
12. Ibid., 165.
13. Kesler, "Statesmanship of Progress," 103.
14. See, for example, Anthony A. Peacock, *Vindicating the Commercial Republic: The Federalist on Union, Enterprise, and War* (Lanham: Lexington Books, 2018).
15. Kesler, "Public Philosophy," 161. Calvin Coolidge's comment on the Declaration provides a notable contrast: "About the Declaration there is a finality that is exceedingly restful.... If all men are created equal, that is final. If they are endowed with inalienable rights, that is final. If governments derive their just powers from the consent of the governed, that is final. No advance, no progress can be made beyond these propositions." Coolidge, "The Inspiration of the Declaration," in *Foundations of the Republic: Speeches and Addresses* (New York: Charles Scribner's Sons, 1926), 451–52.
16. Kesler, "Statesmanship of Progress," 108–9.
17. Wilson, "The New Freedom Chapter Two: What is Progress?" in *Woodrow Wilson: The Essential Political Writings*, ed. Ronald J. Pestritto (Lanham: Lexington Books, 2005), 120–21.
18. Kesler, "Statesmanship of Progress," 105–7, 110–11; Kesler, "Public Philosophy," 156.
19. Harvey C. Mansfield Jr., *America's Constitutional Soul* (Baltimore: Johns Hopkins University Press, 1991). On the differences between Mansfield and the Claremont school on the relationship between the Declaration and Constitution, see Thomas G. West, "Jaffa versus Mansfield: Does America Have a Constitu-

tional or a 'Declaration of Independence' Soul?," *Perspectives on Political Science* 31, No. 4 (2002): 235–46.

20. Kesler, "Statesmanship of Progress," 115.
21. A representative passage can be found in Jaffa, *How To Think About the American Revolution* (Claremont: The Claremont Institute, 2001), 140.
22. Roosevelt, "Commonwealth Club," op. cit., 753.
23. Kesler, "Public Philosophy," 163.
24. Roosevelt, "Commonwealth Club," op. cit., 753.
25. Wilson, "Leaders of Men," in *Woodrow Wilson: The Essential Political Writings*, ed. Ronald J. Pestritto (Lanham: Lexington Books, 2005), 211–29.
26. Wilson, "Random Note for 'The Philosophy of Politics,'" in *The Papers of Woodrow Wilson*, ed. Arthur S. Link et al. (Princeton: Princeton University Press, 1970), vol. 9, 130.
27. Kesler, "Statesmanship of Progress," 116.
28. Aristotle, *Nicomachean Ethics*, 1134b18–1135a15.
29. Kesler, "Statesmanship of Progress," 104.
30. Ibid., 105.
31. Ibid., 123.
32. For a representative example, see Wilson, "Abraham Lincoln: A Man of the People," February 12, 1909, in *Papers*, 19:42.
33. Kesler, "Statesmanship of Progress," 119.
34. Ibid., 121.
35. Ibid., 121.
36. Ibid., 122.
37. Kesler, "Public Philosophy," 158.
38. Ibid., 159.
39. Roosevelt, "Commonwealth Club," op. cit., 747–49.
40. Kesler, "Public Philosophy," 162.
41. Ibid., 162.
42. Ibid., 164.
43. Kesler, "Statesmanship of Progress," 103.
44. For example: Thomas L. Pangle, *The Spirit of Modern Republicanism: The Moral Vision of the American Founders and the Philosophy of Locke* (Chicago: The University of Chicago Press, 1988), 89–111, 124–27.
45. Kesler, "Statesmanship of Progress," 109–10.
46. Kesler, "Public Philosophy," 157.
47. Leo Strauss, *Natural Right and History* (Chicago: The University of Chicago Press, 1953), 294–323.

48. Kesler, "Statesmanship of Progress," 116.
49. Kesler, "Public Philosophy," 156–57, referring to Wilson, "Princeton in the Nation's Service," Oct. 21, 1896, in *Papers of Woodrow Wilson*, vol. 10, 22.
50. Patrick J. Deneen, *Why Liberalism Failed* (New Haven: Yale University Press, 2018), 23–28, 100–2, 141–43.
51. R. Shep Melnick, "Claremont's Constitutional Crisis," *Law & Liberty*, published March 29, 2021, https://lawliberty.org/book-review/claremonts-constitutional-crisis/.

DESIGN & COMPOSITION BY CARL W. SCARBROUGH
WWW.CARLWSCARBROUGH.COM